Creating a College
That Works

Creating a College That Works

Audrey Cohen and Metropolitan College of New York

Grace G. Roosevelt

For Amy and Val – with gratitude
for your commitment to the
city that Audrey Cohen loved –
from Grace ("Jinx") Roosevelt

March 20, 2015

SUNY PRESS

Cover photograph © Estate of David Gahr

Published by State University of New York Press, Albany

For information, contact State University of New York Press, Albany, NY
www.sunypress.edu

Production, Jenn Bennett
Marketing, Fran Keneston

Library of Congress Cataloging-in-Publication Data

Roosevelt, Grace G., 1941–
    Creating a College That Works : Audrey Cohen and Metropolitan College of New
York.
        pages cm
    Includes bibliographical references and index.
    ISBN 978-1-4384-5589-1 (hardcover : alk. paper)
    ISBN 978-1-4384-5588-4 (pbk. : alk. paper)
    ISBN 978-1-4384-5590-7 (ebook)

10 9 8 7 6 5 4 3 2 1

For Dellie Bloom (1920–2006),
Barbara Walton (1924–2008),
and Deborah Allen (1924–2014),
whose careful recording of Audrey Cohen's educational vision
made this book possible.

As I have continued to reflect on our experience, I can raise certain questions about our zeal and perhaps our overly moral approach to the social challenges the program addressed. But that zeal and conviction *did* also help to create change. Rhetoric does help to produce reality.

It *shouldn't* be revolutionary that people's potentials are believed in and challenged to grow. It *shouldn't* be revolutionary to believe that others can learn and perform. It *shouldn't* be revolutionary that service patterns should emerge from patterns of human need. The conditions are, however, for the most part, contrary to this hope. Our society is still too bound up in racism, credentialism, and fragmentation. Yet there are now alternatives, and some of these have been wrought by and from our efforts.

As I look back on the beginnings of the institution, I can see many mistakes—of emphasis, of interpretation, of strategy. But there was an unshakable core of justice, fairness and honesty—in the way we tried to analyze the challenges, in the way we dealt with the world, and in the way we dealt with each other.

We did good work.

—Laura Pires Houston (later Pires-Houston), 12/5/1978, Addendum to "The Women's Talent Corps—The College for Human Services: An Historical Reconstruction. Phase 1—Crystal 3: Institutional Development and Expansion: Pushing the Parameter of the Possible." Volume IV, p. 35.

CONTENTS

gallery of photos follows page 132

ILLUSTRATIONS

CHAPTER 1

INTRODUCTION

Unlike traditional educational approaches that separate learning from its use, [Metropolitan College of New York's] approach links learning directly to action. Students learn in order to use what they learn, and they use what they learn to reach specific goals. This gives them an appreciation for how deeply they can affect the world around them and builds a lifelong interest in learning.

—Cohen and Jordan, 1996, p. 33.[1]

"I'VE GOT THIS IDEA
I WANT TO WORK ON AND
I'M GOING TO NEED SOME HELP"[2]

In a small college library in lower Manhattan, three adult students are busily at work around a large table cluttered with books, papers, and their own laptop computers. Tamisha Tamley is a shy thirty-five-year-old African American woman who has raised three children as a single mom. She works in a homeless shelter in Brooklyn and hopes one day to become a counselor of teenagers so that she can help others avoid the mistakes she feels she made at an early age. Sitting beside her is Bernadette Perkins, a tall, imposing Jamaican woman who has worked as a nurse's assistant at Elmherst Hospital in Queens for ten years but who now wants to become a teacher. On the other side of the table is Juanel Gomez who grew up in the South Bronx, served in the U.S. Army, and has returned to college to take advantage of the Veteran Administration's new GI Bill. Juanel is working on a business degree so that eventually he can open his own company specializing in computer software.

1

Tamisha Tamley, Bernadette Perkins, and Juanel Gomez are composite portraits of students who currently attend Metropolitan College of New York (MCNY). MCNY is a tuition-based, private, urban college with approximately 1,200 full-time students, most of whom are women of color who have jobs and families. Although not well known outside of New York City, MCNY is familiar to many New Yorkers thanks to the college's frequent ad campaigns on major highway intersections and in the subways. As those ads and the college's prize-winning website (www.mcny.edu) make known, MCNY includes a human services unit (the Audrey Cohen School for Human Services and Education), a public affairs unit (the School for Public Affairs and Administration), and a business unit (the School for Business), with daytime, evening, and weekend schedules that allow students to attend college while continuing to work. For working adults, an important MCNY attraction is that by attending full time, including the summer, students can complete an undergraduate degree in two years and eight months. The college's promotional materials make clear, however, that the college is no "fly-by-night" institution. MCNY is accredited by the Middle States Commission on Higher Education, its Masters of Childhood Education program is accredited by the National Council for Accreditation of Teacher Education (NCATE), and its School for Business is accredited by the Accrediting Council for Business Schools and Programs (ACBSP).

What makes MCNY unique is the structure of its curriculum. In a conceptual framework that the college created and that it calls Purpose-Centered Education, each semester has a specific performance goal or purpose to which all five courses taken that semester relate. The courses themselves are then taught as "dimensions" of each semester's purpose, and the course content is often transdisciplinary—combining, for example, readings from literature and psychology or history and philosophy. Most importantly, students are required to use the knowledge gained each semester to complete a specific project—what the college calls a Constructive Action—in a human service agency, school, or business, and to document that process in a systematic way. As one student wrote, "We become immersed in the practical application of what is taught in theory."[3]

MCNY's unorthodox model has achieved positive results. In a recent survey of MCNY graduates, 68 percent of respondents reported that they had full-time jobs and 47 percent reported holding a manager/administrator/supervisor position. Thirty percent of respondents reported having received a recent promotion. MCNY alumni include social workers, teachers, ministers, school administrators, business owners, emergency professionals, psychologists, and lawyers. Most interesting, perhaps, 87 percent of the graduates recommended the Constructive Action process as an excellent learning tool.[4]

Less apparent in the college's promotional materials than its offerings and outcomes is the story of the college's founding. In 1964 activist educator Audrey Cohen and a group of hard-working, highly motivated women associates began with a dream and eventually succeeded in creating a college that, against many odds, continues to provide an academic home for students like Tamisha, Bernadette, and Juanel. As the chapters that follow show, the women who created what is now MCNY were visionaries and pioneers. Like other women of the past whose contributions to the present have been forgotten or neglected, Cohen's and her friends' courage, commitment, and foresight merit historical recognition.

Part biography, part institutional history, *Creating a College That Works* is about how Cohen created a new kind of college that has evolved over the past fifty years. The story records a feisty woman's lasting contributions to the city, but more importantly it chronicles the creation of a unique curricular structure that enables low-income adult students to integrate their academic learning with meaningful work in community settings. What motivated Cohen and her associates to devote their lives to creating an alternative model of higher education? How did they work together and what forces did they have to overcome? What were some of the defining moments in the college's early history, and how did Cohen's vision evolve? What are the lasting legacies of Cohen's leadership in terms of student learning? These questions provide the focal points for the structure of this book. I begin with Cohen's own life story, but her story quickly merges into the history of the educational institution that she founded and presided over for thirty years. In identifying and describing the key moments in the creation and early years of the college, I use the voices of the individuals who participated in the process as often as possible—in part to give life to the narrative but also to show how the fates of both individuals and institutions are often shaped by chance encounters, unforeseen events, and the random play of historical forces.

Intertwining both biography and institutional history, the book's narrative contains a built-in tension. Is this a story about a woman's life, or is it the history of a college, a reader may ask. The answer is "both." Most of Cohen's adult identity was shaped by her creation of a college, and the college's identity was the result of her vision, passion, and hard work. Cohen's life and the college's life cannot be separated. The dominant narrative, however, is historical more than biographical, mostly because of the availability of evidence. Much of Cohen's inner life remains a mystery. She did not keep a diary or write personal letters, so her deepest motivations cannot be fully analyzed. In contrast, the college's history is an open source, thanks to the extensive archives that Cohen arranged to have organized shortly before her death. It is those archives that have provided most of the material for the narrative that follows.

Current concerns about the future of U.S. higher education make the story of MCNY's founding particularly compelling today. At a time when the income gap between college-educated and noncollege-educated young people is growing,[5] Cohen's project has much to teach us about structuring curricula so that nontraditional adult students can complete a college degree. Around 60 percent of MCNY students identify themselves as Black or African American and 20 percent as Hispanic or Latino. More than 90 percent of the students at MCNY receive financial aid, and most come from neighborhoods characterized by low levels of household income and high levels of recent immigration.[6] The story of how Cohen created an alternative form of college experience that meets the needs of inner-city students is instructive for anyone interested in broadening educational opportunities.

In the context of the corporatization of higher education and the loss of its humanistic "soul,"[7] the evolution of MCNY's unique curriculum is also instructive. Bridging the age-old divide between vocational training and humanistic learning, the college that Cohen created demonstrates that the study of Dante and Du Bois need not be abandoned in the quest for gainful employment, and that job readiness need not be sacrificed to the pursuit of a broad-based liberal education. Cohen's story shows how an educational institution can aim to produce both practical learners and reflective practitioners—students who are self-conscious about the purpose of their learning and who connect what they learn with what they do.

Finally, as the twentieth century recedes into our collective rearview mirror, the founding of MCNY reminds us of the creative energies that the social changes of the 1960s released. Along with the civil rights movement, the women's movement, and student activism, the decade from 1964 to 1974 gave rise to hundreds of educational experiments aiming to dissolve the barriers of class, race, and gender that had marked much of the nation's previous educational history.[8] Today, in educational settings from kindergarten to college, we see the integrative impulses of that era being replaced by separatist and utilitarian aims.[9] The story of Cohen's accomplishments can help twenty-first-century parents, educators, and activists reflect on which idealistic experiments of the late twentieth century can be left behind and which ones merit being studied, sustained, and even replicated.

Metropolitan College of New York is perhaps the only institution of higher learning that can trace its origins to a conversation between two young mothers. On a warm day in September 1960, Audrey Cohen and Alida Mesrop met on a gritty sidewalk near a large fountain in Stuyvesant Town, a vast, private housing complex on the east side of Manhattan below 23rd Street. As they watched the toddlers splash in the water from the fountain, the women talked animatedly about their children, their own backgrounds, and their prospects for staying active in the workforce while raising a family. The taller of the two women, Alida Mesrop, had recently worked as the public relations and publicity director at WPIX-TV, a local news, weather, and entertainment channel, but she had had to quit her job when her first daughter was born earlier that year. On a tip from a friend she had arranged to meet the other woman, Audrey Cohen, to talk about part-time work. They had decided to meet at the fountain, because both of them lived in apartments nearby.

At age twenty-nine Cohen was already the co-founder and director of Part-Time Research Associates, a consulting firm employing college-educated women on a flexible schedule to do social science research for government and business. Petite and energetic, with curly blonde hair and blue eyes, Cohen was on the lookout for women with writing skills, which Mesrop clearly had. In addition, Mesrop had had leadership experience with the media, experience that was, as Cohen put it, "unusual" at the time. The two hit it off, and they began a friendship and collaboration that would last for more than three decades.[10] Little did they know that Mesrop would one day replace Cohen as president of the college that grew out of the conversation the two women had on that day.

As a result of her meeting with Cohen, Mesrop was hired by Part-Time Research Associates to take on two writing assignments during the next few months. But by the end of the year she was pregnant again, and she was pregnant again the next year. ("With three children in four years I was drowning in diapers," Mesrop later quipped.) It wasn't until 1964 that she resurfaced and put in a call to Cohen to say that she was back in the world and ready to work. Cohen's voice on the other end of the phone had a new energy. "I definitely will call you," she said. "I've got this idea I want to work on, and I'm going to need some help."[11]

Cohen's idea was to establish a Women's Talent Corps, which would create jobs and provide training not just for the educated middle class women served by Part-Time Research Associates but for a broader and less visible group of women—low income and minority women—who had been left behind in America's postwar economic boom.[12] "I had a mission when I started Part-Time Research Associates, and that mission was to assist other women as well as myself to do something fulfilling," Cohen once said. But as time passed she realized that that the fulfillment gained by Part-Time Research Associates was "insufficient."[13] The business she had co-founded had succeeded in providing jobs for educated, middle-class women but was doing nothing to help low-income, less well-educated women who were also desperately in need of meaningful work.

In the previous year Betty Friedan had published *The Feminine Mystique* highlighting the bias against women in the workforce; Martin Luther King Jr. had delivered his famous "I Have a Dream" speech during the historic march on Washington; and Lyndon B. Johnson had declared a "war on poverty" in his January 1964 inaugural address. Heralding a new concern about gender equity, civil rights, and economic justice, these events and others set in motion a wave of change across the United States. In retrospect, though probably unbeknownst to the two women at the time, Cohen and Mesrop were riding on this wave when they discussed Cohen's idea for a Women's Talent Corps in the fall of 1964.

Over the next decade and a half, a diverse and multitalented group of dedicated women would join Cohen to implement her vision of a Women's

Talent Corps for low-income New Yorkers. An early associate was Barbara Walton, an administrator and writer who had worked on the de-Nazification of Germany and then taken a job with the Institute for International Education. She recommended Sylvia Hack, a Queens resident and activist who contributed political savvy and connections to the project. Another early convert to the idea was Laura Pires-Hester, whose Creole family had immigrated to Massachusetts from the Cape Verde Islands when she was a child and who had recently earned a master's degree in social work from Columbia University. Pires-Hester was the most scholarly and serious of the group and the one with the most knowledge of the communities and social needs that the Women's Talent Corps would directly address.

Inspired by Cohen's energy, other women soon joined the project. Janith Jordan came to New York from Michigan where she had done graduate work in education and had taught for several years in a Detroit inner-city public high school. At the other end of the socioeconomic spectrum was Millie Robbins Leet, a philanthropist and activist whose husband had at one time been the landlord of the East 67th Street building where the Cohens then lived[14] and who provided financial support for the project in its early years. Later on a young journalist named Deborah Allen joined Cohen's administrative staff. She was hired on the recommendation of Alida Mesrop, who had met her through their work together on the PTA in the Pelham, New York public school system. Allen was also a member of the college's board of trustees and continued to serve as the keeper of the vision of the educational model pioneered by Audrey Cohen.

Together, the middle-class, well-educated women inspired by Cohen's idea of a Women's Talent Corps engaged in activities that women of another generation, or even their own generation, might have found improper or even dangerous. They lobbied in Washington, attended meetings in economically depressed neighborhoods late at night, and demonstrated in front of City Hall to push for recognition and support. They testified, petitioned, sat-in, and marched; they were criticized, harassed, and forced out of buildings.[15] In the early years, even within their own institution, the women faced resentment, rebellions, and strikes, and at one point Cohen's own office was occupied by a group of angry students.

But the efforts of Cohen and her supporters eventually succeeded. In 1966 the Women's Talent Corps received funding from the Office of

Economic Opportunity, and in 1970 the institution became the College for Human Services, which, under Cohen's presidency, grew to an enrollment of more than one thousand students over the next two decades. In 1992, four years before her death, the college was renamed Audrey Cohen College, and in 2002 it was again renamed Metropolitan College of New York. Today MCNY includes undergraduate and graduate programs in human services, business, urban studies, and education. The programs graduate more than four hundred students a year, most of whom are low-income, adult women of color and recent immigrants.

The story of a group of women getting together to found a college is itself worthy of historical documentation. As noted earlier, though, what makes the story of this college's founding most significant is the uniqueness of the curricular model on which all the programs offered at the college are based. Central to Cohen's vision from its earliest articulation was her desire to relate educational experience to meaningful work. Decades before the concept of "service learning" became important in academe, Cohen was committed to the idea of connecting academic study to the real needs of underserved people in urban communities. As a result, the social vision that has permeated the college's conceptual framework throughout its history has generated curricular structures, academic requirements, and forms of assessment that are unlike any others in American higher education today.

MCNY's uniqueness as an educational institution will be apparent in the story that follows. An interwoven aim, however, is to record the process by which a group of extraordinary women led by Cohen defied the conventions of their time to found a radically innovative college that has served New York City's underserved populations for half a century. Similar in some ways to Jane Addams and the generation of women who devoted their energies to establishing settlement houses and improving social work practices during the Progressive Era at the beginning of the twentieth century, Cohen and her friends who came to maturity during the upheavals of the 1960s envisioned and created new structures for individual and collective empowerment that have survived the test of time.

The story of MCNY's founding is a 1960s success story.[16] Here at the outset, however, I caution against any easy stereotyping of roles and motivations. Although the tumultuous events of the 1960s provided the context for Cohen's and her associates' achievements, the women themselves cannot be identified as part of the "Sixties" generation. Most of them were born in the 1930s or before. They came of age during the presidencies of Roosevelt, Truman, and Eisenhower; and many of them were already married and were raising their own children by the time that hippies and flower children became media phenomena. An interesting paradox of these women's story is that although the educational institution they created was extremely radical, even for its time, the women themselves in many ways exemplified the life-styles of the mid-twentieth-century suburban middle class.

Nor can the women inspired by Cohen's vision be easily pegged as feminists, at least in terms of the third wave of feminism familiar to us today. Cohen and her associates were firm believers in women's empowerment, but the later preoccupation with sexual identity or gender as a social construction was not part of their education. For Cohen and her associates the empowerment of women was essentially a matter of practicality and common sense. They, and in many cases their husbands as well, felt that the bias against women in the workforce resulted in a huge waste of talent, and that meaningful jobs for women would both improve the lives of women individually and add to the welfare of the community as a whole.[17] As Cohen once stated, the belief that shaped her life was a firm faith that Americans could tap into the vast reservoir of human potential that at that time was being wasted in the United States: "Just as it is said that the average person only uses 10 percent of the brain's potential capacity, so I believed that our society had not even begun to fully use the talents of all its people."[18]

It was the combination of practicality and vision, common sense and "dreams" evident in Cohen's story that first inspired me to write this book. Besides chronicling the successful work of an enterprising group of women, the book may also suggest to others some of the qualities that are needed for successful leadership in any setting. As is apparent in what follows, the achievements of Cohen and her friends did not come easily nor was her particular management style always effective. Over the long term, however, their creation of new structures for educational empowerment is of lasting value and merits recognition.

CHAPTER 2

THE EDUCATION OF AN ACTIVIST
(1931–1963)

When historians look retrospectively at life in twentieth century America, one of the phenomena they will undoubtedly examine is the insistent demand for social justice, and especially for equal opportunity in employment and education. They will note that social critics demanded a world in which, regardless of race, color, sex or religion, talents and abilities were encouraged to develop and then were appropriately rewarded.

At the same time they will note that reality fell far short of this ideal. It is apparent to me that social justice requires power not to be lodged in a disproportionately small number of persons and no group be excluded from the power structure. Social justice will be a reality only when national, State and local goals reflect the needs of all constituencies and when all constituencies have a voice in determining their goals.

—Cohen, 1978, p. 2

"In the beginning was my father," Audrey Cohen once told her close friend Alida Mesrop. He was, she recalled, "a truly good man who consistently stood at the forefront of social change and made me want to stand with him. It was my father's passion that provided the first context for my life's work."[1]

Audrey Cohen remembered her father as a family man who was progressive in his thinking. Long before the Supreme Court's 1954 *Brown v. the Board of Education* decision outlawing segregated schooling, Abe Cohen spoke of the need for racial understanding and for all people to be treated as equals. He was convinced that it was economic background that created social distinctions, and that poverty was the underlying cause of social problems. In her reminiscences Audrey stressed her father's commitment to social change. Whatever he saw as a movement toward social justice, she said, "he would join that movement."[2] She remembered well their walks together, when he would talk to her about his hopes for a more just and equitable world.[3]

Audrey Cohen was born in Pittsburgh, Pennsylvania, in 1931, at the beginning of the Great Depression. As a debit agent for the Met Life insurance company, Abe Cohen's job involved going door-to-door collecting premiums from individuals on their insurance policies.[4] The family was not wealthy, but Abe Cohen had steady and reliable work. When Audrey was a young girl her father took her to see one of the first public housing projects in western Pennsylvania. She remembered his being proud that the government was putting up public housing. "It is a movement in the right direction," he told his young daughter. He stressed that the country had to take action to remedy situations where people were living in unhealthy conditions. How could the human spirit flourish in poverty? she remembered him asking.[5]

The public housing experiment Audrey and her father visited was undoubtedly the cooperative community in Westmoreland County, Pennsylvania, which had been established as part of the New Deal's 1933 National Industrial Recovery Act (NIRA). As authorized by the NIRA, Congress allocated $25 million for the creation of subsistence homesteads for dislocated industrial workers, and Westmoreland Homesteads became the fourth such project. Over the next decade, 250 families, including laid-off coal miners, were provided with houses that they helped build themselves, plots of land for farming, and by the end of the 1930s, a factory for steady employment.[6] As a citizen concerned about social justice, Abe Cohen would have been interested in the project. In light of his daughter's later dream of providing meaningful employment opportunities and training for low-income women, it is interesting that the trip to Westmoreland Homesteads with her father was a memorable one.[7]

Cohen remembered her own childhood in Pittsburgh as being relatively free of fear and want, in contrast to the difficult circumstances faced by farmers and industrial workers in Western Pennsylvania. "I have a nice warm feeling about my childhood, about being comfortable in my world," she told her friends. She described in positive terms the relative affluence of the Squirrel Hill neighborhood where she was raised. Today the north side of Squirrel Hill is, as Cohen suggested, prosperous and secure-feeling, with large homes, ample back yards, and sleepy, tree-lined streets safe for children on bicycles. One of its claims to fame is being a one-time home of children's television host Fred Rogers,[8] and it is featured as an ideal source of stimulation and nurture in Annie Dillard's *An American Childhood*.[9]

In fact, however, the neighborhood that Cohen grew up in has little in common with the cozy innocence of *Mister Rogers Neighborhood* or Annie Dillard's nostalgic reminiscing. Located on the south side of town, Cohen's childhood home at 1040 Flemington Street is a small, two-story dwelling made of faux bricks and cement. The house is attached to a row of similar houses and has concrete steps rising steeply from the sidewalk. Unlike the shaded lawns of the more affluent Squirrel Hill neighborhoods, many of the small front yards on Flemington Street glare harshly in the noonday sun.

The relative plainness of her early physical surroundings was something Cohen never conveyed to her later friends or associates. In a characteristically positive way, she stressed her own good fortune to have been raised in a secure and loving home. She was brought up in a traditional family, with caring parents, she told her friends. She remembered being driven to elementary school by her father while her mother mostly stayed home cleaning the windowsills in a constant battle against filth and soot. Cohen's maternal aunt was an early role model. Bright and energetic, Cohen noted "in another time she would have left her mark."[10]

In her own words, the young Audrey was by no means a difficult child, but she was far less "biddable," as she termed it, than a younger cousin close to her age who was labeled both smart *and good*. Nevertheless Audrey's mane of golden ringlets and her bright blue eyes, at a time when the Shirley Temple look was in vogue, enabled her to get her way. Audrey was always small for her age, but her parents never stopped telling her that good things came in small packages, and she believed them. "I accepted that I was bright and cute," she remembered, and when her brother Carl was born six years later she paid little attention. "I thought he was just a funny-looking inconvenience that my mother had to put up with."[11]

A wiry, boundlessly energetic child in and out of school, Cohen by her own account was something of a pain in the neck to her teachers. She was a frenetic and constant hand-waver, and her parents would occasionally be called to the school to discuss how to get their daughter to quiet down a little. But her high-energy behavior never bothered Cohen herself. She felt well-liked by other children, she said, and those she thought highly of, "liked me back, even though those who were both smart *and* good were better liked by the teachers."[12]

HIGH SCHOOL

The sense of being admired for her energy and intelligence became even more marked when Audrey entered high school. A top-ranking school today, Taylor Allderdice High School had opened in 1927 and was named after a local industrialist who was president of a subsidiary of the U.S. Steel Corporation.[13] Audrey Cohen's first husband, Mark Cohen, who attended the same school, remembers that in the 1940s the school was beset by ethnic tensions among the three groups that made up the school—Hungarians, whose fathers worked in steel mills and coal mines, poor blacks, and Jewish children whose parents were mostly professionals.[14] But Audrey Cohen's own reminiscences omit any mention of such tensions or divisions. Like her tendency in later life to minimize conflict and to emphasize accomplishment, what she kept in her memory were the positive experiences with friends and the stimulation of new learning.

One thrill was to be elected president of GALS, a club that a small group of girls formed in elementary school. Even more important was being chosen one of four cheerleaders once she entered high school. "It was a big deal," she recalled. Being a cheerleader meant freedom and power because the coach often signed excuse notes for whatever the cheerleaders asked for—including getting out of a boring class or puffing an occasional cigarette. "That was possibly the thing I am most ashamed of in my life," Cohen later admitted, "not the class cutting but the smoking."[15] The cheerleading experience may have had a more long-term significance. Sixty years later, in a speech to a graduating class of the college that Cohen had founded, her daughter Wendy Cohen noted that her mother's early experience with cheerleading exemplified her ability to devote energy and enthusiasm to everything she believed in. Cheerleading turned out to be a big part of the woman Audrey Cohen grew into, her daughter emphasized. She always looked for the good in people and herself, and "passionately advocated for change in order to make great things happen."[16]

At Allderdice Cohen also became interested in academic learning. A high point in those years was a newly offered economics class taught by one of the few male teachers in the school. It was one of the only classes where the teacher encouraged discussion and challenged the students to argue about issues with him and with each other. Even though he occasionally criticized students who failed to grasp his ideas, Cohen respected him for being both an intellectual and also a man with real-world experience in business, and she came to love economics as a result. In his class, "I could express my ideas and he would listen."[17] With some embarrassment she proceeded to recount the following incident:

> One day when I was standing in the hall after class with a small group of friends, he stopped in front of me and said in front of the entire group, in complete preoccupied earnestness, "You know, Audrey, you are a genius." It was an incredible thing to say in front of me and my friends. I don't think I heard too much after that. No way to account for it. I had been carrying on the way I usually did in his class, the one we had just come out of. But it meant a great deal to me, especially coming from him.[18]

As might be expected, Cohen's growing sense of self-confidence and security began to make her think about wider horizons beyond the comfortable community that had nurtured her. In later years she recalled that from her mid- to late teens on, the sense of feeling special expanded to feeling that she was important and would do something important in the world. She began to sense that her known world was a wonderful warm place but parochial. She wanted to know more, to get a bigger picture of what the world was like. As the time to choose a college approached, the itch to get a bigger picture resulted in a months-long screaming match between herself and her father. Abe Cohen wanted her to go to the University of Pittsburgh where she had a full scholarship, and Audrey wanted to go elsewhere.[19] In the end she went along with her father's wishes and enrolled as a freshman at the University of Pittsburgh in the fall of 1949.

Before moving on to her memories of college, two memories of Cohen's high school years are interesting to note because of what they suggest about her early intellectual inclinations and later life as an educational leader. In describing her extended family she mentioned an older cousin who had been in the army and then had became a successful surgeon. The young Audrey hero-worshipped him. In his office one day she noticed a book of poetry by Edna St. Vincent Millay. She remembered being very impressed that he, a doctor, also loved poetry.[20] Although the presence of a poetry book in the doctor's office may have been accidental, it is interesting that Cohen as a teenager was cognizant of conventional disciplinary boundaries and the possibility of going beyond them—an impulse that, as we see in later chapters, has always distinguished the curricular model of the college that she founded.

Another anecdote may serve to anticipate more problematical aspects of Cohen's later leadership style. In one high school class the teacher asked the students why drivers should always stop at least six feet from the back of a bus. Cohen answered, "to avoid the effect of gas fumes." Wrong, she was told. The right answer was "to avoid hitting the bus should it stop short." Cohen adamantly refused to be dismissed so lightly. She was certain that her answer was right. It made complete sense to her. Her father had told her that whenever they stopped at a gas pump they should avoid the dangerous fumes. "I still remember my sense of frustration and anger at my answer being so summarily dismissed as wrong, without considering the possibility of discussion."[21]

Cohen's response to the question was in fact quite far off the mark. Gas fumes do not come out of the rear of buses and are not really dangerous to breathe (though exhaust fumes are). Here we see a streak of stubbornness on Cohen's part, a need to be right in all circumstances, even when the evidence was largely against her. "She wouldn't take no for an answer," several of her close associates and friends recalled.[22] In later years her perseverance and fierce assertiveness would be seen as both her greatest strength and her most problematical weakness. She would be referred to as a visionary but also at times as overly controlling by those who knew her well.[23]

COLLEGE

In talking about her earlier life to family and friends Cohen always stressed the extracurricular experiences of her college years and said little about the more formal, academic side of her higher education. Highlighted in the version of her education that Cohen and her friends later constructed were the experiences with movements for social change that she was involved in during the summers and on weekends in the early 1950s—the civil rights movement, women's issues, and community organizing. By her own account her introduction to the political, social, and economic issues that would later come to a boil in the 1960s formed a more significant part of her education than her formal coursework.

One seminal moment of her early college years was to see a notice posted on a bulletin board at the University of Pittsburgh announcing a series of citizenship seminars sponsored by the YWCA that were to be held in the summer of 1952 in Washington, DC. Two young people would be chosen from each state to work during the day in a government office and at night to hear top members of the government discuss how policy was made and how the government actually functioned. Cohen applied and was accepted. This taught her something about not being fearful of taking a step into the unknown. Given that the internship experience was under the aegis of a Christian organization, she later noted that she might have been concerned that she would not be selected because of her name and her faith. But that did not occur to her at the time. One of the best experiences of her life, she recalled, was to really see what it was like to work in a federal agency and then to hear from the policy makers—everyone from the secretary of state to the president of the United States, Harry Truman. She later saw this experience as being tremendously significant in her overall development.[24] The government agency she was placed in was the Department of the Navy, and in the nightly seminars she came to realize that the rhetoric and positive statements made about the responsiveness of government by government leaders such as cabinet officers—and once even the President—did not reflect what she was seeing firsthand in the Navy Department.[25]

One consequence of that summer's work was to meet for the first time an independent woman whose satisfactions in life came from work rather than from a family. In a position requiring great skill, even if not granted much authority, the woman had the job of designing a system to keep track of Navy personnel around the world. She was able to use her mathematical skills to design a system that worked, and her success gave her a sense of accomplishment. The woman was also far ahead of the men in the department, none of whom had the skills to design the system she had developed. Although she had no status and no extra financial reward, she saw herself as a happy person, and, Cohen recalled, "she was an important mentor for me." In fact, this unnamed woman told Cohen that she hoped that Cohen would not devote herself only to raising children—that she would work. Up until then Cohen hadn't really looked beyond the present. "It was interesting that she even raised the idea of work, and I thought about it a lot."[26]

In Washington that same summer Cohen also became aware of racial segregation. The African American students she lived with could eat in only one of two places—across the street in a special club that opened its doors to the students and was willing to let the one or two negro students ("that was the term we used in those days," she told her daughter) join them, or in the Greyhound Bus Terminal. "Believe it or not," she went on to say, "everything else in our nation's capital, in 1952, was quite segregated. I saw this, for the first time up close, and recognized what a horrible injustice was being committed."[27] The need to work for social change and social justice was becoming clear.[28]

Cohen's perception of the need for social change and social justice led her to join two other groups—the Congress for Racial Equality (CORE) and the American Friends Service Committee (AFSC). Here, too, in later accounts of her own self-formation, Cohen emphasized how her work with both organizations had a formative influence on her values and choices in life. CORE had been founded in 1942 by an interracial group of students who had been influenced by Mahatma Gandhi's teachings about nonviolent resistance. It was one of the first groups to stage sit-ins to protest segregation in public accommodations, and by the early 1960s it would become one of the leading organizations in the civil rights movement.[29] Few people had heard of CORE in 1952, but that did not deter Cohen from taking up posters and joining in its demonstrations.[30] Her work with CORE gave Cohen solid ties to African American leaders like James Farmer, one of

CORE's co-founders, and Carl McCall, who later became comptroller for New York State and with whom she later was able to joke about having met on early marches in the civil rights movement. "Our mutual commitment and the links and friendships we forged then exist to this day," Cohen later recalled.[31]

During her college years Cohen also spent weekends with the AFSC, again in Washington, DC. Most of her work was on a special project to paint the frames of the houses of the black people who lived in the shadow of the Capitol "in abominable slums and yet were right there under the legislators' noses and treated as the great underclass of our society." The AFSC group was deliberately interracial, aiming to show by example that racial cooperation could lead to social progress. "We—Blacks and whites working together . . . wanted to show those who lived in poor communities that together we could bring about change."[32]

The range of Cohen's political interests in her college years was not limited to the nascent civil rights movement. The summer when Cohen was working as an intern in Washington she wanted to meet Secretary of State Dean Acheson, then under attack both for his liberal internationalism and for his refusal to engage in the "Red-baiting" tactics of Joseph McCarthy. Cohen wanted to meet Acheson to tell him that she believed in what he was doing. And so meet him she did—by going to the State Department, telling the guard in the lobby what she wanted, and being immediately whisked up to Acheson's office. "Anything other than the most direct route just didn't occur to her,"[33] a colleague commented when recalling this story. Although there is no record of what she actually said when she met Dean Acheson, as we see in Cohen's work as a college founder, her impulse to take the most direct route was often the key to her success.

In terms of Cohen's later founding of an educational institution known for its novel ways of combining of community work with academic study, her own perception of the importance of her extracurricular experiences during her college years is not surprising. As she put it later, her work with the YWCA, CORE, and the AFSC "awakened in me the sense that a powerful kind of learning takes place when you are involved in real life experience."[34] In retrospect, however, the role of formal college instruction in her overall development as an activist must not be underestimated.[35]

Cohen ended up graduating *magna cum laude* from an institution that throughout its history has provided one of the more rigorous settings for academic study in this country. At the time that Cohen was a student, the University of Pittsburgh (or Pitt, as it is often called) was a fully private institution with a reputation for both its research accomplishments and its strong commitment to the liberal arts. In the 1950s Jonas Salk was developing the polio vaccine there, and the college campus was well known for its Cathedral of Learning, a 42-story structure that since 1937 had housed the school's liberal arts department classrooms.[36]

Cohen later put great emphasis on the importance of what is generally known as the "humanities" in the curriculum of the college that she founded—a commitment that may have had its roots in her undergraduate years at Pitt. Her college transcript includes courses ranging from Music Appreciation, a Survey of Fine Arts, and the European Background of English Literature to American Government, Economic Principles, and General Zoology.[37] Typical of the broad liberal education that many colleges offered students in mid-twentieth-century America, the emphasis at Pitt was on breadth and understanding. In fine arts, for example, the College's 1949–1950 *Bulletin* stated that "all courses consider the visual arts largely from the historical and philosophical approach"; in philosophy the courses were "designed to enlarge people's views of nature and history, knowledge and language, morality and society, and art and religion."[38] The two history courses that Cohen elected to take also swept a broad path: a Survey of U.S. History covered, in two semesters, 1492 to 1948, and another was titled simply "History of Civilization."

At Pitt, Cohen pursued a double major—in education, to comply with her father's wishes, and in political science, to satisfy her own growing interests. She evidently did well enough in both subjects to earn high honors. It is interesting to speculate about the education courses that Cohen took at Pitt. Given MCNY's lasting commitment to progressive, hands-on, experiential education, one cannot help wondering about the extent to which Cohen absorbed the educational philosophy of John Dewey. Dewey is known as the father of progressive education in the United States, and his vast output of books and articles on making education more relevant, more social, and more democratic has had a long-term influence on American schooling, particularly in the private sector. Did Cohen ever read *The*

School and Society, Democracy and Education, Experience and Education, or even his short, early piece, "My Pedagogic Creed" that has long been a required text at the college that she founded? Was Dewey's philosophy a significant part of Audrey Cohen's education?

As an education major in the mid-1950s, Cohen was undoubtedly introduced to Dewey's ideas, probably in a course called "General Education Backgrounds" that she took as a junior in the fall of 1951. And clearly Cohen's lifelong commitment to making education connect to the life of a community suggests that Dewey's thinking had some resonance for Cohen. "She took John Dewey seriously, probably one of the few people in the world who has, and used him in her life in terms of the structure of education," one associate, Steven Sunderland, asserted.[39] Yet in her later years Cohen herself was known to make disparaging comments about Dewey and to belittle the influence that his ideas might have had on the college she founded. "Oh we've gone way beyond Dewey," she maintained, and she frequently denied being influenced by Dewey.[40] What explains Cohen's later resistance to such a likely source of her ideas?

Cohen's denials of a Deweyan influence on her thinking might simply be attributed to her well-known desire to take credit herself for the ideas that others gave her—a tendency that shows up in the testimony of her close associates. But there is another possible explanation. Cohen's college studies focused primarily on secondary education rather than on the early childhood or elementary classroom practices that are generally associated with Dewey's influence. The coursework that Cohen was required to complete at Pitt in order to prepare for high school teaching included two courses on "Teaching History and the Social Sciences" and another on "Measurement and Evaluation"—not subject matter generally associated with Deweyan methods. Hence it is possible that in the totality of her college learning Dewey's writings had little immediate importance, and in later years Cohen could conveniently imagine that she had given birth to what was in fact a very Deweyan model of education without any help from him.[41]

During her college years Cohen joined a number of extracurricular clubs and did her practice teaching at George Westinghouse High School. Westinghouse was located in a low-income neighborhood, and while there she was told by a colleague, "You shouldn't teach here. . . . You should be home raising kids of your own who will turn out like you."[42] In a conversation shortly before her death, Cohen told her gathered friends about a more alarming incident at Westinghouse. She was just out of college and looking for a teaching job in Pittsburgh. To apply for an opening, she had to present a lesson to the Board of Education that would then be evaluated. Her topic was, "The Causes and Cures of Crime," and after the presentation she was offered one of only three social science teaching jobs in the city, which happened to be at Westinghouse. During her brief teaching stint there, a student once threatened her with a knife. Cohen was not fazed. She looked the student in the eye and said, "Give me the knife." Several times she repeated, "Just give me the knife," keeping her eyes fixed on him. The young man finally handed over the knife. In retrospect Cohen characteristically saw this as a positive experience. It taught her "to deal with conflict," she told her friends.[43]

Cohen also taught in Jewish Sunday school while in Pittsburgh,[44] one of the few times that her religious heritage is apparent in her overall education as a visionary and activist. Unfortunately, except for the above story, which may be apocryphal, there is no record of how the twenty-two-year-old college graduate who would later become a pathbreaking educator experienced her first ventures into the world of teaching, or how her only slightly younger teenage students responded to her lessons.

Cohen's next educational pursuits would take place well beyond her Pittsburgh neighborhood.

TRAVELS WITH MARK

"My marriage to Mark Cohen proved to be a . . . catalyst for my self-discovery and self-development, and ultimately for the realization that I wanted to spend my life changing education,"[45] Audrey Cohen told her friend Alida Mesrop, years after Cohen had become the founding president of what was then the radically new College for Human Services. Although such a statement might be seen as an interpretation of her past that could only be made retrospectively, the theme of education flickered like a silver thread in the rich fabric of Cohen's early married life.

Audrey Cohen met her first husband, Mark Cohen, at a New Year's Eve party when she was in eleventh grade. He was a sophomore at Temple University in Philadelphia and had come home to Pittsburgh for the holidays.[46] They were introduced by mutual friends, Elaine Chaifeld and Alan Azen. Audrey had been close to Elaine since she was thirteen and was briefly dating Alan, who was Elaine's next door neighbor. Mark was a friend of Alan's.[47]

There must have been plenty of mixing at the party because two new couples emerged from the New Year's festivities that night. Elaine and Alan started dating and eventually they got married, and Audrey and Mark began to see each other that spring whenever Mark was back in town. In the fall of 1948, when Audrey was beginning her senior year of high school, Mark transferred to the University of Pittsburgh for his last two years of college.[48]

Elaine Azen-Lampl described Audrey in those years as "a dynamo," despite her small size. "She had full lips like Angelina Jolie before it became popular, and she always had a smile on her face." She was amicable but serious, and she wanted you to know that she was not to be taken lightly even though she was so small. "And everyone knew," Elaine added, "that Audrey was not going to stay on Flemington Street forever!"[49] Photos show her as more cute than beautiful, with closely cropped hair framing a round, soft face, and a gaze that was open and steady. Her skin was not flawless—a physical imperfection that she later took great pains to hide.[50]

Mark Cohen saw the seriousness of Audrey's intellectual interests early on. He remembers her writing a paper in high school that criticized the postwar American military presence in Okinawa, Japan. Although they rarely discussed political issues in those early years, he could see that she was beginning to think about questions relating to social justice, and he admired her moral convictions. "She was strong in her feelings from the first time I met her, about what was right and what was not right, and beginning to get some thoughts on how things might change." He also admired her gumption. In retrospect, he said, she had what Jane Addams, Lillian Wald, and other reformers have had, which was "the feeling that you never take 'no' for an answer." At least, he continued, you have to be told "no" twice or maybe three times before you go on to something else.[51]

Mark's family was more affluent than Audrey's and lived in the more prosperous northern residential area of Squirrel Hill. Although Audrey once joked that her mother-in-law felt that Audrey had come from "the other side of the tracks," Mark's father was, like Abe Cohen, an insurance agent (though at a higher managerial level), and the two families were close. It was probably no surprise to anyone when Mark and Audrey decided to get married in 1952, when he was in his last year of law school and she was still a senior in college. A newspaper picked up the news that a Cohen was marrying a Cohen, both attending different parts of the University of Pittsburgh at the same time, and, according to Mark, their pictures were in the newspaper.[52] "Being married and going to school seemed a lot to deal with," she later told a friend, but added that many young women of her generation were married within a year of finishing college.[53]

There was little chance that the bright and ambitious young couple would stay long in the tightly knit neighborhood of Squirrel Hill. They loved their parents and their families, but they did not have a strong desire to emulate them. Unlike Audrey's early sense of her father's progressive views, Mark's later assessment was that neither of their families was very active politically nor even very articulate in expressing any views outside of the norm of society. "We had parents who *did* take 'no' for an answer, and I guess we both grew up saying, 'We're not going to do that!'"[54]

The newlyweds were given a convenient push out of their parental nests by the U.S. Navy. In the 1950s every American male was required to complete two years of military service, and Mark's time in law school had caused him to delay fulfilling that requirement. By the fall of 1953, in order to avoid being drafted into the army, he enlisted in the naval intelligence program at the Officer Candidates School in Newport, Rhode Island. While there, he and Audrey shared a house with two other families, and during the day, when the men were in the training program, the wives spent time together. Audrey became a little more political at that point, Mark remembered, but not with any particular focus other than a sort of early feminism that was in the air.[55]

By the spring of 1954 Mark had completed his naval intelligence training and was assigned to a six-month tour of duty in Japan on an aircraft carrier out of San Diego, California. All of the other officers' wives stayed home or returned to their families to wait for their husband's return. But not Audrey Cohen. "She was the only woman relative of any sort, at any level—out of two thousand men on the ship" to follow her husband to Japan, Mark recalls with pride.[56] He first flew to San Diego, and then when the ship had a layover in Hawaii, she flew out to be with him. They were there for two weeks and had a very enjoyable visit.

Photos of the young couple in the early months of their marriage give a sense of Audrey and Mark's mutual attraction and compatibility. In most photos Mark is dressed in a suit or a naval uniform. Not a tall man, he is still several inches taller than Audrey and has a slender, wiry build. He has a handsome, open face, and there is a hint of a playful smile on his lips. She, too, is impeccably dressed—a habit that she kept throughout her life—her tiny waist accentuating shapely shoulders and arms. Her expression is contented and straightforward. Both of them look clean cut and open to new learning—very different from the "Ugly American"[57] who all too often accurately represented the postwar American presence in the Far East in the 1950s.

After their two weeks in Hawaii, Mark continued on the ship to Tokyo, where Audrey joined him (via a freighter, this time) for the next several months. They rented a room in a small hotel near the Tokyo railroad station because Mark had to leave by train at 5:15 every morning to get to his ship at the Navy base in Yokosuka. He would come home in the evening for dinner, spend the night, and then go back in the morning. "I loved Tokyo and so did she," Mark recalled.[58]

Postwar Japan provided a safe and stimulating context for Cohen to pursue her ongoing interest in education while exploring a new culture. She and Mark became enamored of Japan, and she felt comfortable exploring the country on her own. Audrey Cohen found that she could make friends and handle new and unusual situations. "I was learning to be self-sufficient," she later recalled. Together with Mark or on her own, she traveled to remote rural areas to visit potters' communities and elementary schools. She was often as interesting to the Japanese as they were to her, and many went out of their way to please her. One innkeeper, she remembered, piled up dozens of futons to make something equivalent to an American bed, "which I didn't want"; another insisted on preparing a bacon and egg breakfast when she would have preferred a Japanese breakfast.[59]

Through an odd chance meeting Audrey Cohen became acquainted with a Korean woman named Julie Moon who soon became a close friend and useful resource. Moon had been sent to Tokyo by her parents to live with a prominent Japanese family, the head of which was a member of the Japanese Diet. Moon's social contacts gave Cohen a chance to get a glimpse of Japan's evolving education system. Cohen had begun to be interested in the impact that the postwar infiltration of American ideas was having on Japanese schooling, and Moon provided a way for her to visit schools, both in Tokyo and in rural areas. Mark Cohen remembers that Audrey was struck by the contrast between what she referred to as "the traditional and the nontraditional" in Japanese life,[60] but although she was known to take detailed notes wherever she traveled,[61] unfortunately no records remain of her specific impressions of Japanese schools.

The contrast between the traditional and the nontraditional also struck Cohen in terms of gender roles in postwar Japan. In the 1950s and 1960s a Japanese woman was still expected to heat up her husband's bath water, serve him his food, and walk six feet behind him on public streets. Audrey was outspoken in her criticism of such practices. One day she and Mark went to visit the Japanese editor of what was then the predominant English-language newspaper in Japan. The man greeted them kindly and they had a long conversation about current events, and near the end of the conversation he spoke admiringly about his wife. Audrey was impressed and mentioned the possibility of the two couples having dinner together. The editor immediately squashed the proposal. "In Japan we don't mix our business with our family life, and we don't generally have an entertainment dinner . . . with non-Japanese." As the Cohens were getting ready to leave, he said to her, "You know, Mrs. Cohen, the more a woman understands her place, the better off she is." Audrey said, "Thank you. Good-bye!" and quickly walked out of the office.[62]

By the time Mark Cohen's six-month tour of duty in Japan was over and the couple had returned briefly to California, it was clear to Audrey that she could never be happy in the traditional homemaker role that women at that time were generally expected to occupy. She also recognized that she was itching to become somehow involved in movements for social change. After doing substitute teaching in California while waiting for Mark's next assignment, she was convinced that she was "the world's greatest teacher" and was more interested than ever in education. But how she might combine her interest in education with her passion for social change was not yet clear.[63]

Indeed, the way to combine her two consuming passions would not become clear to Audrey for several more years. In the meantime, Mark's next naval intelligence assignment took the couple to Morocco, where they encountered an even more surprising culture than the one they had encountered in Japan. Audrey Cohen later shared little about the eighteen months that she and Mark lived in Morocco, perhaps because she could not travel around the country alone as she had in Japan and because she was pregnant for the last nine months that they were there. For a sense of Audrey and Mark's life in Morocco one must rely on the memories of John Rodgers, who became their close friend at the time and who later became chair of the Board of Trustees of the college that Audrey Cohen founded.

A native New Yorker, Rodgers had attended private schools in the city and had graduated from Harvard College and Harvard Law School. He arrived in Morocco a few months ahead of Mark Cohen, but they were both assigned to the U.S. Navy Fleet Intelligence Center for the Eastern Atlantic and Mediterranean on a base near what is now Kenitra but was then called Port Lyautey. Rodgers had a car, and he drove Mark to the airport to pick up Audrey when she arrived in the summer of 1955. At their first meeting Audrey struck Rogers as soft spoken and charming, though he would later see her tough side. He also remembered that when the three of them stopped for lunch she ordered iced tea, then a novelty that neither he nor the Moroccan restaurant had ever encountered. To his surprise, she got what she wanted, something he would often witness in years to come.[64] Audrey's impressions of John Rodgers were also favorable. She remembered him as different from other intelligence officers, who rarely left the base and had little interest in the country where they were stationed. Unlike most American servicemen, John had learned Arabic and left the base whenever he could to learn about Morocco, its culture, and its people. In Audrey he found both a companion and a student.[65]

Rodgers lived in the bachelor officers' quarters on the base, and the Cohens rented an apartment in the town, but the three often got together to explore the surrounding area in Rodgers's car or in the Cohens' newly purchased Volkswagen. Morocco was moving toward independence from France in 1955, and the political situation was in flux. Not only was there tension between the Moroccans and the French, but the Moroccan population itself was divided among those who had received a French education, those who had received a more traditional Islamic education, and the Berbers who were the original inhabitants of the countryside.[66] Mark Cohen later published a book about the country's political and social challenges during these transitional years entitled *Morocco: Old Land, New Nation*, much of the information for which he gathered during his travels with Audrey and John Rodgers.[67]

Driving around Morocco in the 1950s was not without its risks. One time they traveled to Tétuan, in what was then Spanish Morocco, the northern part of the country near the Straits of Gibraltar. They spent a couple of nights at the Durasau Hotel and by day explored the city with its wide streets, marble fountains, and tile work. The day after they had returned to Kenitra, Rodgers met Mark outside of an intelligence office on the base. "Did you hear that they blew up the Durasau Hotel?" Mark asked. Then with a twinkle he added, "Well, they missed us again!" Another time the three friends were in Marrakesh and had entered the Medina, the old walled city with its complex maze of narrow streets. Suddenly there was a disturbance in the crowd. Mark and John started heading toward what they thought was an exit but Audrey refused to leave. She wanted to go find out what the agitation was all about. "Mark was having a fit, you know, trying to get her out of there," Rodgers remembers. "Getting her out was no easy job."[68]

Rodgers describes another episode that revealed Audrey Cohen's powerful curiosity and fierce will. He and Mark and a friend who sometimes accompanied them planned to drive east into Tlemcen, Algeria, to see what was going on. By now Audrey was several months pregnant, and the men knew that the trip would take them over bumpy roads and through areas where there was political unrest. Without telling her they decided to leave her behind. The trip turned out to be more dangerous than they expected. In Tlemcen the three Americans were arrested and spent a long time trying to explain to French military officials what they were doing there. Eventually they returned safely. That evening there was a cocktail party on the base, and John Rodgers spotted Audrey across the room. She made a beeline in his direction, and he realized rather quickly that Mark had broken the news that they had gone into Algeria without her. Her "beams of light bore down on me!" Rodgers recalled. "All I could do was feel sorry for Mark, because he got it first." Audrey made it clear that if the three of them had been hung in the village square, it would not have been such a terrible thing because that was what they deserved for having left her behind.[69]

In discussing Audrey Cohen's strong personality John Rodgers tells one more story about his months in Morocco with the Cohens. He and another officer had had dinner with Mark and Audrey, and as the two bachelors were walking back to the base the other man was commenting about Audrey's strong character. Then he said, "You know something? I bet we all end up working for her!" As Rodgers often points out, because he eventually ended up as a member of the Board of Trustees of the college that Audrey Cohen founded, the officer's prediction turned out to be true.

During their eighteen months in Morocco, Audrey Cohen continued to pursue her interest in education, at this point not so much by visiting Moroccan schools as by honing her own teaching skills in an elementary school on the base, where she spent most of her weekdays.[70] Interestingly, however, especially given their future joint efforts at the college that she founded, John Rodgers does not recall any discussions about her teaching and never got the impression at the time that she would make a career out of education.[71]

PART-TIME RESEARCH ASSOCIATES

In February 1957, six weeks before the Cohens were scheduled to leave Morocco, their first daughter, Dawn Jennifer Cohen, was born. In March, Mark completed his term of service for the U.S. Navy, and the young family returned to Washington, DC, where Mark got a job as a tax lawyer in the General Council's office at the Internal Revenue Service.[72] In later reflecting on her early years of motherhood, Audrey Cohen recognized that her feelings were mixed. Like most young mothers she delighted in the miracle of Dawn's birth and growth: it was "an enormous source of pleasure," she recalled, to watch her daughter's development. With a copy of Arnold Gesell and Frances Ilg's classic *Infant and Child in the Culture of Today* at her fingertips, Audrey constantly compared Dawn's development with what Giselle and Ilg described as normal at each stage,[73] noting how far ahead of other children Dawn was. Audrey proudly recalled seeing

Dawn struggling to walk and noted that she achieved this remarkable feat "to perfection" by the time she was nine months old.[74]

At the same time, however, Audrey admitted that she felt somewhat unprepared for motherhood. Her younger brother had been born six years after her, and she hadn't paid much attention to his upbringing, so raising a child was a novel experience. Moreover, she noted that both in Morocco and in the United States at that time, there was little done to support a new mother or to help her in understanding her new role. Women with a strong drive and motivation to do everything well, she said, had to assume that they needed both "to give our children the best of ourselves and at the same time to be the perfect woman in the house." She remembered spending most of her time in those early years cleaning and cooking and got nothing out of "spending hours washing the floors, as well as singing to Dawn and helping her to do what she most naturally was doing anyhow."[75]

Like many college-educated women whose lives become focused solely on domestic chores, Cohen began to feel that she needed something more for her own fulfillment. She took some graduate level courses in political science and education at George Washington University, but she did not pursue that path.[76] She started looking for a way that she could work and at the same time take care of Dawn and later also Wendy, her second daughter, born eighteen months after Dawn.

By chance at a Washington dinner party she happened to meet Frances (Frankie) Pelzman, who felt the same way. Down-to-earth and friendly, with a quick mind and an easy laugh, Frankie Pelzman had children around the same age as Audrey's, a deep interest in women's issues, and a supportive husband. While their children played together on the lawn or napped in their cribs, Frankie and Audrey talked at length about their need to work, their own abilities, and what they might do. "We looked beyond ourselves, reasoning that there must be other women, like us, who wanted to both work and raise children," Cohen recalled. They began to speculate about creating a new enterprise. Suppose they set themselves up as a business to carry out various short-term projects that organizations were faced with and for which they had no staff? Cohen and Pelzman envisioned that they could make all the arrangements and bill for their services. The organization might also provide a way to create employment for other talented women.

This germ of an idea, she later said, grew into Part-Time Research Associates (PTRA), an organization that would have a significant influence on her not-yet-imagined and still to be founded college.[77]

Although the two women had never done anything like it before, in late 1958 and early 1959 they set to work to create what was at first an outlet for their own interests but would eventually become a profitable enterprise. They designed letterhead, sent out press releases, and made contacts that they hoped would lead to part-time work for educated women like themselves. "Female Intelligence: Who Wants It?" read the top line on their outreach letters. Services offered included research jobs, rush projects, proofreading, fact-finding, library research, even man-on-the-street interviews.[78]

At the outset there was little to show for their efforts. As Pelzman described the process, she herself was an "inside" kind of person, and Cohen tended to be an "outside" kind of person. Cohen was "very vivacious, very determined, not shy at all, and convinced that she had a good thing going." It was Cohen who went to the Department of Labor and other agencies and made the pitch for PTRA. "We have these wonderful people," she would say to anyone who would listen. "Do you see a place in your agency where we could work out some part-time work for people who you couldn't normally hire?"[79] Despite the women's enthusiasm and hard work, the new venture did not find work for more than a few of its many applicants during Cohen's early years in Washington, and when Pelzman became pregnant with her third child she had to limit her commitment to the project.

Despite struggles with the new venture, the Cohens and the Pelzmans remained close friends. Pelzman later recalled a dinner party at the Cohens' small apartment in Bethesda, Maryland. There were about twelve people, and Audrey and Mark made a circle of little wooden chairs in their living room. People went to the sideboard and took their food and came back. "You were sitting knee to knee with the person on either side of you, and there wasn't any room to move." Yet the beef stroganoff that Audrey had prepared was delicious, and Mark served good wine. There was lots of political talk and an interesting mixture of people. "Our friendships were enriched by no one more than Audrey," Pelzman remembered,[80] and her husband Fred later concurred: "Audrey was a real spark plug."[81] The Cohens had gotten to know newcomers in Washington—young lawyers who had come to work in the Solicitor General's office, in the Civil Rights office, in the Justice Department, or in a Chicago law firm opening an office—"and they all had very smart wives." It was eye-opening for Frankie Pelzman: "Our parents never gave that kind of dinner party!"[82]

Part of the success of the Cohen dinner parties was undoubtedly the attention that Audrey devoted to planning them. Frankie noted that Audrey kept a little file in which she would record what she had prepared for each dinner, who was invited, and what kind of wine had been served.[83] The habit of meticulously recording useful information was noted by several of Audrey's friends, and was one that would come in handy when she was founding a college later on.

By 1959 Mark Cohen's work prospects once again signaled change and opportunity for the couple. Eager to experience new challenges, Mark transferred from Washington, DC to New York City, where he took a job with the U.S. Attorney's Office. The young family moved into an apartment in Stuyvesant Town, very different from the Bethesda, Maryland apartment they had rented while he worked in Washington. The Cohens welcomed the change; New York was where they both had always wanted to live.[84]

Once in New York, Audrey helped set up an organization called Gallery Passport, Ltd. that arranged unique tours of private art galleries led by recognized teachers, writers, and artists.[85] But she continued to devote her main energies to continuing the work she and Frankie Pelzman had begun. They decided to carry on their work with both a Washington office and a New York office, with the Washington office of Part-Time Research Associates being run out of Pelzman's home and the New York office based in Cohen's Stuyvesant Town apartment. She later recalled working there "with Dawn and Wendy constantly at my knee."[86]

Soon after the Cohens' move to New York, a reporter from the *New York Times* took notice of the women's new venture. "Two disgruntled housewives met at a Washington dinner party . . . and an employment service was born," begins the story on the women's unique entrepreneurial venture. "I suppose you could sum us up as qualified women who want to do worthwhile work of a creative nature during the years when our main vocation is taking care of our families," Cohen is reported as saying. As a result of this free publicity, resumes and requests for services flooded in. The research associates for whom they found part-time work included graduates from Swarthmore, Radcliffe, Smith, and New York University; some had completed graduate work and nearly all were married with young children. Clients included advertising and public relations agencies, newspaper correspondents, radio stations, and attorneys.[87] "There was nothing like this at the time," Audrey Cohen later told her daughter, Dawn. "Nothing existed to address the tremendous waste of human power that existed at that time—women."[88] Eventually PTRA could boast of keeping on file the skills of more than one thousand women[89] and having completed research for the U.S. State Department, for Union Carbide, and for Nelson Rockefeller's campaign for governor.[90]

Remembering the experience in later years, Cohen observed that the founding of Part-Time Research Associates was indicative of her thinking and her *modus operandi*. Something that was important to her—doing meaningful work and getting paid for it—reflected a more general social need and was turned into a concept. Moreover, she reasoned, she was meeting not only her own needs but the needs of many women who wanted to work part time while raising their children.[91] Cohen's ability to turn a social need into a concept and to focus on enabling women with children to do meaningful work would underpin many more accomplishments over the next thirty years.

CHAPTER 3

"MY FORK IN THE ROAD PRESENTED ITSELF" (1964–1965)

In light of contemporary events, 1963 and 1964 were halcyon days when the world seemed to be charged with a feeling of hope. I rode on the crest of that hope and harnessed its energy and vision for what became a new institution and a new system of education.[1]

—Audrey Cohen, as recounted by Alida Mesrop

The bright red, black, and white logo for Metropolitan College of New York includes in small upper case print the words, "FOUNDED BY AUDREY COHEN IN 1964." According to the college's own version of its history, the seed for the institution's future growth was planted in that year, for it was then that the idea for the institution first took root in Audrey Cohen's mind. As the story that follows reveals, it took more than two years of hard work before her vision became realized into anything resembling an educational program, and as with any successful planting, the process required the right climate and lots of luck.

By 1963 Cohen's work with Part-Time Research Associates had become successful and was allowing a growing number of well-educated, middle-class women to participate meaningfully in the work force. An article about PTRA that appeared in the *Christian Science Monitor* in early 1964 is entitled "Spare Time Made Profitable."[2] But gradually Cohen began to feel that helping well-off women find work was not enough. She felt a constant pull between trying to run a business and being socially conscious. She noted that only a handful of women were being helped by PTRA. "For every one woman I provided with a social research project, 100 were still unserved." She asked herself what she could do that would involve all of the educated women who had contacted her and at the same time make a difference to women who were poor.[3] "How could these two groups help each other," she asked herself, "the poor who wanted to work and had no chance, and those who had education and skills and wanted to use these to improve people's lives?"[4]

In a speech written later, Cohen's own account of her thought process during those crucial months in 1964 is spelled out in detail. She explained that while PTRA was successful, there were two issues that began to gnaw at her conscience. First, there were many well-educated women who had had training in social services—in health, education, and welfare—and who were looking for meaningful work but were not qualified to undertake the rigorous research-based tasks then required by the corporate firms and government agencies with which she contracted. Second, didn't poor, less well-educated women need jobs even more than those who Part-Time Research Associates was hiring?

Cohen began to see her role as bringing these two groups of women together—those with extensive skills and training, especially within the helping professions, and those less privileged who desperately wanted to learn these same skills in order to use them to improve their own lives and their communities. It was this vision, she goes on to say, to combine opportunities for two major groups of women who had been previously blocked from employment, "to put previously untapped human talent to work building a better society," that led her to establish the Women's Talent Corps.[5] In another context she reiterated this impulse. "I began to see my role as bringing together two groups of women—those with extensive skills and training, especially within the helping professions, and those who wanted to learn these same skills so as to use them in their own communities—and thus focusing their joint efforts on service where so much was needed, and so much was lacking."[6]

In the context of the history of the women's movement, Cohen's impulses at this time are noteworthy. Although she was in tune with what subsequently came to be called the second wave of feminism and was pushing for women to have opportunities in a world dominated by men, Cohen's aim to bring together two very different groups—even classes—of women was unusual. Much of the energy of mainstream feminism in the mid-1960s was devoted to demonstrations, consciousness-raising groups, and the fight for freedom of choice in terms of abortion rights—actions that later on, in the third wave of feminism, often led to splits within the movement, especially along class lines. Cohen's efforts were different. Always more practical than ideological, her stress was on bringing women together to meet a specific need.[7]

In a playfully staged interview with her daughter Dawn that she taped and transcribed (but did not label with a date), Cohen refers to her crucial decisions during 1963 and 1964 in more open-ended language. She admits that Part-Time Research Associates began making a fair amount of money. "Our hard work finally began to pay off in cash," and she probably could have built it into an even larger and more important corporation. But soon she came to realize that her original mission of wanting to assist other women as well as herself was not being realized, in part because she had to reject so many women who had been trained as teachers, social workers, counselors, or for other occupations in the helping professions.[8]

> My fork in the road was presenting itself. . . . [D]id I pursue the corporation making money and employ the best talent? Or did I go back to my original desire to create something valuable for women generally?
>
> I made the decision in 1964 clearly to move ahead and to think about the role of all women and to allow myself to grow and develop into a broader range of activities rather than pursuing the profit motive which would have been one of the exclusive. . . . (the transcription breaks off here)[9]

Cohen's somewhat awkward reference to a "fork in the road that presented itself" (the phrase is followed by the word "fix" in parentheses) raises interesting questions about motivation. How can we understand Cohen's choice to forego the pursuit of profit and opt instead for a more risky path of creating something valuable for women "generally"? What were the sources of Cohen's mission to assist women who lacked the advantages of relative wealth and education that she had been given? Where does the motive to do something good for others come from?

The version of her life story that Cohen passed on to her friends and associates over the years suggests that her values were shaped by her father's social consciousness, by her schooling, and by her formative experiences in the civil rights movement. Chapter 2 has generally reaffirmed that version of her story. We should be skeptical, however, of any unidirectional causality in an individual's personal narrative. Cohen's younger brother presumably experienced the same parental influences that she did, and yet his life took a different path. Other young people in Pittsburgh in the 1940s and 1950s undoubtedly attended the same schools and may even have participated in the same civil rights activities as she did, but they did not end up founding a college for low-income women in New York City or even think about the needs of people beyond their own communities and well-tended backyards. Although Cohen's upbringing, education, and early experiences in the world may have helped shape her values as a mature person, they cannot be seen as defining her. Everyone encounters a wide range of stimuli throughout life; the ways that some of those stimuli influence later actions and some do not remains a mystery that neither biologists nor philosophers have yet been able to solve.[10]

However, in any chance fit between a developing self and its changing circumstances, the historical context may play an important role. Cohen later acknowledged the importance of her own historical moment. "What could I structure so that women trained as teachers and social workers could help women who were low income?" This is followed by the assertion that "the question of how to do this became all consuming," and she ends the paragraph with the statement, "the climate of the times provided the solution."[11]

The climate of the times in 1964 was certainly an important factor in the realization of Cohen's dreams. As Bob Dylan sang out in 1964, "The Times They Are A-Changin'," and foremost among the changes was a new openness about what was possible in terms of addressing the needs of the poor. In 1961 John F. Kennedy had established the Peace Corps as a way for young people to fight poverty in developing nations, and in 1962 Michael Harrington's *The Other America* alerted Americans who had been lulled into complacency by middle-class affluence to the fact that extreme poverty still existed in the United States. In 1963 Martin Luther King Jr.'s "I Have a Dream" speech reminded his audience that one hundred years after Lincoln's Emancipation Proclamation, "the Negro lives on a lonely island of poverty in the midst of a vast ocean of material prosperity."[12] And in May 1964, Lyndon B. Johnson, who had become president the previous November after the assassination of John F. Kennedy, announced the goal of creating a "Great Society" that would aim for the elimination of poverty and racial injustice through new programs in education, medical care, and urban renewal. As Cohen's close friend Frankie Pelzman later remarked, in the early 1960s there was a "fizz" in the air that made almost anything seem possible.[13]

A FOCUS ON JOBS

Interestingly, in light of the future development of the Women's Talent Corps, Cohen's thought process in 1964 focused on the creation of jobs for women even before she began thinking about a training program. Many of the resumes that had been submitted to Part-Time Research Associates were from women in the helping professions, so her thoughts began to turn in that direction.[14] The memories of Audrey's younger daughter, Wendy Cohen, reinforce this view: "My mother didn't start out to found a college. She wanted to help poor women get jobs."[15]

As Audrey Cohen began to think about jobs in the helping professions, more questions came to mind. What kinds of jobs already existed? What kinds of new jobs might be needed? How were the helping professions organized and what did the surrounding power structure look like? Did women have any role in those organizations? Was there something that could be designed to give women leadership responsibilities in the service organizations that controlled their lives? Immediately her thinking "moved from the situation as I saw it to the possibilities that did not at that time exist."[16] Although there were jobs for teachers, social workers, guidance counselors, and psychologists, there were no "assist" roles built into those professions that could be held by people who were not professionals themselves. There were no teacher assistants, no social work assistants, no legal assistants, and no guidance counselor assistants.

In recalling her thought process during these years Cohen makes clear the importance of active participation in any program for social empowerment. Organizations like schools, hospitals, mental institutions, and prisons play an enormous role in the lives of citizens, and they are especially important, Audrey told Dawn, for the low-income citizens, whose very survival depends on the support and guidance and assistance that they can receive from these institutions. Yet these very institutions did not employ people from the community in 1964. Cohen began to see a problem that perhaps she could help solve. "I looked around and saw that in the very professions in which women dominated in terms of numbers, there were huge areas where people could come and begin to work at a level below the professional but above entry level." Once they got involved, she said, these women—these "community people"—could eventually move from a beginning job to a professional job.[17]

Given the eventual evolution of Cohen's vision, it is interesting to see that even at this point her thinking about the possibility of creating new above entry-level jobs for women in the helping professions included thoughts about how one might *educate* women for these new jobs. What kind of education might facilitate entry into such jobs? Moving away from the traditional concept of education, where you take so many courses for so many credits and "when you have served your time you get out stamped with a credential," Cohen asked the question: What if women could go to school and also work and blend their understanding of their work with their theoretical knowledge until finally they achieve professional competence?[18]

Here was the genesis of Cohen's two-pronged approach to the problem of poverty—to create what are now called *paraprofessional* jobs for women *and* at the same time to train women for those jobs.[19] To make this dream a reality, in 1964 she began to travel throughout the city trying to convince leaders (eventually meeting with hundreds of them) that there was a need for new positions in city agencies for women from low-income communities. At the same time she was also working to persuade teachers, social workers, lawyers, and other professionals who had had a traditional education, to work as educators for the women wishing to enter the new subprofessional positions.[20]

To effect change one must work on a wide range of levels simultaneously. For Cohen in 1964 this meant building an organization, getting local support, designing jobs, putting together a group that would eventually become a Board of Directors, and, as she put it, "diffusing opposition."[21]

In all of this work Cohen was not alone; as she stated on the phone to Alida Mesrop in 1964, she was "going to need some help" in implementing her ideas.[22] She would later describe the outreach process as follows:

> After the initial satisfaction of creating a solution to our own problems of juggling roles as wives, mothers of young children and working women, we now were driven to expand, adapt, and build on that experience to solve a larger more critical social problem: creating an education for those other women of talent who lacked our educational advantages but who were no less capable of making a contribution to society. . . .
>
> [Although it was] my idea initially, my co-workers seized it, rallied to it, and it became our idea. . . . They became the crusading core, the proposal writers and rewriters, the researchers, the lobbyists, persuaders, network builders—all unpaid, of course.[23]

Several of Cohen's early collaborators on the project had been involved with Part-Time Research Associates. They shared her view that the talents of educated women were often underused and her social conviction that such underutilization was even greater in the case of undereducated or low-income women. They also shared a desire to see practical results. "All of us were action-oriented. We thought, talked about and researched social issues. Ultimately we wanted . . . to make needed changes happen."[24]

One early source of help was Jane Addams Caulfield, a friend whom Cohen had met in Stuyvesant Town where they both lived and who had worked on projects for Part-Time Research Associates. Caulfield had grown up in Lancaster, Pennsylvania, and was named after the early-twentieth-century social reformer Jane Addams, who was also her godmother.[25] When she and Cohen first met, Caulfield was working alongside Barbara Walton at the Institute for International Education. Caulfield was supportive of Cohen's project in its early years, and it was she who introduced Cohen to Barbara Walton and to Judy Hozore, both of whom became important members of the staff.

Working out of the kitchen of her Stuyvesant Town apartment ("lavender and blue matching my favorite scarf," one early associate remembered[26]),

Cohen began the process of creating a new organization. She and her staff were hemmed in on all sides with file cabinets, boxes, and rolodexes and had to work long days and long nights. But gradually a proposal shaped up that was meticulously researched and thought out and that incorporated constructive suggestions from a wide range of sources. The women were united in their belief that what they were doing was extremely important. "It was so logical," one of them remembered. "As discrimination statutes were being struck down, what we were doing had to be the next step. What the civil rights movement needed now were decent jobs with upward mobility."[27]

COMMUNITY OUTREACH

But what kinds of jobs? A sign of Cohen's genius at this point was to go into low-income communities and simply *ask* what kind of work needed to be done and what kind of work the women in those communities wanted to do to improve their lives. To undertake these investigations she knew that she needed professional knowledge that she did not yet have. She needed to know what to look for, how to listen, and, especially how to record her findings—skills that were outside of the training in education and political science that she had received as an undergraduate at the University of Pittsburgh a decade earlier. In a characteristically gutsy way, she picked up the phone one day and called Margaret Mead, the most famous anthropologist in the world at that time. "I didn't know that you don't just call Margaret Mead," she later commented.[28] Margaret Mead put Cohen in touch with two anthropologists, one of whom was Hope Leichter.

To ask for advice from an anthropologist rather than a social worker or sociologist was an important decision on Cohen's part. Purporting neither to provide services as a social worker would do, nor to analyze the community's social problems as a sociologist might do, Cohen's impulse was to become an activist observer by letting the members of the community identify their own resources and eventually improve the services available to them. Like an anthropologist, her aim was to understand the communities she intended to visit rather than to impose her own views on them.[29]

Leichter turned out to be an extremely important contact. On the faculty of Teachers College, Columbia University, Leichter had received her doctorate in anthropology from Harvard in 1959 and was interested in Cohen's project from the start. "It was important and different, something for women by a woman who saw women as bright, talented, having something to contribute."[30] Through a grant from the Ford Foundation Leichter had worked on a paraprofessional training program at Teachers College and was committed to a collaborative research model that seemed to fit with Cohen's project.[31] Most importantly, through Leichter's expertise as an anthropologist Cohen learned to listen, to ask the right questions, and through listening and questioning to understand more accurately the jobs that people in the communities she was trying to serve were trying to define for her.[32]

Leichter accompanied Cohen a few times on her forays into low-income communities, but most of the time Cohen made the trips alone. (She didn't have the resources to pay Leichter for more.) "I went into Harlem, Bed-Stuy, the South Bronx, and I suppose every major low-income community of this city," Cohen later recalled. "Several nights a week I went to Brooklyn, to the Bronx, to the Lower East Side. I would find these old school auditoriums or these developments where the people had invited me to come talk to a group of women. Then I would find my way back to the subway and come home without the slightest worry that anything would happen."[33]

Cohen felt no fear in situations that others might find daunting. Similar to her confrontation with the student with a knife that was mentioned in Chapter 2 is a story that her daughter, Wendy Cohen, tells about an encounter during these months of groundwork for the Women's Talent Corps. Coming home alone late one night from an outreach event, her mother was suddenly accosted by a mugger. "In that split second she knew she had to stand up for herself," Wendy recalled recently in a speech to the graduating class of the college that her mother later founded. "Although she was barely 5-feet, 1 inch, and 100 pounds, and had no martial arts training whatsoever, she took the stance of a karate expert and yelled 'HI-YA!' Immediately the mugger went running off."[34] When Wendy told this story, the mostly adult, female, minority audience roared with cheers and applause.

How did Cohen know where to go? How did she make contacts? Her later recollections reveal her persistence in what later would be termed *networking*. She would call up a friend and get the name of someone she sensed was a natural leader. That this was well before there were community development agencies and organizations set up to find talent in low-income communities, so she had to do the research herself. She would ask people she knew who had contacts in the local communities, like ministers and priests.[35] The women she reached out to were those local activists who were doing the kinds of things usually done by social workers and teachers with advanced degrees. In every housing development there are women who serve as natural social workers, she told Dawn, who care about their neighbors, who help them get to places that they have to get to when they have a problem and "who are totally supportive and who really knock themselves out to do the kind of service we get trained as professionals to do." She located about half a dozen of these natural social workers and contacted them. She asked them if they would have a few women in for coffee and let her tell them about her idea to open up new kinds of positions in the agencies operating in the community. Some of the women agreed to host meetings, and Cohen would arrive to find four, five, or six women sitting in an apartment. "I would come up, and we would meet after the children were in bed. It was very important, of course, for the women that these meetings be held at night."[36]

How did the women respond? Dawn asked her mother. How did they react to a self-appointed crusader from a middle-class background, "telling them that you could make their lives better by an idea that you had formulated?" In her answer Audrey Cohen pinpointed what was probably the most important factor in her approach: she asked the women how they could *see themselves* working to improve the agencies and institutions that affected their lives. The initial hesitancy that might have occurred was overcome because they could see themselves actually performing in these agencies. "The way I phrased the questions to them," Cohen recalled, "often excited their interest and motivation because I said to them, 'Do you see anything in your community, in these agencies, schools, and hospitals and so on that *you* could do to support the work of these agencies?' "[37]

It is interesting to compare Cohen's community outreach methods with those of Saul Alinsky, generally considered to be the "father" of mod-

ern community organizing in the United States.[38] Alinsky's work was familiar both to Hilary Clinton, who wrote her senior honors thesis on him, and
to Barack Obama, who studied Alinsky's writings in preparation for his own
community organizing work in Chicago in the 1990s. Recent commenta-
tors have even detected Alinsky's influence on the grassroots organizing
of the Tea Party movement.[39] But whereas Alinsky's strategy focused on
agitation—on making a community become aware of its collective resentments and then persuading its members to take action[40]—Cohen's method
put the emphasis on positive *personal* change. By asking active community
women (whom Cohen referred to as the "natural leaders") what they could
see *themselves* doing to improve the service agencies in their communities,
she opened up a new way of thinking that eschewed any sense of victim-
ization or resentment.

Cohen's questions to her listeners brought forth an outpouring of
opinions, as she told her daughter, about how they could help. The wom-
en saw themselves as helping teachers teach, working with children with
reading challenges or with behavioral problems; they saw themselves helping to make the work more tolerable in a clinic or a hospital, getting to
the patients faster and giving them the support and nurturance that they
needed.[41]

In some ways Cohen's methods were not very radical. The women
she recruited saw themselves playing in a more formal setting the roles that
they had already been playing as natural leaders; they envisioned themselves
improving the delivery of services by doing what they had always done as
women with nurturing capacities and compassion. They saw themselves,
Cohen recalled, "using those very fine qualities that many women have been
acculturated to and which men have too although not as great a degree,
and they saw themselves actually doing it to improve service delivery so
that part of their hesitancy was overcome quickly."[42] Here there was no
mention of a glass ceiling that might hinder women's advancement, no
suggestion of gender discrimination in employment.

Yet from another perspective Cohen's method *was* very radical. In
essence she was attempting to bring social services into low-income communities without disrupting them, thus avoiding the condescension ingrained
in most of the practice of social work.[43] And in reflecting on the evolution
of the college that eventually grew out of Cohen's 1964 to 1966 community

outreach, one might note here that her impulse to ask the women she spoke with to imagine what *they* could do to improve the services being offered to them aligns closely with the later institution's emphasis on *empowerment*— a concept that suggests the possibility for radical change. As is shown in later chapters, "empowerment" was a relatively new term when the college first began to use it in the early 1970s, but since that time it has become a guiding principle of MCNY's curriculum. Students every semester are asked to do a "needs assessment" of the human service agencies or businesses where they are working or interning and then come up with a "plan of action" for meeting that need. The documentation of their actions that students are required to submit provides evidence that in many cases the process has, over the years, succeeded in empowering either individuals or communities in fundamental, if not radical, ways. In her early forays into low-income communities Cohen herself was in fact encouraging her listeners to become the kind of change agents that her college would later pride itself on producing.

Throughout her outreach work Cohen approached her listeners thinking of what she shared with them, not what might have separated her from them. Citing her tendency not to let herself be discouraged by what might have been overwhelming obstacles, she recalled that she really didn't dwell on the differences in cultural background, financial background, or educational background that differentiated her from her audience. Rather, she concentrated on "what we had in common, our womanhood, our need to be recognized in society, our need to support each other, our need to improve service delivery, our need to care." By focusing on these commonalities, she said, her own sincerity must have come through, because she never had anybody treat her in a negative way at any of those meetings.[44]

Driving Cohen's sincerity was her personal passion for her work. On one trip to the South Bronx she met Evelina Antonetti, the founder of United Bronx Parents, an organization that began as an effort to improve local public elementary schools but eventually led to the establishment of programs serving homeless mothers, substance abusers, and those infected with the HIV virus. Although Cohen and Antonetti came from very different backgrounds, the two women established a close working friendship that lasted for decades. Antonetti's daughter, Lorraine Montenegro, fondly remembers her mother's and Cohen's conversations about community needs, networking, and fundraising. In her dress and appearance, Montenegro recalls, Cohen always appeared to be very "proper," but once she started talking "her warmth and caring came pouring out!"[45]

Indeed, far from treating her in a negative way at those early meetings in low-income women's apartments, the women invited her back to speak to larger groups. Many of the women had ties with civic organizations or religious groups, and so it was easy for them to arrange for a meeting in a school auditorium or large church. They would send the word out, and dozens of people would come to the meetings. At the larger gatherings Cohen would make essentially the same pitch that she had made to the smaller groups.[46]

In addition to opening her listeners' minds to their own self-empowerment and making them feel comfortable by stressing what they shared, a key factor in Cohen's success in these early efforts was that, unlike many of the other well-meaning activists who were working in Harlem, Bedford Stuyvesant, and the South Bronx in the mid-1960s, Cohen kept her word and *came back* once the money for her project came through. One thing she always did to win trust was to take down names and addresses and assure everyone that when her project got funded she would give each of them the opportunity of becoming participants in the Women's Talent Corps.[47] And, in fact, when the money did come through, when Cohen and her associates finally received a grant from the federal Office of Economic Opportunity in 1966, she followed through on her promise. "When we went back, and we did, to every single person who had ever attended and asked them if they wanted to come in . . . quite a number did apply, and those that were eligible were screened into the program and became part of that first very important first class."[48]

Cohen's recollections of how she built trust in the low-income communities are supported by Laura Pires-Hester's memories of the early years of the Women's Talent Corps. Cohen was very committed, Pires-Hester says, to going back to the people in those communities and making sure that they *knew*. "That was something that made a big impression on those people, . . . not only to take but also to give, . . . not to forget, when you got to a certain point, that that was where you started."[49]

UP AGAINST A MALE BUREAUCRACY

Although Cohen's nighttime forays into low-income neighborhoods were often gratifying in terms of the reception she received, her daytime work of trying to get support for the project from the city was fraught with frustration. One early opponent of her plan was James Dumpson, at the time the first black commissioner of the New York City Department of Welfare and soon to become the dean of the Graduate School of Social Service at Fordham University. Cohen's efforts to persuade him of the need for a program that could train women to become social work assistants were firmly rebuffed, perhaps because he saw such a program as a threat to the social work profession.

The opposition to Cohen's proposal came from an entrenched bureaucracy that was mostly male. In early 1964 the political climate in New York City was not yet hospitable to the idea of women taking a leadership role in the antipoverty campaign. In 1961 Democratic mayor Robert F. Wagner had broken his ties to the Tammany Hall political machine and had won a third term as mayor. By 1964 he had gained a reputation for progressive policies such as building public housing, establishing the right of collective bargaining for city employees, barring housing discrimination, and being the first mayor to hire significant numbers of people of color in the city government.[50] But the liberalism of city's administration did not yet extend to empowerment of women. "Over and over again I was told that I could not be funded," Cohen said, "and all sorts of irrelevant rationalizations were used, many of them around this whole issue of the role of women."[51]

Even including the word "women" in the organization's name was problematical at the time. As Cohen sheepishly admitted to her daughter Dawn, her first name for the organization was W.O.M.E.N—"it stood for 'Work Oriented . . . Now'—I don't remember exactly"—and the name immediately raised the hackles of the city officials whom she approached for funding and support. The organizations having the most influence on the city's poverty programs at that time, such as the Community Service Society, the Protestant Welfare Society and the Jewish Federation, "felt they were doing everything that could be done to overcome the problems of poverty in our town," Cohen recalled, "and they saw what I was doing as a threat and they used the issue of women to attack me." Interestingly, some of the criticism took the form of accusing Cohen and her associates of addressing the needs of women who did not really need help. "They said that my real goal was to do things for middle-income women, and they used that successfully in the city and prevented us from being approved for funding."[52]

Attempts to gain support were met with cold disdain even after Cohen and her colleagues had decided to name the organization the Women's Talent Corps. As Jane Caulfield recalled, the endless rounds of meetings with religious and social service agencies, public and private, where she and Cohen had hoped to find moral support, if not commitment to provide training slots, were often insulting as well as disappointing. "How naive we were!" she exclaimed. The program administrators, mostly men, seemed to have rehearsed their defensive and antagonistic refrain: "*We* are doing what needs to be done about poverty in this city. We don't need *you*, an outsider in every way, to come in and tell us what needs to be done!"[53] In addition to the condescension there were often sexist jabs. She and Cohen were subjected to rude and ribald comments regarding the working name for the organization, Caulfield reported. "Exactly which women's talents were we planning to encourage, heh, heh?" At that time the social policy emphasis was on working with males. " '*He's* the only one who needs to have a job' was the stereotype that prevailed."[54]

But Caulfield also saw strength in Cohen's naiveté. She didn't have sense enough to be intimidated in advance, which even she might have been at that time. The freshness of Cohen's ideas, her approach, her high expectations "jolted the more committed of [the men], energized them to think and dream again as many of them had before they had been ground down by the bureaucracy maw." In fact Caulfield ultimately came to believe that Cohen's energy galvanized those from whom she did manage to get a respectful hearing and inspired them eventually to give their support.[55]

In retrospect, Cohen saw her own persistence as the key to her eventual success. "Naturally there are going to be forces any time that we try to do something different that will serve as a barrier to our making change," she said, referring to the challenges she encountered in 1963 to 1966. "We have to recognize that. But if a woman or anybody persists, it is amazing what can be accomplished."[56]

When the Economic Opportunity Act (EOA) was passed and signed by President Johnson in August 1964, Cohen saw a new opening for her persistence. She learned that the EOA authorized the allocation of government funds to community-based organizations that were addressing the needs of low-income citizens. Immediately she and her colleagues set to work drafting a proposal for federal funding. It is to that effort that we now turn.

CHAPTER 4

SHE WOULDN'T TAKE NO FOR AN ANSWER

Here's another example of what women have to do: I went to Washington D.C. and pleaded my case there until I won. I did not take No for an answer. . . . It was very important that I not be discouraged even though over and over again I was told that I could not be funded.

So while I tried to convince the people who ran the major social service agencies of this city for the need of this new kind of worker and these new positions, and while I tried to convince the hospital administrators, district superintendents, and the social service agency directors of the need for this new position in their very agencies, and while I tried to convince the low-income women of the value to them of these new positions, if we could get them instituted, by going every night to the low-income communities and working with them, at the same time I was going to Washington and trying to get money to begin the Women's Talent Corps.[1]

—Audrey Cohen to her daughter Dawn

In his sweeping overview of the post–World War II period entitled *Grand Expectations*, historian James T. Patterson recounts a story of Lyndon B. Johnson's early days as President. On the evening of November 23, 1963, just one day after John F. Kennedy had been assassinated, Walter Heller, the head of the JFK's Council of Economic Advisers, met with Johnson and told him about Kennedy's plans in the last weeks of his life to battle poverty. "That's my kind of program," Johnson replied. "Move full speed ahead."[2]

"Move full speed ahead" the Johnson administration did. Thanks to Johnson's appointment of John F. Kennedy's brother-in-law, Sargent Shriver, to head the effort, and to Johnson's notorious power-wielding influence with Congress, the Economic Opportunity Act of 1964 was drafted in February and was passed in August with substantial support from the solidly Democratic House and Senate. Included in the final bill were loans to small business and for rural development, funding for work–study for college students, the establishment of VISTA (Volunteers in Service to America, the domestic peace corps), the creation of Job Corps centers and a Neighborhood Youth Corps to create jobs for young people, and finally the development of Community Action Programs (CAPs) that would be worked out in concert with Washington. To coordinate these efforts, the bill established an Office of Economic Opportunity (OEO) that Shriver himself was named to lead.[3]

Diana Gordon (called "Dinni" by her friends) had graduated from Harvard Law School in 1965 and began a job with the OEO soon after the agency was created. She explained the role of the Community Action Programs (CAPs) that the Equal Opportunity Act had made possible. "The idea was that you would infuse these social service programs, these anti-poverty programs, with the participation of the beneficiaries of the program."[4] Built into the Economic Opportunity Act's wording, in fact, was the stipulation that the poor themselves would have "maximum feasible participation" in poverty program planning.[5] To complicate matters, however, local and state economic opportunity offices and antipoverty officials were also drawn into the process. In New York City this meant that funding for a pilot Community Action Program had to be approved by an antipoverty agency set up by the City Council of New York City as well as by the OEO in Washington, DC.

In the archives of the College at 431 Canal Street there is a two-page, single-spaced list of the proposal submissions made by Cohen and her associates over a two-year period to the New York City Council's Antipoverty Operations Board and to the OEO in Washington. The list provides striking evidence of the hurdles that the women faced as they tried to make their dream of a Women's Talent Corps become a reality. In January 1965 they were told by the New York City Council's Antipoverty Board that the proposal for a Women's Talent Corps would clear the NYC Council Vs. Poverty with no difficulty and could be sent on to Washington immediately.

Three months later, however, they were told by the OEO in Washington that there was a concern about the use of the word *training* in the Women's Talent Corps proposal and that more forms would have to be filled out. Cohen and her associates quickly completed the necessary paperwork, but it wasn't until July that they were informed by General Counsel of the OEO that "the proposal is now under consideration in Washington." Then in September 1965, Arthur Logan of the New York City Council wrote directly to Sargent Shriver about the Council's "inability to concur on the funding of the program."[6] This jarring news only strengthened the women's resolve, and they wrote to New York Senators Jacob Javits and Robert F. Kennedy asking them to intervene on the Women's Talent Corps behalf. Still the months went by with no response.

GROUNDWORK

All the while Cohen persisted in believing that her efforts would eventually bear fruit. Throughout the nearly two years of struggle with the city and federal government to get OEO funding, she and her colleagues worked to build the groundwork for an organization that would be ready to go into operation as a training and employment program for low-income adult women as soon as the funding came through. "She told us all never to take 'no' for an answer," an early associate, Sylvia Hack, recalled. "She taught us that if somebody didn't want to meet with us, we were to go to the office and to sit there until they would talk to us."[7] Cohen's community outreach described in the previous chapter continued, as did her efforts to raise funds and interest among community activists. In addition to her nonstop work in the field, she was able in March 1965 to get the Women's Talent Corps incorporated as a nonprofit organization in the State of New York, and by the fall she had put together a Governing Board, which had its first meeting on September 30, 1965.

The first members of the board included close associates of Cohen's such as Jane Caulfield and Hope Leichter from Columbia Teachers College. Reflecting the tenor of the times, all of the women on the Board are listed in the early Minutes under their husband's names—for example, as "Mrs. Mark I. Cohen," "Mrs. Robert Caulfield," and "Mrs. Henry Leichter."

(Cohen later quipped that, "It was very important to do 'Mrs.' in those days, since it was bad enough to be called the Women's Talent Corps!") Also included on the Women's Talent Corps Board were individuals who Cohen knew through prior contacts. Susan ("Mrs. Richard") Medalie was the wife of a friend who Cohen had met in the YWCA program in Washington during her college years, and Harold Taylor, then the president of Sarah Lawrence College, was recommended by a woman who had once applied for a job with Part-Time Research Associates. ("This shows you the interconnection of experiences in one's life," Cohen noted.) Another early board member, Rina ("Mrs. Charles") Mosely also had ties to Part-Time Research Associates, and Father Phillip Hurley, S.J., was an activist Catholic priest who Cohen had met through a friend of her husband Mark.[8]

An important board member who later became its chair was Preston Wilcox, a community activist and a professor at the Columbia University School of Social Work. Wilcox had grown up in Youngstown, Ohio, and attended Morehouse College in Atlanta, Georgia, before being drafted into the U.S. Army. After the war he moved to Brooklyn, New York, and completed his undergraduate studies at New York's City College, where he majored in biology. He went on to complete a master's of social work at Columbia University and began teaching there in the late 1950s. In the mid-1960s he became an activist for community control of the city's public schools and was an advisor to activists in two of New York City's most contentious battles, Ocean Hill–Brownsville in Brooklyn and I.S. 201 in Harlem.[9] A prolific writer, Wilcox authored some two-hundred articles in the period during which he was closely involved with the Women's Talent Corps, mostly on public education and community empowerment.[10] It is unclear how Cohen first became acquainted with him—she may have just introduced herself over the telephone[11]—and in the early years of the Women's Talent Corps Wilcox was a crucial ally in her struggle to create a new educational institution that would provide training and jobs for low-income women and at the same time forge a curricular connection between social work theory and community organizing.

In a slim folder with his name on it in the MCNY archives is a carefully typed eight-page paper that records a discussion Wilcox had with Cohen about the phasing-in of the Women's Talent Corps. The discussion is wide-ranging and includes the possibility of setting up Women's Talent

Corps "field stations" in low-income neighborhoods, recruiting women in "clusters" from each neighborhood, and planning the program so as to coincide with the school year because the first occupational type that the Women's Talent Corps planned to train was teacher assistants. The middle pages of the report focus specifically on the role of these teacher assistants, suggesting that they might grade tests, check workbooks, help with remediation work either on an individual or a group basis, make home visits, and "bridge the gap between the school and the community." In discussing what kind of relationship the teacher assistant trainee would have with the Women's Talent Corps trainer, Wilcox points out that in some situations it might be appropriate for the trainer and the trainee to be sitting in the same classroom because there will be a "common body of knowledge in which both the trainer and the trainee will be in the role of the learner."[12] Here Wilcox is suggesting that teachers and students have much to learn from each other—a concept that was relatively new at the time.

The easy tone of Wilcox's memo veils the contentiousness of the debates over public school control that shook many New York City school districts in the mid-1960s. Despite the Supreme Court's historic 1954 *Brown v. Board of Education* ruling, many New York City schools had become more segregated as a result of demographic shifts, and the bussing of minority children into predominantly white schools had not succeeded in improving academic performance. In frustration, many activist parents and community leaders were pushing for more localized community control over public schools. By 1967 they succeeded in getting the Board of Education, backed by Mayor John Lindsay and the Ford Foundation, to decentralize the control of three schools. The experiment soon led to fierce and lasting hostility, however, between the mostly minority local boards and the mostly white United Federation of Teachers—a hostility that in Ocean Hill–Brownsville erupted into a months-long teachers strike in 1968.[13]

Although neither the Women's Talent Corps nor Cohen herself became directly involved in the turmoil over decentralization during these years,[14] she, too, at one point experienced the wrath of the New York City public school establishment. Determined to provide above entry-level jobs in public schools for low-income women, some of her well-intentioned efforts met with fierce resistance. During a typically long day at 110 Livingston Street, then the headquarters for the New York City Board of Education, she refused to take "no" for an answer and got into an argument with representatives from the United Federation of Teachers. Her unwelcome presence was reported to the Chancellor, who proceeded to have security guards physically remove her from the building. At the time she did not publicize this event, but in later years, when her own educational projects had become well established and her presence was welcomed at 110 Livingston Street, she retold the story to a trusted colleague.[15]

Eventually, the Board of Education did listen to Cohen's plan, and the teacher assistant position in city schools became well-established. As some participants in those school struggles have recalled, Cohen's main contribution was to lobby simultaneously with the United Federation of Teachers (UFT) and with the Board of Education for this new paraprofessional role. "She was the first to bring the UFT around," asserts Nicholas Juravich, who has studied closely the history of paraprofessionals in schools, communities, and the labor movement during these years. "She got Al Shanker [the president of the UFT] on board."[16] "UFT Hails Breakthrough Program of Teacher Assistants," announced the February 17, 1969, issue of the *United Teacher*, the union's newsletter.[17]

Besides her advocacy for teacher assistants, Cohen worked to promote other "assist" jobs that Women's Talent Corps trainees might fill once the institution got its funding. Welfare agencies, community centers, hospitals, and city departments as well as schools were approached as possible sites for women to learn useful new skills while contributing to their communities.[18] In the minutes of the second meeting of the Women's Talent Corps Board, held in early November 1965, is a list of twenty-one individuals who Cohen contacted in her efforts to drum up suggestions and support. Included in this list were Robert Chandler at the Ford Foundation, Dr. Mamie Clark at the Northside Child Development Center, Professor Richard Cloward at the Columbia University School of Social Work, Father Joseph Feeney from the Archdiocese of New York Catholic Schools division, Messrs. Hays and Raverra of the New York City Urban League, Mrs. Christian Herter of Volunteer Opportunities, Inc., Mrs. Honig and Mrs. McFadden at the Public Nurse Association—the list goes on and on.[19]

Among the dedicated public servants who Cohen contacted at this time was Herbert Bienstock, the regional Commissioner of the U.S. Department of Labor's Bureau of Labor Statistics. Although he was not able to offer Cohen's project any direct financial support, he, like others, was struck by her commitment to her vision. "There are many phonies in this field," he once said, "who are looking to get money for their projects." But although Cohen was obviously seeking funding, it was clear that she was motivated by an important social purpose. "You could just feel it from her. She *oozed* sincerity. She was *authentic*. And if you were that kind of person yourself, you tended to respond to her." And, he added, she was "tireless," working day and night.[20]

In February 1966, Cohen could report one very positive outcome of her efforts. The Marshall Field Foundation, led by its executive director, Leslie Dunbar, had agreed to grant the Women's Talent Corps $15,000 "to support further location of community service jobs for nonprofessional aids and the scheduling of meetings with local women indigenous to slum areas to elicit their interest in training and employment."[21] This good news only increased the pace of Cohen's work. Attached to the minutes for the February meeting is a list of forty-five more individuals and agencies that Cohen contacted—including the Bronx River Neighborhood House, the Women's City Club, Planned Parenthood, the Federation of Protestant Welfare Agencies, the Labor Department of the NAACP, the Convent Avenue Baptist Church, the Hudson Guild, Mobilization for Youth, and the South Brooklyn Settlement House. Still, however, there was no word from Washington about the fate of the Women's Talent Corps's proposal to the OEO.[22]

THE OEO GRANT

Meanwhile back in Washington Dinni Gordon was learning the ins and outs of poverty program funding from her boss, Sanford Kravitz, who was in charge of the Community Action Research, Demonstration, and Training Programs within the OEO. "I was very much of a novice," Gordon recalled, "and so he sent me to look at the programs that he thought would go nowhere."

One day in the late fall of 1965 Kravitz came into her office with a thick folder in his hand. "We have this application from a society woman from the Upper East Side of New York City—apparently a kind of dynamic person who has this idea that she could form a college for welfare mothers," he told Dinni. "And it's called the Women's Talent Corps and, uh, would you please just go up and help me figure out how to get rid of her?"

"Basically that's what he said," Dinni recounted, "though I've put it a little crudely."[23]

By now Mark Cohen had gotten a job as an attorney for Mobil Oil that enabled the family to move from Stuyvesant Town to a duplex on East 67th Street. The rental apartment was a bargain and had looked unpromising at first, with a broken skylight, old appliances, a black fireplace and two kitchens. But on their first visit Audrey had scraped off a little paint from the fireplace with her fingernail and saw that there was beautiful marble underneath. "You know what? I can turn this into something," she said. She could see past the ugliness, her two daughters recalled.[24] The fireplace was restored to its original marble, the second kitchen was turned into a bedroom, and the girls' rooms opened out onto a terrace. With artwork from Japan and Morocco on the walls, the apartment was soon transformed into a spacious, comfortable home.

At the age of thirty-four, Audrey's demeanor and dress were well suited to her new Upper East Side Manhattan address. No longer as tiny-waisted as she had been in her prechild-bearing years, she was still trim and fit, and wore well-tailored clothes, fashionable shoes, and appropriate jewelry. In many photos she is wearing pearls. Even when she was dressing down, one colleague remembered, her clothing was relatively "upscale."[25] Her hair was longer than it was in her early twenties, but its natural curliness was still tamed and under control. It wasn't until the late 1960s that Cohen, like many other women of her era, let her curls fly free.

Following her boss's suggestion, Gordon went to New York and met with Cohen. "I got there, to her beautiful apartment, and she laid out this idea of a program for low-income women with very few educational or material resources," Gordon remembers. With dynamism and evident determination ("she was short and solid and just bursting with energy!") Cohen enthusiastically described to Gordon a curriculum that would be practical and oriented toward problem solving. Every course would take real-life situations and move from the concrete to the abstract, but the idea was that they would be academically challenging courses. "I remember thinking, 'you know, there are some good ideas here.' It sounded very sensible. It also sounded kind of radical."[26]

Gordon went back to Washington and told Kravitz her impressions. She made it clear that she did not want to write an evaluation that would kill the program. The ideas were very compelling. Besides, she told him, Cohen was "somebody who is probably going to carry through with whatever she wants to do."

" 'Well,' he replied, 'let's move it along.' And that was that!"[27]

By mid-July 1966, Cohen and her colleagues finally got the word that they had long awaited. A Western Union telegram from Shriver himself addressed to Audrey Cohen "c/o Mrs. Mark Cohen" was delivered to her doorstep. "PLEASED TO INFORM YOU OF APPROVAL OF GRANT OF $314,000.00 TO YOUR AGENCY TO ASSIST IN FINANCING YOUR COMMUNITY ACTION PROGRAM UNDER TITLE II-A OF THE ECONOMIC OPPORTUNITY ACT OF 1964," the telegram read.[28] Although the grant was for much less than the amount that she had asked for (the proposal had been for $875,000[29]), she and her friends were jubilant at the news. "When the College received its first federal grant in 1966, after two and a half years of planning and anticipation, I was so overjoyed that I literally began to dance around my office," she told a group of women college presidents and administrators in 1980. The hopping around and shouts of hooray were "an appropriate and exhilarating release" after so many months of struggle.[30]

Other forces besides Dinni Gordon's timely insights were at work in the effort to get seed money for what has been a successful institution for nearly fifty years. Among the other forces at work, as Cohen herself was quick to recognize, was the election of reformer John Lindsay as mayor of New York in the fall of 1965, which made the political climate more receptive to the kind of project she was trying to organize. Lindsay's combination of conservative roots (he was nominally a Republican) and liberal commitments (he was in favor of Medicare and the Civil Rights Act) worked well during the mayoral race,[31] and among his supporters were Mark and Audrey Cohen who actively campaigned for him.[32] Soon after Lindsay's election, the City Council's Antipoverty Committee came around on the Women's Talent Corps proposal. Some pressure on the OEO might also have come from Senators Jacob Javits and Robert F. Kennedy, whose support Cohen assiduously cultivated in the crucial months leading up to the final decision.[33] And although the "grand expectations" (as James Patterson called them) of the mid-1960s did not last long, the Women's Talent Corps proposal was, as Dinni Gordon pointed out, "of its moment." "You know," she said in our interview, "I think we were aided in that the idea was that we should be adventurous. Even pilot programs now, I think, don't get the message that we got then, which was, 'Be bold.' "[34]

FAMILY MATTERS

With the grant for her program finally secured, Cohen turned to the education of her own daughters. Perhaps anticipating that she herself would have little time to devote to supervising their homework and school life, she sought out what she felt would be the best educational opportunities available. Dawn Cohen Margolin speaks with some ambivalence about her mother's desire to send her and her younger sister Wendy to the Chapin School, a private, all-girls school known for its homey atmosphere but rigorous academic curriculum. At that time the school was perceived as having a largely WASP student body. As Dawn remembers (though the story is true only as she remembers it, she said, and may not be the whole story), Mayor John Lindsay felt "beholden" to her mother, and so told the headmistress, Mrs. Barrison, that she should accept the family, even though they were Jewish. "So, in the end we were accepted."[35]

Dawn resisted the change. "I went kicking and screaming." She had already completed third grade in public school and loved it. But, she said, her mother tricked her into changing schools. One day Dawn came home from public school and said that she hated the food. "That's it! You're going to Chapin!" Audrey exclaimed, and enrolled her for the following fall. Dawn recalled that for her the transition to Chapin was a big change, mostly because of the affluence of the families that she encountered at the school. Although she and Wendy often had an *au pair* helper to help take care of them, they didn't have a nanny ("nannies were too expensive") like many of the other Chapin girls did. Nor could they expect a Porsche for their sixteenth birthday or a horse because they wanted one. "I think my mother was disgusted by that kind of behavior, and understandably so, since she didn't have those things growing up herself." Her mother, Dawn continued, wanted her and Wendy to get "the education and the connections," but she didn't want her children to turn into snobs.[36]

In their early childhood years Dawn and Wendy's father Mark Cohen was an involved and reliable presence, in some cases more than their mother. "Dedicated" and "unwavering" were words Dawn used to describe her father,[37] who, at a time when it was not yet fashionable for dads to share childrearing tasks, was very involved in his daughters' lives. Wendy remembers that when their mother was "out doing her thing" and their father saw that something needed to be done, "he stepped in, stepped up." It was he, she continued, who was the one helping them with their homework, chaperoning them to parties, and staying up late waiting for them when they were out on dates.[38]

In response to his daughters' praises, Mark Cohen demurs, stressing instead his wife's role in Dawn's and Wendy's upbringing. Because his job as a tax lawyer with Mobil required him to travel abroad frequently, it was Audrey who "managed both to keep them in line and also to keep her dream going."[39] In discussing his wife's courageous ventures into neighborhoods that others might have deemed unsafe, he contrasted her fearlessness for herself with her protectiveness of her daughters. "There was one incident where I went a little overboard, at least in her mind." He was driving the girls back from a weekend in Massachusetts and got a flat tire in the middle of Harlem. It was a hot summer day, and the car did not have air conditioning, so he let the girls sit on the curb while he changed the tire. When he got home he told Audrey what happened. "You did *what*? You let those little girls sit out on the curb?"[40] Apparently her own forays into dangerous neighborhoods at night aroused in her less concern than her daughters' experience of having to spend a few minutes sitting on the curb of 125th Street in full daylight.

Tensions would develop within the family when the girls reached adolescence in the early 1970s. But in 1966, with her hoped-for dream becoming a reality and her children safely cared for, Cohen could look forward to the future with gratitude, confidence, and hope. "It was a very good year," she later concluded.[41]

CHAPTER 5

THE WOMEN'S TALENT CORPS
(1965–1967)

In many instances today, the classroom and the world remain very separate, and a majority of students receive inadequate exposure to addressing real challenges and learn skills that have little application toward meeting the needs of their social environment. Purpose-Centered education, however, links education and life, bringing the classroom into the community and the community into the classroom.

—Cohen and Jordan, 1996, p. 33

Once the grant from the Office of Economic Opportunity came through, one of the first and most important decisions that Cohen made was to hire Laura Pires-Hester (then Laura Pires) to lead the community outreach effort. Tall, with black wavy hair, dark sparkling eyes and a radiant smile, Laura is openly proud of her Cape Verdean heritage. She speaks thoughtfully, in well-developed paragraphs, her calm intelligence and broad knowledge giving weight to her words. Yet there is nothing condescending or imperious about her. A practicing Christian, she exudes trust and care. She comes across as someone who is well-organized, reliable, and very kind.

In an interview in her bright and comfortable apartment in Riverdale, New York, Pires-Hester recounted how she decided to join Cohen's new organization at its inception. A young graduate of Smith College and the first of her Cape Verdean family to attend college, Pires-Hester had attended the Columbia School of Social Work and had been working since 1963 at Harlem Youth Opportunities, Unlimited (HARYOU)—a precursor of community action programs that were soon to appear around the country. By 1966 she had decided to move on, but just before leaving HARYOU she received a call from Preston Wilcox, who she had known at Columbia and later had met professionally in the Association of Social Workers. Wilcox told her about Cohen's project and suggested that she meet her.[1]

Pires-Hester telephoned Cohen right away, and after meeting with her and discussing her project, Pires-Hester agreed to work part time to help develop the field placements for the first class. Pires-Hester was impressed with the clarity of Cohen's thinking and with the originality of her plans, and she liked the idea of identifying and recruiting low-income women to become new kinds of human service workers.[2] She remembers Cohen as being precise, serious, and quietly urgent about her project. To Pires-Hester, the proposal was carefully thought through, and it laid out general parameters as well as very specific strategies. "I think it was that that hooked me."[3] From their first meeting Cohen also knew that she had found a gem in Laura Pires-Hester. "She had this experience on how you act. She had done training programs. She knew exactly what we were going to be getting into. And she knew the pitfalls."[4]

By October 1, 1966, Pires-Hester had been hired to work full time as the field training director. Together with Cohen, Anne Cronin (the staff training director), and Barbara Prem (hired to recruit new staff), the women set to work building and putting into place the systems that would be directed toward accomplishing the Women's Talent Corps' mission.[5] They quickly moved into rent-free space in a federally owned building at 346 Broadway[6] with orange crates, a few government-issue desks, and a whole program to set up. In what became standard practice, Pires-Hester continued, "we worked fast, collectively—at first almost everything was participated in by all of us—and purposefully."[7]

"Fast" may be an understatement. When the Board of Directors (no longer referred to as the Governing Board) met on October 26, 1966, less than a month after she had been hired, Pires-Hester had already made contact with sixteen schools, hospitals, neighborhood centers, and conservation bureaus in Harlem, lower Manhattan, the Bronx, and Brooklyn; and she had received highly favorable responses to the Women's Talent Corps' proposals. Most of the agencies had accepted the idea of sharing the costs of paying the trainees during the last twelve weeks of the program, an idea that had been part of the plan from the beginning. The minutes of that first board meeting state that possible placements for Talent Corps women included teacher assistants and guidance-counselor assistants in public schools, and social service assistants in hospitals. Specific jobs for such assistants had already been identified at Bellevue Hospital and other agencies as well.[8] By early November more than one-hundred trainees had been interviewed by Pires-Hester and her colleagues, nine coordinator-trainers had been hired, and the orientation sessions for both groups had been launched.[9] Cohen's dreams were coming true.[10]

CORPS WOMEN

Women's Talent Corps training was for career positions in education, health, and social welfare. As Cohen explained in an article she later wrote for the *Teachers College Record*, the Corps aimed to prepare women for socially useful, paid jobs that they were uniquely suited to fill because of their firsthand knowledge of community life and their own experience of what it means to live in poverty. The new preprofessional jobs would include teacher assistants, guidance assistants, research assistants, library assistants, social work assistants, occupational and recreational therapy assistants—jobs that Cohen and her colleagues had deliberately pushed agencies in the service sector to create. "A basic aim of the [Women's Talent Corps] is to develop new career lines in community agencies representing a new entry level for neighborhood women which does not require the B.A. degree."[11]

Cohen's writings about the Women's Talent Corps suggest that she was alone in envisioning new career paths for low-income adults in urban communities. But in the mid-1960s other activists were thinking along similar lines and working to promote new subprofessional or paraprofessional jobs in service-related agencies and organizations. In a 1967 pamphlet entitled *New Careers: A Basic Strategy Against Poverty*, Cohen's friend Frank Riessman, a professor of educational sociology at New York University, made an eloquent case for exactly the kinds of employment opportunities that Cohen was working to create. Building on an introduction by Michael Harrington, Riessman argued that the hiring of "nonprofessional" workers could be used to:

Provide millions of new jobs for the un-employed.

Create human service positions which cannot be automated out of existence.

Rehabilitate the poor through meaningful employment.

Provide more and "closer" service for the poor.

Reach the unreached.

Reduce the manpower shortage in education, health, and social work.

Free the professional for more creative and supervisory roles.[12]

In the pamphlet Riessman refers to efforts to create new careers being developed in Baltimore, Rochester, Seattle, New Haven, San Francisco, Sacramento, Washington DC, and Eugene, Oregon.[13] Surprisingly, Cohen's project is not mentioned. While Riessman suggests the need to involve institutions of higher education in training workers for these new career roles, he includes no specific suggestions about how this might be done.

What clearly distinguishes Cohen's project from other mid-1960s efforts to meet the employment needs of low-income women was the rigor of the training program that she and her colleagues set up.[14] The initial program was set up as thirty-week "cycles" of training for each incoming group of students (called "Corps Women" in the organization's evolving lingo). Students could begin a cycle in September, January, or May. Each training cycle consisted of three phases, the first being an eight-week classroom orientation, the second a closely supervised ten-week period of on-the-job training in a school or community agency, and the third an additional twelve weeks in the same workplace during which the trainee would work more independently and become assimilated into the school or community agency. The agency would pay a share of the Corps Woman's salary at this point and she would return to the Women's Talent Corps base for advice and guidance as needed.[15] As had been planned from the start, the Corps Women received an allowance of $2 per hour ($13.75 in today's dollars) for their participation in the program, and the Coordinator Teachers received $4 per hour.[16]

The first trainees, or Corps Women, were recruited ("exclusively," a 1967 report reads), from low-income neighborhoods, and inquiries about the program from potential trainees reached as many as two-hundred per week that first fall. To be eligible for admission, women had to meet OEO poverty criteria (one of them being that they had an income below $4,000 a year[17]), be over twenty-one years of age, and able to read and write. For admission they also had to participate in a group interview and pass a written test developed specifically for the purpose (no preexisting standardized test was found adequate). Crucial factors in the final selection were "personality, attitude, and commitment to community service."[18]

Attached as Appendix B in a 1967 report on the Women's Talent Corps' first year accomplishments are three profiles written in their own words by the first group of Corps Women. All were heads of their household (two had husbands who were ill or hospitalized), and two out of the three were welfare recipients. One fifty-four-year-old woman (F.L.) remembered a brutal childhood in Texas digging potatoes, picking citrus fruits, and enduring "eternal beatings" by her parents who eventually abandoned her. She was then taken in by another family, who brought her to the Bronx and taught her to read and write using their own children's schoolbooks. From there she was placed in the care of members of the Seventh Day Adventist Church and began spending time in a nearby public library. "It was there that I received my education," she wrote. After six miscarriages she successfully had a son who was now twelve years old, but her husband was ill and could no longer work. She applied to the Women's Talent Corps, was admitted, and loved the experience. "I am looking forward to a new, more secure way of life, through the help of the Women's Talent Corps." Now in her fifth week of the orientation phase, she wrote in the final sentence of her profile, "I am happier than I have ever been in my whole life."[19]

Another trainee, a younger woman (L.C.), was born in Brooklyn, New York, and moved to Harlem as a young child. A "church-going child" who didn't go to movies or parties, she attended Central Commercial High School and majored in bookkeeping. After a long illness that forced her to quit her job, she became active in community organizations and tenant associations, was a tenant captain of her building, and became a member of the Democratic Club in the South Bronx. "I have helped people as best I can. I feel that this is service each one should give to others who can't find themselves." She too expressed hope for her future in the program: "What I learned from the Women's Talent Corps should give me a brighter future."[20]

The third woman (G.C.) profiled in the report was born in Puerto Rico and brought to East Harlem as an infant. She was a voracious reader at a young age (she claimed that her favorite authors were Pearl Buck, Edna

Ferber, Louisa May Alcott, and Ayn Rand), but in adolescence she decided to "have fun," and ended up, in her own words, "relinquishing even the pretense of a serious student by indulging myself in all the frowned-upon activities prevalent in a mixed school for boys and girls." She was soon in what she called "the League of Unwed Mothers." After being on welfare for several years she joined the Women's Talent Corps and reported finding "ultimate fulfillment" in her new role. Her on-site training was as a teacher assistant at Benjamin Franklin High School, where many of the young people on the block where she lived were students. "They are used to seeing 'their people' as lunchroom workers and workers with hallway duties," she wrote, so seeing someone like themselves working with "the higher echelon" often provoked questions. "This affords me a wonderfully opportune way of reminding them of the value of their own education and aspirations,"[21] she concluded.

The above three profiles were undoubtedly selected for their value in persuading bureaucrats in Washington to continue federal support and hence might be thought of as not typical of most Women's Talent Corps trainees. But in conversations with people involved in the Corps in its early years, and from my own acquaintance with women enrolled at the college that evolved out of the Women's Talent Corps, the profiles selected do seem representative of the kinds of women who have been drawn to Cohen's project since its inception. An article published in the *Christian Science Monitor* on January 23, 1967, supports this view. Under the headline "Talent Corps graduates sent afield," the author reports that of the first group of forty women selected for the program thirty-seven were unemployed, twenty-two were heads of households, and eighteen had been or were currently on welfare. The reported racial breakdown was (in the terminology of the time) thirty Negroes, seven Puerto Ricans, and three "other." Almost as an afterthought it is noted that "There was not a single dropout in the Women's Talent Corps's first six-week community-service training program."[22]

CTS

The high retention rate of the program was surely due at least in part to the commitment and tireless work of the coordinator-trainers (CTs) who Cohen and her associates hired that first year. What kinds of women were they? The OEO funding allowed for hiring staff only on a part-time basis (17½ hours per week), so the first group of nine CTs was made up mostly of white, middle-aged women whose husbands were the main breadwinners of their households. With backgrounds in teaching, social work, volunteerism, and church outreach (two women were married to ministers), they were hardworking, interesting individuals with perseverance, commitment, and a willingness to take risks.[23] Later publications referred to the women as "hard-headed do-gooders."[24] Few had advanced academic training. Indeed, in its early deliberations, the Board of Governors had decided that people with administrative experience in education or social work might prove to be "more able and energetic workers" than those with advanced academic degrees.[25] Although this policy became problematic later on, the hiring of people without specialized training may have served the project well in its early years.

Among those on the original list whose commitment to Cohen's project was ongoing were Sydelle ("Dellie") Bloom, Barbara Buchanan, and Doris ("Dodie") Younger.[26] While other women of her age and social strata were working on their tennis skills, Dellie was making her way into the city on the Long Island Railroad to put in long hours of work at the college. She loved the job, her colleagues (Audrey and Laura, in particular), and the students.[27] For Barbara Buchanan the experience was "in some ways a disaster and in some ways glorious." But she was a firm believer that people could find their own way if they could be taught how to start, and she was proud to be part of "that particular thing we invented"—the unique educational system of the Women's Talent Corps.[28] As another early associate recalled, it was an adventure to work for Audrey.[29]

Dodie Younger later recalled her first interview for the job. She had been in what she called a classic housewife depression, feeling "neglected, martyred, unappreciated" as a stay-at-home mom whose husband was a busy minister. She had answered the Women's Talent Corps' ad with some trepidation The setting was not what she had expected. "I entered this kind of rusty, crumbling old Federal building, went up in a badly tarnished, creaky elevator, and found the office lined with crates and boxes." She was interviewed by Laura Pires-Hester and Anne Cronin, and to her dismay was denied the job. She "did a fair amount of crying," she later said. But a few months later, after a chance meeting with Pires-Hester at a conference, she was invited to come in for another interview, and this time she got the job. Her mood immediately lifted. Now, she said with knowing irony, "I could throw myself into this exhausting, tension-filled job and feel absolutely marvelous!"[30]

In the Women's Talent Corps' first year of operation many of the coordinator-trainers developed their own curriculum for the first phase of the training cycle, the academic orientation. This phase was designed to introduce the Corps Women to the "facts, skills, and attitudes" required of a preprofessional in community service. Visiting experts provided background information on city agencies specifically those relating to health, education, and welfare. In what was later referred to as the *core curriculum*, trainees were introduced to concepts in the fields of psychology, sociology, and education that could be applied to urban issues. Some class sessions were focused on individual challenges encountered by the trainees; others dealt with the kinds of human relations problems that could be expected to arise in the field. Role-play was often used to model professional interactions. All of the lectures were followed by small group sessions directed by CTs, in which trainees could discuss the meaning and implications of what they had heard. Students were required to keep a record of their learning in what was called a *Student Progress Workbook*.[31] Remedial work in basic skills was also an important part of the curriculum and was handled on an individual basis at the end of the day.[32] Not surprisingly, the question of how to provide effective remedial work became increasingly urgent as the program expanded.

As Cohen later explained, the term *coordinator-trainer* was explicitly chosen to emphasize the faculty's dual role as teachers in the classroom and coordinators in the field. Each CT generally supervised up to ten trainees, with the aim of permitting a maximum of individual instruction and counseling. Because they were expected both to provide academic instruction and to follow the Corps Women into the field, the job was a demanding one.[33] Again Dodie Younger's recollections are illustrative. She remembered putting on psychological armor to brace herself when she went into a school in the Ocean Hill–Brownsville section of Brooklyn. Her only previous experience with schools was her interactions with her own children's teachers; she had never had to deal with principals or administrators. "I had been brought up to be a very good girl, and good girls did not question higher authorities—ever!" Not only were the personnel issues challenging, the whole setting was new. She was familiar with the Lower East Side because of church work, but nothing had prepared her for Ocean Hill–Brownsville, "a bombed out country." She was not worried about her own safety, but about what she could teach the Corps Women that would help them become teacher assistants. So she taught herself. "I went up to Teachers College, bought books on teaching, on phonetics, pamphlets on anything that sounded remotely relevant" and set to work learning about elementary school education.[34]

Despite feeling overwhelmed by new challenges, the coordinator-trainers often saw positive learning outcomes that justified their belief in Audrey Cohen's vision. Laura Pires-Hester recalled some of the transformative moments that she observed or heard about during the Women's Talent Corps' early years. A book that one CT assigned in her orientation class was Edith Hamilton's *Mythology*, a classic compendium of Greek, Roman, and Norse myths and legends. One student became so enthralled by the material that she stayed up all night reading it—something she had never done before. "It was an opening up, a transformation of the women which occurred. You could see the transformation in them, physically," Pires-Hester reported. The students began to dress with more care and became better able to speak out in public sessions. Several shared with the CTs issues that were occurring in their families, including their husband's negativity. Some of the Hispanic women had never worked outside of their homes before, and that was a new challenge for their husbands.[35]

It was also evident that the momentum gained by the first cohort of Corps Women during the orientation phase of their training served them well once they began their supervised work in the field. Placements of Corps Women from November 1966 to June 1967 were at Bellevue and Harlem Hospitals, Benjamin Franklin High School, the Hudson Guild, and Fountain House (a home for adults with mental illnesses) in Manhattan; the Bronx River Neighborhood House, and Public Schools 25, 146, and 6 in the Bronx; and the Willoughby Houses in Brooklyn.[36] The Corps Women's work ranged from helping teachers with attendance sheets and lunch lists in public schools to writing reports and business letters in hospitals. In a 1968 article Cohen listed the range of tasks undertaken by Corps Women and supervised by CTs as follows:

In the hospitals no such position as Social Work Assistant existed. Now Women's Talent Corps Social Work Assistants are touring the wards to obtain information for the social worker, talking with children to decrease their sense of trauma at being in the hospital, collecting data for a special research project on asthma, participating in group discussions and seminars concerning hospital and personnel problems, serving as hostess to visitors, working with the Welfare Department to arrange for a family to move, hunting for an apartment with the client, and making school visits on behalf of a hospitalized child.[37]

EARLY SUCCESSES

For both the Corps Women and their CTs, the hard work brought gratifying results. By September 1967, of the initial 120 women 113 had successfully completed the thirty-week program. They "graduated" from the year-old Women's Talent Corps as teacher assistants, guidance assistants, social work assistants, research assistants, occupational and recreational therapy assistants. According to Pires-Hester, more than 75 percent were employed either in their field placement sites (22 of the 28 agencies hired graduates) or in related agencies.[38] The results were outstanding, especially given that the program was brand new, that many of the students had not had full-time jobs before, and that their trainers were women without advanced degrees. As an outside report on the program later observed, even if one looked at the Women's Talent Corps as a job training program for welfare recipients, "its achievement is extraordinary."[39]

The achievement was extraordinary, and given the inexperience of the program's trainers, much of the credit for its early success should be given to the tactful, wise, and diligent work of Laura Pires-Hester. As noted earlier, she had established the initial ties between the Women's Talent Corps and dozens of community-based organizations around the city, and it was she who was ultimately in charge of coordinating the placement and supervision of Corps Women. (In her reports the term is written as one word, "Corpswomen.") The "Historical Reconstruction" that she wrote about the Women's Talent Corps' early years assiduously avoids any showcasing of her own role. Nevertheless, her references to the need to intervene in the difficult situations that occasionally developed between the agency personnel and the trainees, or between agency personnel and the trainers, demonstrate that her ability to listen, mediate, and sort things out was essential to the smooth functioning of the program's operation. In some situations she would speak to the participants individually and then encourage them to work the problem out on their own; in other situations she would hold a joint conference to help them "accept the strengths that each of them possessed" as a starting point for the discussion. The process would be repeated until a mutually acceptable way of working together was arrived at.[40]

Pires-Hester's sound insights and clear vision extended to the Corps Women as well as to their trainers. One of the titles of her early presentations to new trainees was "To Do Is To Be." This idea, she wrote, came from her growing conviction about the role of *work* in building one's personal identity and competence. "I was trying to help Corpswomen (and jointly with CT's) to reach for and develop their capacities for learning, judgment and performance," for those capacities would eventually enable them to become the kind of person they wanted to be. Her message clearly hit home. Pires-Hester remembered the excitement about learning that she often felt in the room as she gave this speech.[41]

Pires-Hester's idea to require regular group meetings of the coordinator-trainers was another significant factor in the program's overall success. Scheduled originally for two hours on Friday afternoons, the group sessions were eventually extended to four hours to allow for more discussion and mutual learning. Some of the time was spent on sharing knowledge. Coordinator-trainers who had not had training in social work, for example, were interested in gaining more understanding of the discipline's vocabulary and basic assumptions. Others found that the weekly discussions enabled them to find solutions to problems they were facing in the field on their own, without the intervention of Pires-Hester—a development that she saw as a major breakthrough.[42] As Dodie Younger recalled later, "we were overloaded but we had a sense of community."[43]

NEW CAREERS

Behind the first year's success was the active presence of Audrey Cohen herself. Continually networking to promote her cause, she soon became a consultant to the New York State Education Department, a member of the Manhattan Borough President's Advisory Committee on Health Careers for the Disadvantaged, and an advisor to organizations on New Careers development in health, education, and welfare.[44] In January 1967, while the forty Corps Women from the fall cohort were about to move from the orientation phase out into carefully supervised field placements, a new group of forty enrolled for the orientation process. In addition to giving opening orientation speeches and publicizing the successes of the program in speeches at the New School and elsewhere, Cohen was planning ahead. Characteristically she and her associates set to work even before the year was out to assure that the successful pilot project the OEO had provided seed money for could take root as a lasting institution.

By now, however, the climate for bold initiatives on the part of the federal government had cooled. In the summers of 1966 and 1967 riots had broken out in urban ghettoes across the country. Impatient at the pace of change and caught in a contagious mood of anger, gangs of young people broke into storefronts, slashed car tires, and set piles of trash on fire. In 1966 there were thirty-eight outbreaks of violence from Brooklyn to San Francisco, and in the spring and summer of 1967 the rage spread even farther, reaching into 164 communities over a nine-month period.[45] Newark and Detroit were the cities hardest hit, with scores of injuries and deaths that prompted the intervention of Federal troops and the National Guard, which in some cases aggravated local tensions.

The summer uprisings raised fears among many, including members of Congress, about the benefits of LBJ's attempt to create a "Great Society" through federal legislation. "How long are we going to abdicate law and order—the backbone of any civilization—in favor of a soft social theory that the man who heaves a brick through your window or tosses a fire bomb into your car is simply the misunderstood and underprivileged product of a broken home?"[46] Gerald Ford of Michigan, then the House Republican leader and later President of the United States, asked accusingly. Clearly by the 1966 session of Congress a backlash was already brewing.

Among the members of Congress who resisted the backlash and continued to support LBJ's War on Poverty was Representative James H. Scheuer, Democrat of New York. In 1966 and 1967 Scheuer co-sponsored an amendment to the Economic Opportunity Act of 1966 called the

Scheuer-Nelson Subprofessional Career Act. Generally referred to as the New Careers Act, the legislation seemed fortuitously designed to support the Women's Talent Corps. In a speech to Congress defending the Act, Scheuer referred to "the creation of new or restructured positions for subprofessionals in public services and private nonprofit agencies," producing new occupations for the unemployed and underemployed, and "tying together training, work, and continuing education."[47]

Cohen and her associates jumped at the chance to tap into the $70 million Congress had appropriated for the New Careers Act. Not surprisingly, the Application for Extension of OEO Contract that the Women's Talent Corps submitted to Washington in April 1967 contained multiple references to "New Careers" in its wording. The project's subtitle was "An Institute for Training and New Careers Development in Community Service for Women of Low-Income in New York City," and the terms *career training* or *new career positions* were peppered throughout the carefully written, 67-page document. The application also provided ample evidence of the Women's Talent Corps successes. In the first year the program succeeded in training nearly all of its enrollees, and because of the close professional supervision provided, the program had worked "with remarkable smoothness."[48]

In addition to containing a glowing report on the Women's Talent Corps' present achievements, the application for New Careers funding also contained a section on goals that hints at Cohen's and her colleagues' ever-expanding vision for the future. Under a subheading entitled "Developing a New Careers College," the application makes the first reference in print to the possibility that the Women's Talent Corps might one day become a degree-granting college. A push for more formal academic preparation came from the trainees themselves, the application states, many of whom were capable of further career development in the general area of community service. In elaborating on this far-reaching idea, the application describes the goal in terms that were remarkably prescient:

> The new college would be built on the foundation already established by the training institute, in part by modifying and expanding the present curriculum. The service concept of education will continue to be stressed, and . . . [a] major part of the

college program will be field work to provide practical experience, integrated with academic work. . . . The students would be given an opportunity to study in greater depth those aspects of education, psychology, social work and guidance most closely related to needs in the fields.[49]

The heady vision ends with a bold assertion: "The second year program will lead to an Associate of Arts degree. . . . An accrediting system for the two-year program will be developed."[50]

Unlike the long, tortuous process required to secure the original application to the OEO, the application for additional funding of $570,000[51] under the aegis of the New Careers legislation succeeded quickly and with little fanfare.[52] The funding now originated with the Department of Labor and subsequently came under the direction of the Comprehensive Employment and Training Act (CETA) of 1973.

FOR THE *RECORD*

Cohen and her colleagues were delighted to be able to proceed with their plans, including plans for creating a college, and they soon moved into a larger space in an old federal office building at 201 Varick Street.[53] Quick to capitalize on her new venture's successes, Cohen wrote an article for the prestigious education journal, the *Teachers College Record*, trumpeting the achievements of the Women's Talent Corps and setting forth her plan for a College for Human Services. The article serves both as a summary of the Women's Talent Corps' achievements and as a clarion call to what Cohen hoped the future would bring.

The article begins with references to the lack of educational opportunities for low-income women that the Women's Talent Corps had aimed to address. Acknowledging that new educational opportunities had opened in recent years—including evening high schools, special programs for high school dropouts, and compensatory programs—Cohen proceeds to point out that neither they nor the existing experimental colleges like Antioch, Bennington, or Goddard effectively addressed the educational needs of "mature working people of our cities." Such people deserved more. "Men and women

of the inner city have every American citizen's right to equal opportunity for
higher education . . . and many are clamoring for it," she asserts.[54]

Cohen then describes the lack of "assist" jobs in human service
agencies and the need to bridge the distance between professional workers
and the people they serve. She recounts the rise of the Women's Talent
Corps and stresses the organization's aim to develop new career lines in
community agencies and in preprofessional jobs so as to improve the
services of the community and benefit the program clients. Here she
narrates in some detail the Corps' successful efforts to create Teacher and
Guidance Assistants in the New York public school system. At first there
was reluctance on the part of the slow-moving educational bureaucracy
to create new positions, she says, but soon some of the more imaginative school superintendents like Bernard Donovan saw the benefits in the
plan. Summarizing the advantages of the new assist roles, Cohen refers
to a letter of support from a principal who had had Corps Women in
his school. Pupils were provided with more individual attention from the
teacher, and the morale of the teachers was raised because with a teacher
assistant in the classroom the teacher could now devote herself more fully
to professional pursuits. Equally important, a closer relationship developed
between school and community since the assistants "are recruited from
the members of the local community."[55]

Gradually pressure from supporters ranging from the Corps Women
to Mayor Lindsay and Cohen herself led to the Board of Education and the
United Federation of Teachers agreeing to create new lines of employment
for teacher assistants. A resolution supporting this innovation was passed
by the UFT on February 14, 1967, and in April the Board of Education
agreed to share the cost of the final twelve weeks of training in the schools.
"Thus the battle was won and a miracle accomplished." A breakthrough has
been achieved, Cohen wrote, in establishing new, meaningful jobs in the
schools, "which will benefit hundreds of talented people in the low-income
areas of New York City and improve public education for thousands of
the city's children."[56]

At the end of the article Cohen announces her future plans. Near at
hand is a two-year College for Human Services that will serve the poor in
new ways and provide a new institution of higher education "that breaks
the mold" of the traditional college. Anticipating the unorthodoxy of the

proposed College for Human Service's curriculum, she makes a prophetic claim. In a sharp departure from traditional undergraduate curricula, "all compartmentalizing partitions [between the disciplines] will be removed."[57]

The tone of Cohen's *Teachers College Record* is triumphant and optimistic. The successes of the Women's Talent Corps were very real, and her hopes for ongoing achievements were well-grounded. Little did she and her colleagues know, however, that when they described their grand proposal for a College for Human Services in 1967 and 1968, how many hurdles, roadblocks, and obstacles they would confront in the road that lay ahead. Before confronting the more problematical events of late 1960s and early 1970s, a glimpse at the new college's social life can give a sense of the euphoria that many young people experienced in those hopeful years.

DELLIE BLOOM'S SOCIAL NOTES

Perched on top of a metal file cabinet in the MCNY archives room is an old cardboard box with Barbara Walton's name on it. In a folder labeled "History, '89–92" are three pages of impressions of the social life of the College for Human Services in the 1960s and 1970s written by Dellie Bloom. Bloom was a member of the Women's Talent Corps faculty who later returned to the college to work on a proposed history of its early years.

Entitled "Social Notes," Bloom's evocative text gives a sense of the spirit of the times, not only at College for Human Services but at other innovative institutions trying to break through the boundaries of class, race, and gender that had defined the 1950s and before. In the world that most adults at that time had grown up in, women never wore pants to work, the faces in television commercials always had Caucasian features, and jazz was a radical form of musical expression. Even by the mid-1950s the social barriers separating WASPs, Catholics, and Jews were almost as formidable as those separating blacks, whites, and Hispanics. But in the 1960s the rigid social conventions of the earlier decade had exploded into a heady mix of exploration, experimentation, and play. While giving a sense of the exhilaration of the times, Dellie Bloom's social notes also suggest some of the complex nonacademic learning that Cohen's project made possible and that remains an aspect of the college's social environment even today.

The notes begin with Bloom's memories of the parties that were held at the college in those euphoric years. Everything was an excuse for a party, she remembered. A birthday, the overcoming of an institutional obstacle, the end of the program year, the coming of spring, the not-yet-coming of spring ("so let's cheer ourselves up—it is Valentine's Day!") became a reason for students, faculty, and staff to get together for music and dancing. Favorite records were brought in, shared, and played by volunteers or self-appointed disk jockeys. A party also meant food—couscous, noodle pudding, ribs, jelly doughnuts, rice and beans, sweet potato pies, fried chicken, pizza, heroes, egg rolls—"standard American fare."[58] Dress was informal. Some students wore the same clothes they always wore—tight jeans, short skirts, slinky sweaters, expensive leather boots, caftans, dashikis. Others took a risk and wore clothes they had never worn in public before.

If College for Human Services students were using drugs (and rumors abounded, Bloom admits), it never showed up on the dance floor. Those in the know among administrators, faculty, and students, were aware that at nearby hangouts the social contacts were less innocent. But on the college's premises, policy was clearly enunciated and consistently enforced: no dealing, no using. If a student nodded out, it was clear that she was not "attending to business," which was class participation, critical for successful completion of the program.[59]

Bloom observes that while the parties were well attended, some of the students remained on guard against all this mixing with faculty and administrators. Others welcomed it as another opportunity for them to get to know the staff. As for the faculty, there, too, the motives were varied. Some faculty members fell into the partying with great abandon, as though they had been "waiting all their lives for these artificial barriers between colors and creeds to come down, allowing an enriched mix based on free choice." Others may have come with more complex needs, looking for total acceptance too soon, "needing it too much," forgetting the common goal of education for independence and social empowerment.[60]

Bloom's observations of the students' reactions to faculty are particularly acute. She notes that the students were good at detecting the phonies—both on the staff and among themselves. They could quickly sense which faculty members were uncomfortable with the rupturing of boundaries, and which ones were pursuing admission to students' lives "in pursuit of needs of their own." Students could at first be angered by the cool and distant members of the faculty and might charge them with an "inability to understand us, to relate to us." But over a comparatively short period of time they came to value these "square-looking seniors" for what they had to teach, how respectfully they treated the students, and their knowledge of an outside world so different from the student's world. These generally older members of the faculty and staff, "uncompromising in their standards, endlessly flexible in their methods," came to be respected by the majority of students for the great men and women that they were: "wise in the ways of the world, unconfused in their own identities, generous, committed, soft-spoken—steady battlers for a changed society."[61]

The older black women on the faculty and staff had a special significance for the students, Bloom remembers. Although not from families of wealth, the mature women exuded older standards of manners and courtesy. They served as models of an earlier time, before the students themselves had grown up or, in some cases, before they had learned to "sharpen their elbows and their voices growing up in this big, noisy, macho city." These competent, take-charge women brought to mind the small Southern towns that some students had grown up in, with churchgoing parents and grandparents, aunts and uncles, "where good manners were as expected as the sunrise," or from other cities, where life was not idyllic but neither was it as raucous, belligerent, and dangerous as New York seemed to be.[62]

For students who were not African American, other dynamics were at work in the social life of the college. Bloom notes that those from Puerto Rico thrived on the noise of the street and the family parties, but nonetheless had a sense that life seemed "more good-natured and less guarded back home, at least in recollection." Puerto Rico was their own turf and the turf of their families. Those from the West Indies or Trinidad were, some for the first time, experiencing the mix of envy and resentment from less well-educated African Americans. In general, however, family outcasts of any color—the ones from middle-class upward striving families, who couldn't or wouldn't fit in when they were younger—found at the college an acceptance and encouragement that they missed from their own families the first time around. Here at the college "they flourished and were looked up to."[63]

After describing the social scene on the premises at the college Bloom reminisces about staff parties that Cohen held at her home. Organized around an institutional victory or the departure of a valued staff member, these social events brought together perhaps the most disparate mix of all. Only a decade after the staid 1950s, when social events were relatively homogeneous gatherings of people from the same class, race, and even religion, now in the same room were people of different colors, from all walks of life, and fitting no conventional stereotypes. In one corner of the room might be the Hispanic secretary who moonlighted as a go-go dancer in a Times Square nightclub and who was preparing to take the police officer's exam, talking with the quasi-social wife of a successful Wall Street broker who co-directed the field office and could negotiate a wide range of leads to training slots and job openings. In the middle of the room might be the Yale-educated Baptist minister and his College for Human Services faculty-member wife who most of the year lived the simple life of good works in lower Manhattan and during the summer lived "the good life" at their Maine cottage, talking with a Puerto Rican school activist from Brooklyn and her husband, a dedicated black teacher in the public schools who was working toward a position as an assistant principal and having his plays produced. The list could go on and on, Bloom noted. "It was exciting and soul-searing, this still new mix of colors, styles and backgrounds. We were a rainbow coalition and a gorgeous mosaic before the phrases were coined."[64]

CHAPTER 6

TRIAL BY FIRE (1968–1972)

We always felt that we had the responsibility to demonstrate the fact that the rhetoric, our rhetoric, is our reality. What that means is that we don't talk about anything we're not clearly intending to make happen. But one of our biggest problems is dealing with gaps between our rhetoric and where we are at the moment. And our students have always had to live with that.[1]

—Audrey Cohen in self-recorded tape

The late 1960s and early 1970s were among the most turbulent years of twentieth-century America. By 1966 the civil rights movement became more militant, with Floyd McKissick taking over the leadership of C.O.R.E. from James Farmer, and Stokely Carmichael replacing John Lewis at the Student Nonviolent Coordinating Committee (SNCC).[2] Calls for "black power" now competed with the earlier refrains of "black and white together." Student protests against the war in Vietnam metamorphosed into protests against any form of university involvement with the military, including ROTC recruitment and federally supported research to develop chemical warfare. The women's movement burgeoned out from the workplace into the home, gaining momentum from the founding of the National Organization of Women (NOW) in 1966. A series of deeply disturbing events— the assassinations of Martin Luther King Jr. and Robert F. Kennedy, campus uprisings at Columbia University, shootings at Kent State University, the arrests of demonstrators at the Democratic presidential convention in Chicago—all combined to make the period from early 1968 to late 1972 one of the most unsettling eras in American history.

Surprisingly little mention of the outside world's turmoil appears in the MCNY archives at 431 Canal Street, perhaps because the college's key actors in those years were so preoccupied with the institution's own external and internal challenges. During the years from 1968 to 1972 Cohen and her associates fought opposition from New York City and New York State as well as confronted two serious crises within the institution itself. The women faced demonstrations, strikes, and accusations of racism. Yet in the face of these upheavals, the institution's leadership succeeded in developing new ideas that by 1974 resulted in a bold new structure of higher education.

GROWING PAINS

As with any retrospective analysis, it is difficult to pin down the causal elements in the institution's history during these years. As was mentioned in the last chapter, by the end of 1967 the Women's Talent Corps had succeeded in getting renewed funding from the Federal Government through the Scheuer Amendment to the OEO. This funding enabled the training program to expand quickly from 120 to 200 students. The expansion was gratifying, but it put an additional burden on the staff. In addition to supervising the full complement of the original Corps Women in their field placement settings, there was now a need to begin training a much larger incoming class.[3]

Along with the expansion, a change was made to move from three cycles of forty students each to two cycles of one-hundred students each, so that each major learning group became one hundred instead of forty.[4] To accommodate this change, the administration devised a new system for the academic component of the training. What resulted was a three-tiered model of instruction consisting of lectures delivered to a whole group of one-hundred students and then class discussions and skills development workshops for smaller groups.[5]

The new expanded system provoked dissatisfaction on the part of the coordinator teachers, all of whom now had more responsibilities both in the classroom and in the field. The need occasionally to lecture, to lead small discussions of the material covered in the larger lectures, and to be engaged in overall curriculum development proved challenging. There were complaints of having too little time, of coordinator teachers being unable to sit in on all the lectures, of individual group discussions not being consistent, of students gradually "turning off."[6] Pires-Hester's personal notes covering the period from the late 1967 to 1968 suggest a gradual building up of tensions among the CTs and increasing disgruntlement about the demands of the job.[7] Her observations are illustrated by Dodie Younger's reaction to the transition: "Why in the second year none of us yelled our heads off at being asked to teach a course to 100 people in the auditorium I do not know," she said in an interview. Yet she admitted that she learned from the experience: "We struggled with how we could hold the attention of 100 people—we were ingenious—and we developed the ability to do it—no matter what we were teaching."[8]

Another problematical consequence of the renewed federal funding was a shift in the way the money was to be distributed to the growing institution.[9] By 1967 New York City had created a Manpower and Career Development Agency (MCDA) that was designed to take over the funneling of employment-training money to the city. Meanwhile, the person from the local office of the federal Department of Labor who had been assigned to administer the funds to the Women's Talent Corps was heard to say that the "DOL would rather not fund the WTC if it didn't have to."[10]

Rather than becoming accountable to a local agency, Cohen and her associates wanted to maintain the relative independence that federal, rather than local, oversight gave the institution. Letters and phone calls had not worked, so the women decided to make their demands public by taking the kind of action that many other groups were taking in those years. They organized a demonstration. On Friday, September 28, 1967, the Women's Talent Corps led a march of about 150 people, including faculty, students, and other supporters, from the Talent Corps's classrooms at 346 Broadway to the MCDA. Many of the women who joined the march had never participated in a demonstration before ("Can you imagine, these middle class women demonstrating?" Alida Mesrop asked, when remembering the march[11]). But the demonstration succeeded. The Women's Talent Corps was permitted to continue receiving funds directly from the Department of Labor rather to go through the MCDA—a position that was retained until the federal structures became reorganized under CETA.[12] Little did Cohen and her associates know at the time, however, that within three years similar but more radical protest tactics would be used against themselves.

With the independence of their funding secured, Cohen and her colleagues began their next initiative, which was to make the Women's Talent Corps into a degree-granting, bona fide academic institution to be called the College for Human Services. This aim had been hinted at in the 1967 application for the renewal of the OEO funding and had originated in the Women's Talent Corps trainees' own expression of need for more academic learning. In 1969 the program also began to admit men,[13] which pointed to the need for a change in its name. The institution recognized more forcefully as each day passed that it had to become a college.[14]

Becoming a college was easier to wish for than to achieve, however. As a later article by Gerald Grant and David Riesman reported, the Department of Higher Education of New York State rejected the Women's Talent Corps' first application on the grounds that most of its students had not graduated from high school, its faculty did not possess advanced degrees or sufficient college teaching experience, and it did not have an adequate library or endowment. The reviewing officers praised the "social effectiveness" of this dedicated and imaginative group of women but concluded that the Talent Corps lacked "the essential characteristics of a degree-granting institution."[15]

The initial rejection only strengthened Cohen's and her colleagues' resolve. "Audrey Cohen chose to ignore the door that had been shut in her face," Grant and Riesman wrote.[16] Similar to her end run around New York City's blockage of her initial funding proposal for the Women's Talent Corps, she and her colleagues set to work summoning the evidence needed to appeal to the higher level Board of Regents for a reversal of the Department of Education's decision. A group called the Academy for Educational Development was invited to assess the program and ended up approving it. Cohen hired a lawyer to contest the Board of Education's endowment requirement, and she hired more faculty members with specialized degrees. In response to the criticisms of the program's admissions standards, Cohen and her colleagues argued that job performance did not correlate with previous credentials and that students should be admitted without regard to previous formal education if they could pass basic reading and math tests.

In response to criticism of the institution's assessment procedures, Cohen and her colleagues contacted the Educational Testing Service to ask if tests had been developed that could be adapted to the college's program. When the ETS experts could furnish none, the college cited this as evidence of the need for the program to develop its own measures of student performance.[17]

Perhaps the most impressive group to support Cohen's efforts was a team of three respected academics led by Louis Menand from the Massachusetts Institute of Technology (the father of today's well-known Harvard-based historian, Louis Menand). Menand's team spent two days at the Women's Talent Corps visiting classes, observing students at their field placements, interviewing faculty, field supervisors, and administrators, and, as they wrote, of greatest importance, interviewing students. The team's glowing report concluded that the academic program and its supporting co-curricular activities "qualify the Talent Corps to call itself the College for Human Services and to be empowered to recommend the Associate in Arts degree to be awarded by the Board of Regents."[18] By now the curriculum for the Talent Corps included impressive selections from Jean-Jacques Rousseau's *Social Contract*, Plato's *Republic*, Alexis de Tocqueville's *Democracy in America*, and George Orwell's *Animal Farm*.[19] Indeed, the assessors wrote on the final page, the appropriate question "is not whether the quality of the work being done by the proposed college is comparable to that being done in existing community colleges, but rather whether the work in the existing community colleges is comparable to that being done by the proposed college." After examining the performance record of graduates, attrition rates, and employers' evaluations, the team members were moved to wonder if many existing community colleges "could measure up to these standards."[20]

As a result of the well-focused campaign by Cohen and her associates, the Board of Regents of the State of New York provisionally approved in May of 1970 a five-year charter for the new college. To Cohen's great joy, she could now know that she was providing low-income women with a way to earn an associate of arts degree that was a tangible sign of accomplishment.[21] "Regents Charter School for Poor," read a *New York Times* article noting the event. The article quoted Dr. Kenneth B. Clark, a member of the Board of Regents, agreeing that "this is an unusual situation, and the people running this college are unusual people. My admiration for them is practically unlimited." At the end of the article is a quote from Cohen herself that suggests the grandeur of her vision: "I think we have developed a model . . . for moral commitment expressed through social action."[22] Later on, when reflecting on how the college asked of its people to do the most difficult of all things, "to put your trust in something that has not happened," Dodie Younger recalled the moment. "I remember the first time I heard Audrey saying that we were going to become a college and thinking, 'she's crazy . . . this is no college.' And then the next thing I know, I am driving a carload of people to Albany to pick up our charter!"[23]

Having become the head of a bona fide college, Cohen herself began to gain recognition for her work. Even as early as October 1968, *Vogue* magazine featured Cohen as the founder of the "radically proposed College for Human Services" and in a glowing article referred to the college as a "standard-bearer" in education. "Our courses are action oriented for people who can reach out and interpret the community in its own terms," Cohen is quoted as saying.[24] In 1969 she received the Stanley M. Isaacs Award of the American Jewish Committee for "imaginative leadership in expanding the relevance of higher education for disadvantaged mature women, enabling many to lead fulfilling lives in careers of community service"; and in 1970 the college received the George Champion Award given by Chase Manhattan Bank for "dedication to helping disadvantaged people by offering new opportunities for greater self-realization."[25] In July of 1970, a short article about the new college appeared in *Time* magazine hailing Cohen's "vision and tenacity."[26]

The most prestigious recognition, however, was Cohen's being asked by educator Frank Newman to become a member of the Committee on Higher Education. Sponsored by the Secretary of the federal Department of Health, Education, and Welfare and funded by the Ford Foundation, the Newman Committee was formed to study the problems of higher education in the 1960s and early 1970s and to propose solutions and alternatives.[27] Cohen was the only woman appointed to the Newman Committee, and at first the other members, having never heard of the College for Human Services, looked at her somewhat condescendingly. But, as one member later recalled, "she was feisty, gave as good as she got, was not a shrinking violet, and in the end made more friends than enemies." She was gifted, this observer noted, at finding ways to do something that needed doing.

"She was inspirational and charismatic and could keep the pieces together when it looked as though they would fly apart."[28] As a consequence of Cohen's valuable work on the committee, the committee members came to see that the College for Human Services, while nontraditional, filled a vital niche in the academic landscape.

That she was not a "shrinking violet" is clear from a position paper she wrote for the Newman Task Force and that was later published in *Phi Delta Kappan*, a widely read magazine for professional educators. For Cohen personally, the experience of being part of an all-male think tank seems to have strengthened her awareness of the need for more educational opportunities for women. Entitled "Women and Higher Education: Recommendations for Change," the article forcefully lays out the roadblocks to women's full participation in higher education at that time, including the scarcity of women on university faculties, differentials in pay scales, and the lack of child-care facilities. Among her recommendations are for colleges and universities to establish campus health services for women and to institute "female studies" programs. Given that today women outnumber men at many colleges and graduate schools, and that health services for women and women's studies programs have become available on most campuses, much of her critique now sounds dated. Nevertheless, Cohen's general call for institutions of higher education to "help all students develop a new image of women as human beings, capable of substantial contributions to the academic, scientific, and political world around them" continues to resonate. Uncharacteristically Cohen's article does not mention her own institutional groundwork, but the byline refers to her as "the creator and president of the unique new College for Human Services . . . recently chartered by the state."[29]

Although the college's new charter brought status and recognition to Cohen's fledgling project, the overall morale of the faculty and students continued to sour. One source of disillusionment that later received some negative publicity was the failure of the legal service assistant program, a joint venture that the college arranged with the Columbia University Law School. College for Human Services students in the program spent one-third of their time in the interdisciplinary curriculum at the college, one-third in courses in legal skills and analysis at Columbia (with special emphasis on poverty-related law), and one-third working as legal aides in neighborhood law offices. The program was terminated after only two years, mostly because the wide range of time-management and writing skills that the College for Human Services students brought to the program made their overall performance unpredictable. Almost half of the students dropped out after the first year, and by the end of the second year only six out of the original twenty-three students were actually hired as legal paraprofessionals.[30] Neither Cohen nor her associates dwelled on the failure of this closely watched educational experiment, but for faculty and students the experience raised questions about the viability of the college's program as a whole.

Complaints about their workload, about a lack of communication, and a growing ferment among some faculty members and students over questions about race and power led Cohen in the summer of 1970 to hire Preston Wilcox's consulting firm, Afram Associates, to lead a two-day series of sensitivity training sessions. There was also an altruistic motive behind the decision: Preston Wilcox had been chairman of the college's Board of Trustees since 1966, and, as Cohen remembered later, she wanted to give him some opportunity to learn more about the college. "I wanted to be helpful to him."[31]

Faculty and staff were invited to participate in the sensitivity training process. After a plenary session the participants were broken down into smaller groups and encouraged by a group leader to share honestly their feelings about the functioning of the college, their roles and responsibilities, their hopes and fears. As Cohen later observed, the kinds of problems that began to surface during those two days were crucial to understanding what happened later. From hearing faculty and students openly express their grievances, Cohen learned that there were factions within the college that did not believe in the mission and "considered their own black students and fellow workers and themselves as inferior, and could not see them playing a prominent role in bringing about needed change in higher education."[32] Students felt that they were not getting enough support from faculty, and faculty felt overwhelmed by the responsibilities of meeting students' needs both in the field and in the classroom.

Interwoven with these stresses were questions coming from the larger urban context about race and power. In the previous year, even the relatively mainstream *Ebony* magazine had given voice to some of the newfound assertiveness regarding race and identity that Stokely Carmichael's leadership had brought to SNCC and that the Black Panther movement was beginning to exhibit. "Liberation is impossible if we fail to see ourselves in more positive terms," an article about black liberation in the arts by Larry Neal proclaimed. "For without a change of vision, we are slaves to the oppressor's ideas and values—ideas and values that finally attack the very core of our existence." Black Power, the article goes on to say, "teaches us that we must have ultimate control over our own lives."[33] In a position paper that had been circulated earlier in the decade by SNCC, white liberals and radicals who were trying to organize in black communities were specific objects of criticism. "The problem is not in the black community. The white people should go into white communities where the whites have created power for the express purpose of denying blacks human dignity and self-determination."[34]

As participants in an educational experiment headed by a white Jewish woman, many students at the College for Human Services in the early 1970s were inspired by the Black Power movement's logic, as were many faculty members. At the sensitivity sessions organized by Afram Associates, their challenging questions about race and power were juxtaposed with equally provocative questions about the role of human services providers. "What are the consequences of serving your own people justly? Is this your goal? Or is your goal to make it in the system? Does one try to make change or does one just try to 'make it'?" The intensive two-day event left Cohen somewhat dejected, as she said later, and aware that the college needed a "major overhaul if we were going to realistically attack the kinds of problems we had set ourselves up against."[35]

THE STRIKE

The major overhaul that Cohen first saw the need for during the sensitivity sessions in mid-1970 would not occur until three years later, in 1973. Simmering dissatisfaction on the part of the faculty, confrontation with city and state agencies, and the need to create the academic foundations for an AA degree were minor challenges compared to the disrupting institutional crisis that Cohen and her associates were faced with in the late summer of 1970. The trouble started on Tuesday, August 11, when, after nearly two weeks of deliberations,[36] the administration terminated the employment of Robert Jackson, a black member of the staff who had been hired to direct the second year of the college's two-year program. Reasons for the termination—communicated to him both orally and in writing—were his failure to integrate his component of the curriculum into the total program of the college and his failure to adhere to the college's budget guidelines, "thereby jeopardizing the financial stability of the institution."[37] In a taped recollection of the event afterward Cohen elaborated on the specifics of the charge: Jackson had not been forthcoming in discussing budgetary issues with the rest of the staff, and by midway in the semester he had already spent $13,000 of the total $19,000 allocated to the program.[38]

Jackson refused to leave the premises of the college and began to spread the word that he had been treated unjustly.[39] By August 12, a group referring to themselves as Black and Brown Faculty and Students had coalesced to protest the firing. Terming it an example of the "arbitrary, unjust and racist practices of the administration," the group wrote up a list of eight demands ranging from the provision of free office supplies and giving students a voice in all hiring procedures to the immediate reinstatement of Bob Jackson.[40] Cohen and Pires-Hester met with the students that same day and in response sent out a memo and a letter addressed to them. The administration agreed to bring the students' issues before the Board of Trustees but also explained in detail the procedures that had been used in Bob Jackson's termination. The letter included an acknowledgment of Jackson's right to appeal the termination to the Board of Trustees (which by now had representatives from the student body) and his right to seek further legal recourse if necessary.

As Cohen herself recollected, Bob Jackson was meeting with students at this time and giving them questions to ask. On Thursday, August 13, the students requested to meet with Cohen, but somehow the message did not get to her. In retrospect she said that she had no idea that students were ready to walk out and was thus surprised when, on the next day, the students had formed picket lines in front of the College for Human Service entrance at 201 Varick Street. Cohen contacted the Board of Trustees and scheduled a meeting for the following Sunday. On Sunday, August 16, the board met, and as Cohen recalled, the meeting lasted for twelve hours.[41]

During the meeting Board Chairman Preston Wilcox telephoned and then wrote to Robert Jackson inviting him to meet with a committee of the board. Jackson refused to meet, claiming that since he had not requested such a meeting, attending it might jeopardize his legal rights. Wilcox wrote again, saying that an appeals committee had been formed to meet with him if Jackson decided to follow the "due process" course. Wilcox ended the letter with "Liberation, then peace" and signed it "Brother Preston Wilcox."[42] Still Jackson did not respond.

The situation continued to deteriorate. By early the next week, a number of faculty members had joined the movement and resolved to strike to support the students' demands. A petition dated August 18 and signed by eight faculty members affirmed the students' aims and added the demand that Cohen resign as president and be replaced by "a competent Black or Brown administrator." The petition referred to its aims as being consistent with the college's mission: "Implicit in the goal of the College is also the goal that Blacks and Puerto Ricans no longer advise the decision makers but actually make those decisions which vitally affect their lives." The petition ended with a stinging quote from a speech by Preston Wilcox himself: "If you are white and you have a need to make decisions about how to manage Black people, . . . you are a racist. If you are white and you are working in a Black community or sitting on top of an organization that is serving the Black community, you are a racist."[43]

For Wilcox, the irony of seeing his own words used against him must have been very painful. Here he was, working hard to lead the Board of Trustees of an institution that he felt was empowering his own people, but now those people were claiming that the head of the institution herself was the enemy. At this point in the crisis his response was to shoulder on. By the next day he and the board had composed a five-page carefully written memo addressed to faculty, students, staff, and administration laying out what the college had already done and was preparing to do to respond to the strikers' and picketers' demands. Entitled "Report to the College for Human Services Family," the memo deals with the eight demands point by point and ends with a carefully worded assertion that the board had the sole right to select the college's president and vice president. Wilcox ends with an invitation to all the addressees to contact him at his office "if they have *specific* suggestions, complaints, and actions they feel that the Board should hear and/or act upon."[44]

The strike continued for the next two weeks. About sixty students and ten faculty members participated.[45] Despite the daily picketing, Cohen and her associates continued to keep the college open and functioning, although classes were not held. Meeting late at night and frequently in the early mornings, she later recalled, they wrestled over whether the nonstriking students could be guided inside the building and offered protection so that they could get beyond Bob Jackson and the people carrying the picket signs outside. It was decided only to encourage the nonstriking students to continue their field work at the agencies so that they would not be faced with more intimidation than was necessary. Administrators also wrestled with the payroll questions. The end of the month was coming up, and, because the college was still being federally funded as a New Careers program, the students were being paid $62 per week to attend. A decision on student funding was not reached, but it was decided that faculty who were out on the picket line should not be paid.[46]

The ongoing crisis took a tremendous toll on Preston Wilcox. Again, Cohen's memories of the period give a sense of the personal struggle that the official documents from Board of Trustees files do not reveal. Cohen spoke on the phone with Wilcox's wife Marilyn, who said that he was physically exhausted. There were even demonstrations at the office of Afram Associates in Harlem aimed at him. Cohen later heard that having black people march on his office in Harlem was too much for Wilcox to bear. "The students had posters calling him names, had my picture at the top and his picture further behind. They ridiculed him before his friends and admirers on 125th Street, and . . . he was in a state of shock."[47] The event would have life-changing consequences for Wilcox's relationship to Cohen's project.

The strike reached its climax on Wednesday, September 2, when Cohen's own office was taken over by the striking faculty and students. Cohen's later reflections on this moment focus mostly on the individuals involved and are not very useful. More telling is the media coverage of the occupation, although Cohen and her colleagues later called some of the reporting distorted.[48] According to a *New York Times* article on the episode, about thirty students and faculty members entered Cohen's office shortly before noon and demanded her resignation. "The president sat, without saying a word, as female students taunted her and waved in front of her a letter of resignation,"[49] the article reads. " 'You blue-eyed devil, sign this,' Brenda Scurry, a 24-year-old student, screamed at her." A faculty member told the *Times* reporter that she was supporting the president's dismissal because "she is racist, paternalistic, and has manipulated the poor since this college was founded." The demonstrators milled around the office; one student took over the phone. Robert Jackson, according to the *Times* account, sat reading *History Will Absolve Me*, by Fidel Castro.[50] Cohen did not dispute these facts later on, but did argue that there were twenty, not thirty, demonstrators, and as many as half of them were in no way connected with the college.[51]

Finally at 6:30 P.M. the demonstrators left the building and Cohen returned home. She had agreed to meet with them in the auditorium the next day, Thursday, September 3, to discuss their demands. Under the headline, "Students Decide to End Strike at College for Human Services" the *New York Times* reported that at the noisy, six-hour meeting the administration agreed to grant three of the demonstrators' nine demands. It would expand the college's appeals board to include students and faculty members and would let the new board try the case of Robert Jackson. It also promised to take no reprisals against strikers, and, surprisingly perhaps, to pay them for the three weeks that they were on strike from classes. The demands not granted were a public accounting of all college funds (although, Cohen later told the *New York Times*, detailed accountings of all federal college funds are always available to individuals on request), an equal voice in hiring the president and faculty (a decision that is the responsibility of the Board of Trustees), and use of the college's mimeograph machine and clerical supplies. (The article states that the documents that the strikers had been handing out during the demonstration were printed at the nearby office headquarters of Congresswoman Bella Abzug.) Thanks to the administration having invited *all* enrolled students, not just the demonstrators, to attend the event, at the end of the meeting, by a vote of 70 to 3 the students decided to drop their demand for Cohen's resignation. They also voted to return to classes the following week.[52]

THE AFTERMATH

Throughout the strike Cohen had maintained a courageous demeanor, at least in public. At the height of the demonstration in her office, she told the *New York Times* reporter afterward, "I was more afraid for the program than I was for my physical safety. Trouble like this could cause us to lose our funding."[53] At home her daughter Dawn saw a more vulnerable side. She remembers her mother coming home in tears and her father, Mark, comforting her. They barricaded themselves away from their daughters, because Audrey "certainly wouldn't want to cry in front of us." Dawn was struck by her mother's deep hurt. As she understood it at the time, her mother's motivation for putting so much work into the college was *not* a self-righteous act of charity. It was not like a social worker or a wealthy philanthropists' attitude. "Her attitude was more like, 'Let's do this together,'" and that's why she felt so surprised and betrayed by the hostility.[54]

Conversations with Laura Pires-Hester helped Audrey Cohen understand the students' anger and put the event into a larger context. Pires-Hester had worked with Dr. Kenneth Clark at HARYOU and had studied many of the issues covered in Clark's pathbreaking 1965 work, *Dark Ghetto: Dilemmas of Social Power*. Both during and after the strike she gave Cohen a way to process the students' actions. "Remember that for all those years we were taking in students and at the same time struggling for some recognition in status," Cohen explained to Alida Mesrop later on. "It was always easy to attack us . . . to say 'you're a dreamer' or 'you're moving ahead but you're using us.'" Added to that uncertainty was a deep sense of inferiority that most of the students came to the college harboring. "I am incapable of doing what you're talking about—graduating from a college, reading and writing on a sophisticated level—how dare you!' So on the one hand there was this tremendous self-hatred and on the other these dreams that I was sending out."[55] The combination of uncertainty and insecurity caused resentment and became contagious, Cohen concluded.

Back at the college the following week Cohen and her colleagues set to work to try to make the structure of the institution more transparent and to address some of the deep tensions that the strike revealed. Several of the faculty members who had been involved in the strike left the college voluntarily, and one was fired. The staff began a series of meetings to try to pull themselves together, Cohen recalled, and worked to develop a system that allowed student input from the ground up.[56] Out of the meetings came what Cohen proclaimed was a "totally participatory" system of committees and subcommittees, and Cohen was energized by the prospects for improvement. It was a trial period, she admitted, but exciting. It was also a period of hard work, for in November the first cohort of students to be awarded the associate of arts degree would graduate.

For Preston Wilcox and the Board of Trustees, however, the wounds inflicted by the strike continued to fester. Wilcox's leadership of the board became more erratic as he increasingly identified with the Black Power movement. The board minutes of a meeting on November 13, 1970, for example, refer to the "Resignation of the Chairman" in the previous meeting's minutes but add as a correction that Wilcox "did not tender his resignation to the Board." There followed a two-hour discussion of Wilcox's status, with nothing resolved except the need for improved communication between the college's various constituencies. The minutes end with the statement, "Preston Wilcox is able to give the Board the leadership it needs."[57]

Wilcox's ambivalence about the college became more evident in a December 22, 1970, letter addressed to Professor Kalu Kalu, a black member of the faculty who was the first male to be hired by the college. A leader of the Biafran independence movement in Nigeria, Kalu had immigrated to the United States and had studied economics at Yale and Berkeley. At the College for Human Services he was perceived as a dignified, loyal supporter of Cohen's vision and had been elected to be the faculty representative to the board.

Written on Afram Associates letterhead, Wilcox's letter to Kalu focuses on the college's curriculum. Wilcox lists three areas about which he is particularly concerned. The first is the need for students to get credit for past experiences and the second is for them to be involved in curriculum development. The third item is more inflammatory. Here Wilcox states that he is concerned that racism is included only "as *one* of one of many 'reality conditions and limitations,' as against being *the* basic underlying condition." He goes on to say, "I am prepared to state that the College for Human Services is a white racist institution and that its major mission should be to confront itself *first* as a means to deal with that reality." The aim, he continues, is not to try to make blacks and Puerto Ricans "equal" to whites but to enable them to acquire the "skills, desire, and knowledge to refuse to participate in their own oppression."[58]

Included in Wilcox's examples of how to educate students for resistance to their own oppression is what was in 1970 an almost unheard of aim. "Black and Puerto Rican students must be educated as members of their communities of origin; heavy inputs must be made as to the authenticity of their own cultures." Twenty years prior to the Afrocentric curricula that scholars such as Molefi Kete Asante made popular in the 1990s, Wilcox suggests that colleges offer courses that are specifically aimed at celebrating the history and cultures of the African diaspora.

In the final paragraph of his letter to Kalu, Wilcox's ambivalence over his relationship with the college becomes clear. "I have a feeling that you will receive my concerns as an 'order' largely because I am Chairman of the Board. This is not the case. I am a member of the Black community *first* and have a non-negotiable right to be concerned about its destiny. As such I speak from the perspective of one whose destiny is effected by such outcomes." Somewhat disturbingly, he signs the letter, "Power to the correct people—Preston."[59] There is no evidence that Kalu responded to Wilcox's December 22 letter. But later Kalu spoke about his repeated efforts to get Wilcox to support the college's mission. "If you believe that the students are getting an education geared to their needs and their experience, stay and defend the institution," he told Wilcox.[60]

Despite Kalu's efforts, board minutes and Cohen's memories of the period document the growing breach between Wilcox and the college. The minutes for a meeting on May 20, 1971, for example, end with a statement by Wilcox that, "Possibly my goals and those of the Board are in direct conflict."[61] As Cohen remembered it, Wilcox began acting confrontational and several times threatened to resign. Despite his contentiousness, she said, she repeatedly requested that he remain as chair. But finally one day she and Wilcox met together at Millie Robbins Leet's home on Riverside Drive. Leet had recently become a member of the board and had contributed financial support to the college as well as good advice to Cohen. It was just the three of them and they were talking about some issue and Wilcox got very upset, Cohen recalled. At one point he said, "I'm walking out. I'm leaving." In the past Cohen had always responded, "Preston we need you. You are the leader of this Board." But this time she refrained. "It was everything I could do to keep my mouth shut, and Millie kept her mouth shut. We just stood there and looked at him and he looked at us." Cohen felt that it had been the right thing to do. "It meant that he left. He was the one who had just done it."[62]

Reflecting on Wilcox's resignation many years later, Cohen appeared to be still trying to understand it. "He was absolutely so distraught about our relationship . . . and always created situations until that big blowup at the meeting at Millie's." It was a complex relationship. "Preston was actually convoluted about what to do. . . . He wanted to cut his ties with whites. He wanted to go and serve blacks."[63] And yet, she reflected, "Preston was always very taken with my ideas, what I wanted to do, and he was very supportive." So he was torn. "Could he support this good work or did he cut himself loose because this was a White Woman, a Jewish White Woman" who was in charge?[64]

Wilcox did cut himself loose and officially resigned from the board in the spring of 1972.[65] In the extensive biographical materials that can be found online about Preston Wilcox and his important work as an academic and a community leader, there is no mention at all of the Women's Talent Corps or its later incarnation as the College for Human Services—an institution whose foundations he so carefully worked to build for six crucial years. As Kalu Kalu sadly recalled, "He could have been a major player in an important institution instead of just a footnote. He truly suffered. I never understood how he could do that to himself."[66]

FACULTY OVERHAUL

Wilcox's replacement as chair of the Board of Trustees was Lionel F. Payne, a program coordinator of the Bedford-Stuyvesant Model Cities program, who took office in 1973. Payne's chairmanship of the board gets us ahead of the story, however, for by mid-1973 the College for Human Services had entered a new phase of "restructuring," which is the focus of the next chapter.

Between 1971 and the end of 1972 the college continued to suffer from internal tensions. In the aftermath of the strike, despite Cohen's rosy assertions of having come up with a "totally participatory" system of committees that would keep lines of communication open, the overall morale did not improve. Many students continued to express confusion about what was expected of them, faculty complained of overwork, and staff sometimes doubted the ability of the college to meet external expectations of measurable performance.[67]

Once again the institution's achievements may have contributed to the unrest. As the College's Fifth Annual Report records, in 1971 the college was awarded "Recognized Candidate" status by the Middle States Commission on Higher Education, the first step toward accreditation; a new Mental Health Careers project began to be implemented; and the U.S. Office of Economic Opportunity approved a planning grant to enable the college to develop a model for a two-year "professional institute."[68] The buzz about a new professional institute was particularly unsettling. "What did this mean for students?" many asked. "What about the AA degree?" In November 1971 the faculty submitted a report listing their ongoing grievances. They were dissatisfied with their salaries, they were still not clear about whether the place where they were teaching was a college in the traditional sense or a job-training program, and they faulted the administration, once again, for "lack of communication."[69]

Another source of tension was the growing realization that the associate of arts degree was not enabling students to enter the lines of professional advancement that they came into the program expecting. Many service agencies were now expecting their employees to have at least a bachelor's or even a master's degree. Cohen and her associates at first tried to solve this problem by attempting to develop articulation agreements with Columbia University and New York University that would enable College for Human Services students to transfer to those institutions to complete their degrees. But the linkage effort was only successful on a very small scale.[70] As Cohen later wrote, "Four-year colleges were not interested in undergraduate programs that blended theory and practice." The National Association of Social Workers, for example, actively opposed the college's efforts to gain accreditation for professional training at the undergraduate level. As a result of these setbacks, the administration began to realize that it needed to develop its own full "continuum" of baccalaureate and master's degree programs, without which the population that the college aimed to serve would be "at a dead end."[71]

In June 1972, Cohen tried to address some of the faculty's concerns about the college's future in a speech that acknowledged how unsettling change can be. "We have never been an institution which is satisfied with what it has achieved; we have always worked to become something more," she said, and added a philosophical note, "We have always been in the process of becoming." But, she acknowledged, this very process-oriented existence creates tremendous stresses and strains. The college's continuing efforts to make changes in higher education, in credentializing standards, in job opportunities, in its efforts to become the country's first two-year professional institute, mean that those associated with the College for Human Services must be prepared to "face questions and challenges as individuals."[72]

The faculty may not have realized it at the time, but Cohen's charge to the faculty to face questions and challenges as individuals foreshadowed a difficult decision that she made before the end of that year. As it became more and more apparent that the fledgling institution required a major restructuring, it also became apparent that it could not continue to conduct business as usual during the period of change. In October 1972, the Board of Trustees announced that in order to complete its restructuring goal within the timeframe stipulated in the OEO grant for the process, the college would phase out its associate of arts program, not accepting any new students and only maintaining a minimal teaching staff to allow the second-year students to complete their degree. The college would begin six months of intensive planning on January 2, 1973, with only a small, specialized group, a "skilled task force," retained for the restructuring process. "The Board gives full authority to the President of the College to restructure the College staff, with such reductions as may be deemed necessary, into such a specialized planning body," the statement read.[73]

An audiotape that Cohen made of a conversation about her own thinking at this time and that was later transcribed reveals the shifting dynamics of her difficult decision. "Looking back it seems inevitable that we should make this decision, and yet it portends difficulties for a number of people and therefore raises questions that cause me great concern." She proceeds to describe the previous "disruption" of the college and the sense of depression that had gripped the college in the past year. Two alternatives had been suggested. One was for her to leave the college and to allow it to die; another alternative was to continue to do what she had been doing and fighting to keep the college alive. Cohen was not comfortable with either of these alternatives. To simply allow the college to fade away would mean to waste of all the energy that had gone into it and to neglect all the good that had been accomplished. But the second alternative, to continue on as it was, would only mean keeping the college alive "rather than to let it grow." After a brief digression, Cohen's thinking gravitates suddenly back to the subject of growth. What she wants to do next, she says, is to create colleges for human services *all over the country.* "The perfect plan, the plan I'm working on, is to build the two-year professional institution; simultaneous with that to begin spreading it across the country, *spreading it as the College for Human Services.*"[74]

Evident here in the unpolished transcriptions of Cohen's conversations is the extraordinary resilience of her thought processes. At a moment when everyone around her was seeing only the college's demise, she was thinking in terms of national outreach. When it looked like her institution's future was doomed, she was planning for its expansion. The doggedness with which she pursued her grandiose plans would at times infuriate her colleagues, but as the following chapters show, the results often justified the persistence of her vision.

On October 20, 1972, Cohen sent letters by registered mail to all members of the college staff indicating whether they were to be retained or terminated. Nine members of the faculty and six members of the clerical and fiscal office staff were let go, effective December 31. The dismissals caused consternation and resentment, and several faculty members resigned in protest. Others brought complaints against the college through the National Labor Relations Board (NLRB) and through the American Association of University Professors (AAUP).[75] These were not sustained, but some of the people who were terminated harbored resentment against the college for decades.

Having terminated the employment of many veteran faculty members, Cohen quickly turned to the restructuring and teaching tasks that lay ahead. The story of how the College for Human Services used a year of intensive discussion to create a new conceptual framework for teaching, learning, and assessment is the focus of the next chapter. At this point, however, it might be useful to try to make some sense out of the institutional crisis that has been described thus far. One interpretation is that until the 1970 strike, the college's loosely structured two-year program was able to reflect the social justice currents at work in American urban society as a whole. But when a rift developed between integration and black power in the nation at large, these tensions were reflected internally, and at that point Cohen saw that in order to create an institution more immune to local pressures she would need to start over with a more tightly structured four-year college.[76]

To see the evolution of the college primarily in terms of a response to racial currents, however, is to overinterpret Cohen's decisions in racial terms. Racial tensions of the early 1970s were certainly forces to be reckoned with. The strike by College for Human Services students and faculty occurred on the very same day that a warrant went out for Angela Davis's arrest for allegedly supplying the guns used in a shootout at the trial in California of George Jackson, a Soledad Brother and Black Panther. The demonstrators in front of 201 Varick Street and Cohen herself were undoubtedly aware of these events at the time. Yet central to Cohen's commitments throughout her adult life was meaningful work for women, not racial integration. Although most students enrolled in Cohen's program then and now have been members of minority groups, a discourse focusing on race was never her primary concern.[77]

For Cohen, reform of the human services professions and preparation of practitioners of all races for humane and useful work always took precedence over identity politics. A brief chapter that she contributed at this time to a volume entitled *Public Service Employment: An Analysis of Its History, Problems, and Prospects* makes clear her guiding principles. All of our economic and ecological concerns, she begins, are ultimately rooted in the understanding that "we must allow people to be useful, to develop to their fullest capacity."[78] Cohen proceeds to argue that to achieve such development we need to replace the old concept of *civil service* with a new policy of *public service*. Such a transformation would require the collaboration of governmental and educational institutions. "Experiential new humanpower schools and colleges should be established with federal funding," she asserts. With an uncanny hint of what the college would later call a Constructive Action, she adds that in such settings both skills and knowledge would be "constantly related to practical situations in a work-study orientation."[79] Noting the general bias against women at that time, she stresses that the new public service roles would require a blending of male and female qualities as well as new ways of thinking about assessment. "If we can construct a society wherein public service truly means serving the public good," she says, where the educational system is designed "to make full use of each individual's potential at every age," and where service delivery is both "competent and humane," we will have achieved much. So, she concludes, "let us begin with the educational process—it is certainly worth a try."[80]

Indeed, in many ways the strike at the college and its aftermath can be seen as simply giving Cohen the chance to expand the college in ways that she was leaning toward even before the summer of 1970. In this regard one must remember that the strike in 1970 at the College for Human Services was by no means an anomaly. In that year more than 450 university, college, and high school campuses were shut down, mostly in response to the May 4 killing by the National Guard of four students at Kent State University who were protesting the American invasion of Cambodia. The upheavals at the College for Human Services were not inconsistent with what was happening on other campuses; the difference was that Cohen was able to use the crisis as an opportunity for restructuring, something other college presidents were generally unable to do. The events should be seen not as determinative of the college's future path but rather as providing the occasion for an open-ended process that resulted in its path.

DISSENT AT HOME

Given the tenor of the times, it is not surprising that during the period covered by this chapter Audrey Cohen was facing acts of mild rebellion at home in addition to the more serious uprisings at her place of work. In 1969 the Cohens' older daughter Dawn turned twelve, and having always been a precocious child, began an early period of adolescent self-assertiveness that lasted well into her twenties. As Dawn tells the story, her confrontations with her parents were mostly based on disagreements over religion. Mark Cohen's father had been active at the prestigious Temple Emanu-El on Fifth Avenue, and although Mark and Audrey were not particularly observant Jews (they ate pork, celebrated Christmas as well as Hanukkah, and did not regularly attend synagogue), out of respect for Mark's father they sent their young daughters to Sunday School at Temple Emanu-El. When Mark's father died, Audrey saw no use of continuing the practice. Dawn's version of what happened is that her mother said, "OK, good! Now we can quit. I don't want to pay the dues anymore." Dawn's angry retort was, "You want me to quit? *I won't!*"[81]

Dawn wanted to experience more of her religious heritage, not less. She proceeded to choose her own synagogue, insisting that Wendy go to a different one. Her father fell for the idea that Dawn needed her own space and didn't want to have her younger sister tagging along. But the choice regarding which synagogue she would attend marked the start of ongoing conflicts between the headstrong twelve-year-old and her parents. Dawn joined the Temple Israel where she became involved in a Zionist youth movement called Hashomer Hatzair. "It was the beginning of an incredible Israel-centric existence," she recalls. Within a couple of years she was attending Jewish youth group meetings in the Bronx and, she says with a knowing smile, her parents were "*horrified*."[82]

Dawn's early embrace of a more Israel-centered Judaism than either of her parents had dreamed of for their children caused tensions at the time. But Dawn's choice also enabled her later to speculate about the religious roots of her mother's social activism—a source of influence that Audrey Cohen's friends and associates generally dismissed.[83] Although Cohen's Jewish faith was nothing that she spent much time trying to cultivate in her children, Dawn says, her mother's awareness of blacks and Jews having both been ghettoized gave her a sense of connection with the minority, low-income women whom her college aimed to serve. Much of the Torah's message, Dawn points out, is about the responsibility to *tikkun olam*, to repair the world, to make it a better place,[84] and probably those teachings seeped into her mother's consciousness at an early age.

Since 1974 the ultimate goal of improving the world is an explicit aim of every constructive action performed by students at the college that Audrey Cohen founded. The process of building a curriculum that would make that aim possible began in 1973 and is the focus of the next chapter.

CHAPTER 7

REINVENTING HIGHER EDUCATION (1973–1974)

> For all of my adult life, I have struggled conceptually with the idea of blending theory and practice.
>
> —Cohen, 1978, p. 37

Periods of social change are often accompanied by innovations in education, and the 1960s and 1970s are no exception.[1] Along with the civil rights movement, the women's movement, and student activism on college campuses came passionate calls for fundamental changes in elementary and secondary education. A.S. Neill's *Summerhill: A Radical Approach to Childrearing* (1960), and Paul Goodman's *Growing Up Absurd: Problems of Youth in Organized Society* (1962) led the way in the early 1960s. Best-sellers in the decade that followed included John Holt's *How Children Fail* (1964), Herbert Kohl's *36 Children* (1967), Jonathan Kozol's *Death at an Early Age* (1967), George Dennison's *The Lives of Children* (1970), and Ivan Illich's *Deschooling Society* (1970). Although based on a wide range of personal experiences with schools and with children, the books had in common a vision of educational settings in which students had a voice, teachers were psychologically savvy, and the curriculum was relevant to the changing times.

Like bean seedlings sprouting up after a rain, a number of independent schools were founded in this period that echoed or tried to put into practice the liberating educational vision of the reformers. In New York City, for example, Augustus and Martha Trowbridge founded Manhattan

Country School, a conscious effort to bring together John Dewey's progressive educational ideals and Martin Luther King Jr.'s dream of a community that transcends race and class.[2] The Children's Storefront School opened as an alternative for parents in Harlem dissatisfied with the regimentation found in their local public schools. The Calhoun School, though founded in the nineteenth century, was rebuilt in 1975 to house an "open classroom" model of movable walls within each floor. In neighborhoods throughout the city, parent cooperatives, free schools, and daycare centers were set up to create an open and tolerant setting for children in their early years.[3]

Less well publicized at the time and less obvious to the general public than the 1960s experiments in elementary schooling were similarly bold new experiments in higher education. Indeed, as sociologists Gerald Grant and David Riesman make clear in their 1978 book *The Perpetual Dream: Reform and Experiment in the American College*, innovations at the college level in the 1960s and 1970s were as widespread and often as radical as the innovations in elementary schools. For their survey of the changes in higher education that they saw occurring in the "decade of experiment" of the 1960s, Grant and Riesman visited more than four-hundred colleges and universities where recent changes had occurred, and they then made return visits to more than thirty.[4] In their book they chose to focus on six colleges that they felt best represented the educational innovations of their era.

Cohen's founding of College for Human Services is one of the six college experiments of the 1960s that Grant and Riesman showcase in *The Perpetual Dream*. The first half of the book, entitled "Models of Telic Reform," focuses on new structures for higher education that the authors found to be based on an overarching and distinctive *telos*, or purpose. These are models, they explain, that "have generated a productive dialogue about distinctive or competing purposes of undergraduate education."[5] Under that heading the model that they use to exemplify the era's "Activist-Radical Impulse" is the College for Human Services.

What was it about the College for Human Services that drew Grant and Riesman's interest? In what ways was the college an example of the "activist and radical impulse" of the 1960s? In addition to its unique combining of academic study with human service training, what has always distinguished the college that Cohen founded from other colleges in the United States is the structure of its curriculum. Before describing the historical process that in 1973 resulted in the college's unique curricular model, it may be useful here at the outset to introduce the essential components that prompted Grant and Riesman to feature the college so prominently in their book.

The college's curriculum is based on a conceptual framework that has its own unique vocabulary. In contrast to most colleges and schools where there are "semesters" of study, each term at what is now MCNY is identified with reference to its *Purpose*. Instead of a "senior thesis" that traditionally educated students must complete only at the end of their senior year, MCNY students must produce a *Constructive Action* document every semester, systematically recording a significant, purposeful action that they undertake at an agency or workplace and that in some way aims to improve the world. And in place of the array of isolated "disciplines" of learning within which most American students must pursue their studies, the curriculum at MCNY is presented as a set of integrated *Dimensions* of learning that are required for all students and that thread across the whole sequence of semester Purposes.

Purposes, Constructive Actions (or "CAs" as students invariably call them) and *Dimensions* are terms unique to the college and are the main components of the Purpose-Centered curricular model that has provided thousands of low-income adult students with a meaningful college education ever since the restructuring process that began in 1973. The college's terminology will be further defined in the next chapter. At this point, however, it may be useful to provide an outline of the model that emerged from the restructuring process.

Purposes

As a carryover from the Women's Talent Corps, students at what is now Metropolitan College of New York can begin their college experience in the fall, winter, or spring. Whenever they choose to start, students go through a structured sequence of courses, with each semester's courses having a specific focus or purpose. In the human services program (which provides the exemplary model for this overview), Purpose I, the name given to the student's first semester, focuses on "Self-assessment and Preparation for Practice." In that semester the student is introduced to the skills necessary for college success and for upcoming responsibilities in a human service agency or workplace. The second semester, Purpose II, focuses on "Developing Professional Relationships." By this point students, with the help of the college's field placement services, have settled into an internship or job where they will work two or three days a week. The coursework for Purpose II relates to developing an understanding of that specific agency and the history of the human services profession.

Purposes III, IV, and V (i.e., the student's third, fourth, and fifth semesters in the program) focus on the skills and knowledge necessary to become a human service professional. Purpose III's focus is on working in groups, Purpose IV's focus is on "Teaching and Communication," and Purpose V's focus is on "Counseling." The final three semesters of the program (Purposes VI, VII, and VIII) move the student into wider spheres of responsibility. Purpose VI requires the students to act as a "Community Liaison," Purpose VII requires that they undertake responsibilities of "Supervision," and Purpose VIII requires them to plan a project that "Promotes" positive institutional "Change." Underlying the overall curricular structure is the developmental aim of moving the student from an emphasis on the self to an emphasis on the larger society.

CONSTRUCTIVE ACTIONS

At the heart of each semester's curriculum is the requirement to complete a Constructive Action in the field. As currently defined, a Constructive Action is a "planned effort to use knowledge in effective action."[6] It is a project undertaken in a field setting that has a specific, constructive, aim relating to that semester's purpose. The setting may be as obscure as the Paradise Transitional Housing Program or as well known as the New York Hospital for Special Surgery. The action may involve counseling sessions with one individual or a restructuring project for a whole organization. The scope may be as small as teaching a paraplegic how to use a toothbrush or as large as establishing a daycare center in Haiti. In general the project needs to be an action that can be completed within one semester, although there are some exceptions to that general guideline. As mentioned earlier, in some way, a Constructive Action should aim to improve the world.

Regardless of the specific project a student undertakes for his or her Constructive Action each semester, the process must be documented in a substantial (50- to 100-page) written report that includes a needs assessment, a literature review, a plan of action, a record of the implementation of the plan, and an assessment of the results. Most importantly, in each section of the Constructive Action document, students must refer to content knowledge that is relevant to the project. This may include case studies, theories, or databases; the content knowledge may come from sociology, philosophy, history, psychology, economics, or literature. Where do the students acquire this knowledge? What is the academic framework that enables them to effectively complete a constructive action and to document it?

DIMENSIONS

Here is where the uniqueness of the college's curricular structure becomes most apparent. An even more radical feature than giving each semester a performance-oriented purpose is the college's replacement of traditional disciplines (sociology, philosophy, history, literature, economics, sociology) with what it calls *Dimensions* of learning. The five Dimensions—Values and Ethics, Self and Others, Systems, Skills, and the Purpose Seminar (where the Constructive Action is assigned)—are transdisciplinary conceptual categories through which knowledge for action is learned. Listed vertically in the matrix below, these Dimension courses provide the academic substance for each semester's work. Originally they were conceived as kinds of "awareness" that every human service provider should have—awareness of values, awareness of self and others, awareness of systems, awareness of needed skills[7]—but they can also be thought of as approaches to learning or perspectives on knowledge that remain constant from one semester to the next. As Cohen herself expressed in an early article on the model, the five dimensions are the "different aspects of their performance that we want students to be aware of at all times, no matter what competency they are focusing on."[8]

The names of the semester-long Purposes appear along the top of the following two-sided matrix or grid (see Figure 7.1), and the names of the transdisciplinary Dimensions appear down the left side. The specific courses

	Purpose I: Self-Assessment and Preparation for Practice	Purpose II: Developing Professional Relationships	Purpose III: Working in Groups	Purpose IV: Teaching and Communication	Purpose V: Counseling	Purpose VI: Community Liaison	Purpose VII: Supervision	Purpose VIII: Promoting Change
Purpose Seminar								
Values & Ethics								
Self & Others								
Systems								
Skills								

Figure 7.1. A Curricular Grid for Purpose-Centered Education. Note how each semester (across the top row of the grid) has a designated purpose (in this case, a purpose related to necessary competencies in the field of human services). Students then take five required courses that are taught as dimensions of that Purpose. *Illustrative curricular grid created by the author.*

that fit into each section of the grid may change from time to time to meet accreditation standards or changes in students' academic needs. (The skills dimension courses, for example, have over time been adjusted to include more math and more uses of technology.) But the overall structure of the curriculum has remained constant over time.

What the model allows is a breadth of learning rarely achieved in programs based on discreet academic disciplines. A Values dimension course may include selections from philosophy and literature; a Self and Others course may assign both plays and case studies; a Systems dimension course may include readings from both anthropology and economics. In the Purpose II Self and Others dimension the assigned texts include David G. Myers, *Exploring Psychology*, Matt Ridley's *Genome: The Autobiography of a Species in 23 Chapters*, and August Wilson's 1983 play, *Fences*. In the Purpose VIII Values dimension the syllabus includes Chinua Achebe's *Things Fall Apart*, Oliver Goldsmith's "The Deserted Village," George Orwell's *Animal Farm*, and selections from Adam Smith's *The Theory of Moral Sentiments*, all in addition to the main assigned text, McConnell and Brue's *Macroeconomics*. In another course Aristotle's *Politics* is read back-to-back with Stephen R. Covey's popular *The 7 Habits of Highly Effective People* and a contemporary textbook on *Changing Human Service Organizations.*[9] In the Purpose-Centered Education model, the customary walls between literatures and social sciences become porous; knowledge is approached for its use value rather than for its identification with a specific discipline.

As Cohen later stressed, the model also serves to overcome the traditional divide between vocational education and liberal learning.[10] Students experience the world of work while being introduced to classic texts; they are preparing for a profession at the same time that they are engaging with materials drawn from the humanities. The emphasis throughout all courses is what a former faculty member referred to as "connective thinking."[11] At each phase of their learning students are asked to connect their academic studies with their performance in the field as well as to connect the material covered in the Dimension courses with that semester's overall Purpose. The Constructive Action document, assigned in the *Purpose* dimension seminar, provides the tool for assessing the degree to which connective thinking has taken place.

THE PROCESS

Where did MCNY's unique model for adult education come from? How was the curricular grid invented?

In the light of today's preoccupation with the assessment of teaching in the nation's public schools, it is interesting to note that a concern about performance assessment in the spring of 1973 was what drove forward the search for a new conceptual framework for the college. Teachers and administrators at the College for Human Services sensed that they were producing good results, but how could those results be accurately measured? Or, as Barbara Walton expressed it, "How do you look at somebody doing something and then evaluate the degree to which that person is doing it competently?"[12] Is there any way, beyond a conventional pen and pencil test, to evaluate a person's performance on a job?

Barbara Walton was put in charge of finding a professional organization that would provide the research for the assessment challenge. Walton had been a close associate of Cohen since 1966 and had provided the Women's Talent Corps and then the College for Human Services with much of its institutional research and record keeping. Tall and willowy, with deep-set eyes and a quiet demeanor, Walton was born in Brooklyn, graduated from Swarthmore College, and had received an MA in sociology from the New School for Social Research in 1951. She sent her children to Quaker schools, was a committed pacifist and feminist, and had arranged to prevent any of her tax payments to support military spending. At the college Walton was known for her lucid, well-structured writing; it was she who had faithfully taken the minutes of every board meeting and who, for decades, wrote the institution's annual reports.

With efficiency and a clear focus, Walton set to work on her assigned task to find institutional support for the restructuring process that lay ahead. Just as Cohen's instinct in the 1960s had been to *ask* the women in low-income neighborhoods how they might envision improving the service agencies that affected them, so now, a decade later, her team wanted to *ask* professionals exactly what qualities were needed for successful service delivery.[13] In the fall of 1972 the college received a grant from the Foundation for the Improvement of Post Secondary Education (FIPSE) to fund the research process, and after reading through 125 proposals and making trips to Washington to validate their claims, Walton chose McBer and Company, based in Cambridge, Massachusetts, to undertake a survey of how professionals actually performed when they were in situations that tested their ability to deal with a problem. McBer had been founded by Harvard professor David McClellan, who was known for his work on competence testing, and he assigned one of his associates, Charles Daly, to the project.[14] The McBer team began the survey by asking a wide range of professionals to describe their thoughts and actions during a "critical incident," a research technique that had been developed in 1954.[15] They also used three other interviewing instruments: "scenarios," which dealt with goals that those being interviewed had for their future, a "time when," or memory of a significant event, and "highlights," or descriptions of the professional's feelings about the past year's successes.[16] Early in the year the McBer team began interviewing sixty-two human service professionals and eventually produced a substantial report on its findings.

The college did not wait for the results of the McBer survey to begin its own restructuring process, however. The tensions and dissatisfactions of

the early 1970s resulted in a plan to cut back on the college's daily operations for six months and, starting on January 2, 1973, to engage in what
it referred to as a "think tank" mode[17]—an intensive series of meetings to
develop a workable structure for teaching, learning, and assessment that
would be performance-based, humanistic, and coherent.

The kickoff event for the process was a three-day staff and faculty
retreat at Sterling Forest State Park in Tuxedo, New York, in early January.
On the first day Vice President Laura Pires-Hester presented a summary
of the historical constants or operating principles that had shaped the college since its early days as the Women's Talent Corps. The institution had
always worked both inside the system and outside it, she observed. It had
always gone "against the tide" in terms of its educational practice, and it
had always been committed to experimentation, learning, and change.[18]
Pires-Hester's presentation was followed by a wide-ranging talk by Cohen.
Uncharacteristically metaphorical, the speech invited the audience to think
in terms of a future child named Humanity who lived in a utopian world
where technology could take care of basic needs, and where service on
behalf of others was the norm. "People did not see the distinction between
work and study. . . . Power was distributed to those who offered the most
constructive solution to problems. War was dead." In this heady mix was a
reference to "joy crystals" as the basic units of learning. Cohen ended her
speech with a call for collaboration. "I offer this simple vision as a useful
way for one to think about our role in shaping some small part of a future
that will be a better place. I hope it will inspire you to see further and
perhaps deeper than I, and to share [that vision] with us all."[19]

Although some members of the audience, including her close friend
and associate Alida Mesrop, rolled their eyes at Cohen's references to
Humanity and crystals,[20] the retreat did set in motion a process of creative
collaboration that lasted for more than a year. Barbara Walton later wrote a
fully documented summary of the planning group's work entitled "Origins
of the Human Services Performance Grid, 1973–1974" that provides a
useful overview of the process. Walton begins with a comment about the
general tenor of the year's work. It was essentially a planning year during
which the distinction between faculty and administration dissolved and an
atmosphere of cooperation and teamwork prevailed, she wrote. Although

admittedly there were tensions between individuals based on their different assumptions about the procedure, these differences did not interfere with the creative process. Indeed, "perhaps they enhanced it."[21]

Walton's report starts with a description of the cast of characters who were involved in the planning. Newly hired as dean of planning was Steve Sunderland. Sunderland held a doctorate in organizational behavior from Case Western Reserve and had been director of the higher education program of the National Training Laboratory. Recently he had been involved in preparing a master plan for the City University of New York, and with his fast-moving mind, sense of humor, and ample beard he seemed well credentialed for the role. Among the participants who would eventually be teaching the new curriculum was Ruth Messinger, then known only as a Radcliffe graduate and social worker who had directed an experimental school on the Upper West Side. (This was years before she became borough president of Manhattan and later ran for mayor of New York.) Also involved were Don Hazen, a Princeton graduate who had experience in community development and had taught social studies at the high school level; Doris Richmond, a former elementary school teacher; and Ellen Blum, a lawyer and community organizer who was responsible for the legal implications of creating a new profession and licensing human service professionals.[22]

Though not mentioned in the report, another newly hired participant was Tom Webber. Webber was hired mid-point in the process to contribute to the planning and to teach the incoming students once the new curriculum was rolled out. Webber had grown up in East Harlem, had worked as an administrative intern at Park East High School, and was in the process of finishing a doctorate at Teachers College, Columbia University. Blonde, blue-eyed and boyish-looking even today in his early sixties, Webber was only in his mid-twenties when he joined the College for Human Services faculty and was often teased for being younger than many of his students. Although he was somewhat critical of Cohen's single-minded leadership style (and remembers her asserting, in his interview, that unlike the participatory processes he may have experienced at the Park East School, she was the one "in charge" at the college[23]), he later came to admire her tenacity and was grateful to be part of her exciting project.

Veteran members of the college's staff who were involved in the planning process included Laura Pires-Hester, Jan Jordan, Dellie Bloom, Barbara

Walton, and Deborah Allen. Deborah Allen had joined Audrey Cohen's administrative team in 1971, primarily at the recommendation of Alida Mesrop, who had been impressed with Deborah's organizing skills when they both had worked together on projects in the Pelham, New York public school system. Slightly built, with a careful way of speaking, Deborah was painfully shy as a young adult, the result perhaps of having attended eleven different schools as a child. But one of the schools she happened to attend was Riverdale Country School in the Bronx, and the education she received there allowed her to matriculate at Smith College, where she thrived and developed writing skills that enabled her to be a successful magazine editor before coming to work with Audrey Cohen.[24]

Also involved intermittently, although not part of the planning group because they were teaching the remaining AA students, were Kalu Kalu, Adele Brody, and Yolaine Armand. Walton also notes the important contributions of Kathy Hoffman, a graduate of Sarah Lawrence College whose creative thinking was an important stimulus to the group but who was tragically killed in an automobile accident half way through the process.[25]

Walton's report includes a subsection entitled "Planning Style" that gives a good sense of the way the process worked. After each meeting, members of the planning group would produce a flood of ideas, reports, proposals, and position papers "into which much thought and passion poured. Poetry was in, clarity was out." To the discomfort of some, Sunderland often arrived up to forty-five minutes late to the meetings and seemed constitutionally adverse to any kind of closure.[26] Walton cites Sunderland's support for a deliberately open-ended process: "We should tolerate the possibility that we are going in the right direction and that we are not yet sure of the right road map for getting there." Sunderland continues with a simile that undoubtedly made the more product-oriented participants cringe. The approach we are now moving on is brand new in terms of training, he said, "something like learning how to fly with a bag over our heads but our hands on the gears. We are the wind and know we are moving, but is it up or down and is it forward or backward?"[27] As Dellie Bloom noted in another context, Steve talked like this.[28]

A unifying goal for the group was to rethink the new curriculum in terms of assessment. What *is* a competent human service worker? While McBer and Company was researching this question with its purportedly scientific methodology, the task force at the college undertook its own process of exploration. The first concept the group could agree on was that the curriculum should be based on *competencies*, and everyone also agreed that a College for Human Service student's competencies would be somewhat different from the competencies expected at traditional colleges. Walton stated the consensus as follows: "The College for Human Services curriculum must reflect humanistic values, not just technical skill; it must be described and assessed in terms of actual performance, and it must be holistic, both in the sense of educating the whole person and of responding to the needs of the whole client."[29]

In the effort to come up with a list of the competencies necessary for positive results in terms of the human service profession, there was a wide range of input. Kathy Hoffman, who was studying Chinese philosophy at the time, argued that for every quality a human service worker needed in one context, a very different quality was needed in another. "The worker must be both tender *and* tough, imaginative *and* analytical, cooperative *and* independent." Laura Pires-Hester argued for including both the *purpose* of the service and the underlying *values* involved. At every point, with every decision they make as they pursue their purpose, students must understand that those decisions are based on values, and they need the habit of weighing those values. Ruth Messinger's contributions focused on the competency of self-consciousness. She wrote that students should become familiar with "the base from which they operate" and learn to use self-consciousness dynamically, with attention to both potential and actual change in oneself as a model for helping others.[30]

Steve Sunderland reveled in the experimental nature of the planning process. "It was an absolute delight to try and figure it out, and to name these babies [i.e., the competencies], and to watch them spin around. . . . Do we want five, or do we want nine, or do we want ten, or do we want seven? It was joy, unmitigated joy." He stressed the group's growing self-confidence and intellectual integrity. "We were not accepting the final thing until we really felt like it really was a final thing." And he was scathing in his low estimate of the research that the McBer team was carrying out at the same time. Their process, he opined, "was a total fraud."[31]

What turned out to be a fortuitous push for the planning group was the administration's need to submit to Albany by June 1 a definitive proposal to raise the college's standing to a bachelor's degree–granting institution. Given that the college's curriculum was still in the process of being invented, this was, as Barbara Walton put it, "a little like trying to get a firm grip on a jelly fish."[32] Cohen put Allen in charge of writing the proposal, part of which needed to include a list of characteristics essential to human service workers. Listed in what Walton refers to as the *Albany Document* were twelve characteristics essential to human service workers. The Albany document was shared with the planning group, and as Walton notes, this list prefigured the list of competencies that eventually became Purposes and Dimensions on the college's curricular grid.

Another key step in the process was a list of competencies that Steve Sunderland came up with in September 1973. Sunderland's list combined what Barbara had sent to Albany in June and what the planning group had come up with during its discussions. Phrased in terms of *abilities*, the list ranged from the ability "to know oneself as the prime instrument of conscious delivery of human service," to the ability "to plan, conduct, and evaluate human service research and to apply the results of research to improve the human services." But as members of the planning group were quick to see, the September list contained as many problems as it tried to solve because it included items that were not really *behaviors*. Such phrases as the ability to know, to identify, to recognize, Walton noted, plunged competency straight back into the cognitive area because they emphasize "knowing rather than doing." Moreover, on Sunderland's list the idea of purposeful, value-oriented service had somehow gotten lost, and in terms of teaching the content, there was little sense of any developmental sequencing of the abilities. In the view of some participants, even the fact of having a list compromised the goal of creating a holistic curriculum.[33]

THE BREAKTHROUGH

Throughout the fall of 1973 Deborah Allen continued to push the group for a more performance-based product. She repeatedly sent out memos stating the need to phrase competencies so that they would not only lead to a logical curriculum but also would identify the kind of performance expected of the students. What was needed to go along with each stated competency, she pointed out, was a task-focused method of assessment that would provide an all-inclusive means of evaluating student performance. The word "task" was not accidental: it signified that student evaluation would include "putting theory into action."[34] By November Allen had drawn up her own list of competencies that she presented to the planning group. This list marked a major step forward in that it separated out those items that lent themselves to direct observation and those that did not, and reduced the number of competencies to eight. But still the planners could not reach a consensus on the final form that the curriculum should take.

The final breakthrough occurred at a meeting of the planning group between February 4 and February 7, 1974, more than a year after their deliberations had begun. The need to come to a resolution was urgent, for the first students in the new professional program were due to arrive in two weeks, and there was still no agreement on the final form of the curriculum. Something was needed to break the stalemate, so Cohen decided to attend the meeting. Other members of the planning group in attendance that day were Steve Sunderland, Laura Pires-Hester, Jan Jordan, and Deborah Allen—a smaller group than usual.[35]

As with much of historical and personal memory, the recollection of how the breakthrough happened differs from one participant to the next. Jan Jordan remembered (and other accounts agree with her on this) that she was the first to perceive that the lists of competencies the group was working with included both attributes and skills. "We had apples and oranges mixed up together and I knew we had to separate them." So the group put on the blackboard a list of all the "do-able" things and set the others aside. She then remembers suggesting that they put what they had left out across the top of the board. The group realized that these intersected in some way but didn't yet see them as Dimensions of each semester's work. She also remembers coming up with a developmental sequence for the main competencies using the work of a 1960s theorist named Bill Schwartz as a guide. "We ended up with eight competencies in all, the same as today. This was the [origin of the] Grid."[36]

Deborah Allen remembered the process differently. She pointed out that the beginnings of a two-sided curricular structure were already contained in the document she wrote for Albany. "I remember that the day before the breakthrough I was meeting with Audrey and I said, 'There is a solution. We can have both kinds of competencies and have them go in opposite directions.' "[37] Allen realized that the five competencies she had set aside could become *aspects* of each of the eight main ones on the list. She, too, acknowledged that at the meeting they didn't yet use the term *dimensions* for the horizontal frame, but the basic model was there.

Yet another memory of the breakthrough comes from Tom Webber. Webber is currently a member of MCNY's Board of Trustees, and he attributes the breakthrough to Steve Sunderland. He remembers that one day they were getting it down to fifteen or twenty different groups of characteristics and Sunderland saying that some of these cut across all the characteristic areas while some of them were unique to a different given profession or a given time period. Webber acknowledged that he and Deborah Allen, who was also on the board, often talked playfully about how their memories differ. "Are you kidding? It was not Steve who came up with that," she told him.[38]

Although Audrey Cohen later also acknowledged Deborah Allen's seminal contributions, Cohen's account of the process stressed her own role at the breakthrough moment. As she remembered it, Jan and Steve were putting notes on the blackboard and the structure was becoming clearer, but no one knew what to do with the items which had been set aside. "Couldn't we have the structure go both ways?" she remembers asking. Deborah Allen then spoke about the difference between the two kinds of elements that emerged from the research. "She had not been going on too long when I saw it," Cohen later recalled.

> It was so exciting a vision that I could feel that marvelous quickening of the pulse and exhilaration that I never fail to sense with the conceptualization process. A new idea, a glorious birth, a tingling, an explosion, a race to pull the star-burst together, which is the result of all the whirring and spinning and rockets going off![39]

As all these emotions came together, she continued, she found herself saying that clearly they had a design. The new design would permit a listing of the major areas of work that a professional performed on one axis of a grid, and have the five common elements weaving their way through those areas of work on the other axis. "I knew that we had made the breakthrough, that right there in that room we had turned out the new design that would influence our future and hopefully the future of all of higher education."[40]

In notes written the next day, Deborah Allen summarized the results in a less-effusive way and put the emphasis on assessment. The sequence of competencies, she noted, could be assessed in terms of the dimensions, while the dimensions could also serve as guidelines for instruction. The grid that the group had created "represents the interrelationship between the competencies, . . . and the dimensions, which apply to all the competencies and will be considered throughout the program."[41] The college's unique curricular grid had been born.

Later the same day, shortly after the planning group had experienced its breakthrough moment, the college received a report from McBer and Company outlining the results of its study of sixty-two professionals in the human service field. The report confirmed much of what the more informal planning group had come up with as essential to successful practice, with one difference. Many professionals reported that they often lacked a sense of progress or *purpose* in their year-to-year work. McBer's conclusion was that the college should seek out applicants with "a high tolerance for work that didn't seem to go anywhere," as Cohen quipped in an article summarizing the report a few years later. Such findings only reinforced the planning group's sense of their own triumphal accomplishments, for "Purpose with a capital P" was the cornerstone of the curriculum that they had invented.[42]

In further meetings later that year, the assessment function of the new model was fine-tuned to include the documentation of a Constructive Action that students would be required to complete in their internship or job each semester. The specific form of Constructive Action documents evolved over the next decade, but it may be useful to note that the idea of students having to record their work in the field had been part of the college's conceptual framework since the early days of the Women's Talent Corps. An abiding feature of the Women's Talent Corps' educational program had been the student progress workbooks where students recorded their learning in the areas of knowledge, skills, and attitudes at each phase of their education. Once the new curricular framework was established, the student progress workbooks disappeared and Constructive Action documents became the major instruments for assessment every semester.

Years after he had left the college, Steve Sunderland articulated the significance of the curricular design that the planning group came up with. The process produced "a model of higher education that redefined learning, so that learning was based on a blend of theory and practice and not on memorization and the accumulation of useless courses." In fact, he asserted, "we developed and implemented a successful new model of learning." As for his own contribution as the leader of the process, he said, his role was basically to enlarge the ideas. He took the ideas that the group came up with, put texture and structure into them, and "wrote them up as a good propagandist might."[43] Although some members of the group became impatient with the open-endedness of Sunderland's planning style, Tom Webber remembers Sunderland's role in positive terms. Steve was disorganized but brilliant, Tom recalled. He played "a pivotal role" in creating the new curriculum.[44]

EARLY IMPLEMENTATION

"When change like that envisioned by the College for Human Services is attempted, there are obviously crisis points, barriers, and problems," Cohen and her colleagues Laura Pires-Hester and Alida Mesrop wrote at this time, in a chapter for a book entitled *Managing Academic Change*. Among the challenges that the new College for Human Services had to face were tensions between traditionalists and innovators and between the college faculty and agency supervisors. Such tensions require ongoing efforts of understanding and collaboration, as well as a built-in "theory and method of change," the chapter concludes.[45]

For a firsthand account of the tensions that Cohen and her colleagues described in *Managing Change*, a useful resource is the transcribed voice of Yolaine Armand. Armand had been a coordinator-trainer at the college since 1969. She had been critical of the 1970 strike, and she was one of the few faculty members retained by Cohen in the 1972 shake-up. As noted earlier, she actively participated in the planning for the new curriculum even while continuing to teach the remaining second year AA students. When the new curriculum was rolled out in 1974, she, like the other faculty members, was now designated a coordinator-teacher[46] and took on her new role with enthusiasm. Armand stayed on at the college until 1980, reluctantly leaving only after her husband's work required a move to Haiti. Armand had watched the college's evolution from a training program to a fully fledged bachelor's degree granting institution, so her comments are noteworthy.

A native of Haiti, Armand had received a traditional education. In the French-based system "the teacher teaches, the students learn, and you do what the teacher tells you to do. You take the exams and you're out."[47] Even though she had had some administrative experience at the New School for Social Research before coming to the College for Human Services, the participatory model was new to her. After several years of teaching at the college, however, Armand became a convert to the idea of active learning. "Active learning is where the student is applying what he's learned to reality. Active learning is where students are attaching their experiences to whatever they are learning," she said. She later took the initiative of using some of the college's ideas in her teaching and administrative experiences both in Haiti in the 1980s and then at the University of Cincinnati, where she became an associate professor of sociology in the early 1990s.[48]

Armand remembered the challenges of teaching the new model once it was implemented in 1974. As the competencies were being developed, especially with the addition of the Constructive Action later on, there was resistance from faculty, field supervisors, and students. Why? "Because it was unknown, because it was wide open, because it had to change with each semester." The Constructive Action had to be performed at the agencies, and some faculty members had difficulty understanding how theory could be integrated with practice, "how you can bring about what you have learned into that kind of work." Sometimes people at the agencies also had a hard time understanding the nature of the tasks that the students were being asked by the college to complete. The fourth semester, that is, Purpose IV, which was focused on teaching, was perhaps not so difficult for a student practitioner to implement at a human service agency, but what about the seventh semester competency, which was supervision? "How does the student do the supervision? It took a lot of resourcefulness." Armand mentions the challenge of responding to a student who complained, "There's no way I can do my Constructive Action at my agency. All I do is bring coffee for everybody."[49] To figure out how to make the field experience fit the sequence of competencies demanded of the new model was, she acknowledged, a constant challenge.

Overall, however, Armand appreciated both the tension and the inventiveness generated by the new model. Most importantly, she recalled, the faculty provided both support and impetus. "You're forced into being resourceful, being innovative, looking at different angles, as if [the other members of the faculty] are pushing you against yourself, as if they are saying 'swim, you can swim, go ahead.' Soon I would feel like getting into the water, and I'd end up doing it,"[50] she remembered. The sense of self-confidence she gained those years was important in her later educational achievements both in the United States and in Haiti.

Tom Webber was another faculty member involved in teaching the new curriculum in its first year. He was responsible for teaching the Systems dimension courses, and he remembers that for the first semester he would have his students do an analysis of the College for Human Services as an educational system. This had the advantage of enabling the students to learn some of the tools for analyzing an organizational structure and its management at the same time that they were learning about the curriculum they were engaged in. It was not just the philosophy of the system. "It was the actual organization of it—who was in charge, who made the decisions, what a Board of Trustees is, what relationship different schools have to each other." For the second semester's Systems course, Webber would have his students analyze the human service agency where they were placed for their fieldwork, and for that course they could apply some of the analytical skills developed the previous semester. He remembers the exhilaration of those early years. He and other faculty members felt like they were on the forefront of something new. "Performance-based education, teaching people how to do, not just to think, having to demonstrate everything that you were able to do, having a constructive action that you didn't just have to write about but had to actually show that you had done it—it was a very exciting time."[51]

Steve Sunderland's memories of the early implementation of the new model were even more effusive. When the first students arrived the end of February and the new curriculum was rolled out, Sunderland became a supervisor of the teaching faculty. Once again the word "joy" appears in his reminiscences. "The doing of the first year of the curriculum was absolutely a joy," he said. "It's one thing, as a propagandist, to write this stuff; it's another thing to see it!" His past experiences at City College had made him see the teaching that went on there as a "fiction." But at the College for Human Services, he said, "faculty were attempting to teach and learn, and that was a major difference." Sunderland mentions in particular Yolaine Armand's teaching. "You could actually see her students taking the dimensions and mixing them in together, and developing Constructive Actions that were truly *constructive* and *actions*."[52] Some of the Constructive Actions at the College for Human Services in those early years included such projects as organizing and running a seminar for foster parents to work for improvements in the foster care system, helping a recently retired disabled man through the New York City bureaucracy so that he could collect a disability pension from his former employer, and helping a community center become aware of the needs of the children using the facility so that the center could initiate programs based on those needs.[53] Many Constructive Actions were modest, but they all in some way aimed to fulfill the college's aim of enabling students to "improve the world."

Sunderland also saw the response of the students. "It was beyond my wildest imagination." He describes one student, Benita Gomez, who came into the program knowing very little even about her native Puerto Rico, but who after a year was "spouting C. Wright Mills, making her way to the New York Public Library for the first time, and coming back with tears in her eyes saying 'I didn't know that there were buildings with rooms with books that you could just take out. I didn't know that.' And she was 48 years old!" Another student, Matilda Culpepper, was a housekeeper before coming to the college and had occasionally worked for Sunderland, helping to take care of his kids. He remembered her coming to him and saying, "John Rawls had some very good things to say about social justice," and pointing to a specific sentence saying, "That sentence, I read it and I wrote a little paper on it and used it in my Constructive Action." To see her at the end of two years, Sunderland continued, "with tears streaming down on her grown children and grandchildren, coming to the graduation . . . that's the biggest area of joy in my life." Although the students were overwhelmed by the work, "they rose to the challenge. Over and over, and over again. . . . I mean, it was the invention of Israel!"[54]

At one point Sunderland suddenly mentions the name of John Dewey. "John Dewey never did a damned thing!" Sunderland says. Dewey was a great philosopher, and a great source of integrity for the field of philosophy, he continues. "But in terms of action, Audrey did more in a minute of her life than John Dewey did in eighty or ninety years! . . . Here was thought and action, here was practice, here was every cliché and academic jargonized stuff, actually working!"[55]

Sunderland's ebullient assessment of Cohen and her college became more ambivalent over time. External economic factors, as well as growing tensions in his and Cohen's relationship, caused him to leave the college and New York City in 1978. Although some members of Cohen's inner circle later criticized his leadership style, the archival record makes clear that the year-long process Sunderland's group engaged in did create learning outcomes that have made a college education possible for thousands of low-income students. On balance, the work of the planning group was itself a Constructive Action.

A DEWEYAN MODEL?

Sunderland's impulsive comparison of John Dewey's and Audrey Cohen's accomplishments prompts a deeper questioning about the extent to which Cohen's project aligns with Dewey's conception of progressive education. Sunderland's assertion that Dewey "never did a thing" is obviously unfair. Dewey was the founding director of the Laboratory School at the University of Chicago, and throughout his life he actively worked to support institutions such as Jane Addams' Hull House, the New School for Social Research, Bennington College, and the Barnes Foundation Art Collection. He was active in these ventures even while delivering hundreds of addresses, writing dozens of books, and teaching at Columbia University.[56]

But Sunderland's point about the alignment of Dewey's educational principles with Cohen's vision merits further discussion. Was the new structure for adult learning that the college's task force created in February 1974 completely new, as Cohen herself often maintained? Or did it represent, albeit for an adult constituency never envisioned by Dewey, a curricular model that embodied many of Dewey's most consistently held educational ideals? Here Sunderland's comments provoke a digression from the story of the college's founding to probe more closely the extent to which Cohen's work relates to seminal themes in twentieth-century progressive educational thought.

Many people associate Dewey with the child-centered, private (some would say even elitist) elementary and secondary schools that were founded in the Progressive Era, at the time when Dewey's ideas about education were first becoming popular. Following the model that he had instituted at the Laboratory School at the University of Chicago in the late 1890s, the private progressive schools founded in the early twentieth century (many of them in New York City) emphasized creativity, individuality, and free choice. At the Walden School, Dalton, the City and Country School, and Putney, children were encouraged to learn at their own pace, pursue their own individual interests (even, at Dalton, planning their own studies for the year[57]), and integrate art, wood-working, plays, and music into their academic learning. Many educators during those years appeared to give primary importance to Dewey's statement in "My Pedagogic Creed" that although education has both a psychological and a sociological side, it must begin with "a psychological insight into the child's capacities, interests, and habits" and must "be controlled on every point by reference to these same considerations."[58] This aspect of Dewey's thought, and the private, arts-oriented, child-centered, elementary schools that spun off from it, clearly have little in common with the highly structured curricular grid for low-income adult learners that Cohen's team came up with in 1974.

There is another important theme in Dewey's thinking, however, that goes beyond the child-centered elementary schools of the Progressive Era and relates more closely to Cohen's project. Dewey's lifelong aim was to bridge the conceptual divide between individual and social aims, and much of his writing can be seen as an effort to synthesize those competing aspects of educational experience.[59] Even as early as 1892, when he was a young professor at the University of Michigan, his lecture notes show this effort. "Individuality cannot be opposed to association," Dewey told his students. "It is through association that man has acquired his individuality and it is through association that he exercises it. The theory which sets the individual over and against society of necessity contradicts itself."[60] Dewey's discomfort with what he saw as an overemphasis on the individual and a neglect of the social importance of education is evident in Chapter 9 of his classic

Democracy and Education (first published in 1916) where he criticizes the educational philosophy of Jean-Jacques Rousseau. Dewey's main argument with the eighteenth-century philosopher is the weight that Rousseau gave to the child's own "nature" in any educational encounter. *Contra* Rousseau, Dewey argues that the social context is at least as important as the child's individual nature, for the "social medium" is what is responsible for putting the child's powers to their best possible use.[61] Dewey took this point even further in his final educational work, *Experience and Education* (1938), where he tried to distinguish his own educational philosophy from the child-centered theorists and practitioners who by then had come to dominate the Progressive Education Association. Here Dewey attacked educational romantics who wanted simply to emphasize the freedom of the learner. Most children are naturally sociable, he argued, and hence "education is essentially a social process."[62]

Dewey's emphasis on education as a social process is the main overlapping concept in any comparison of Dewey's and Cohen's educational visions. In Cohen's sequencing of the semesters, for example, Purpose I begins with self-knowledge and taking stock of one's own preparation for practice, but then the succeeding Purposes move outward into ever-widening social spheres—from the workplace, to professional groups, to the community, and finally to the completion of positive, constructive social change in a human services agency. Although Dewey was not referring to the education of adults, in his early writings there is an intimation of a similar movement toward empowerment and service. "I believe that the only true education comes through the stimulation of the child's powers by the demands of the social situations in which he finds himself," he asserts in "My Pedagogic Creed." Through these demands, he continues, the child is stimulated "to emerge from his original narrowness of action and feeling and to conceive of himself from the standpoint of the welfare of the group to which he belongs."[63] Getting students to move from the narrowness of self-limitation, through a series of demands coming from a socially educative environment, into a more committed life in the community is in essence a very Deweyan vision of human development, and it is at the heart of the college's curricular model.

Another interesting commonality found both in Dewey's educational philosophy and in the curricular model that the College for Human Services invented in 1974 is the new framework that the task force gave to academic subject matter. Dewey was always skeptical of the way that academic institutions divided subject matter into discrete disciplines, and in his early work at the Laboratory School he encouraged teachers to integrate math, art, and literature into their social studies lessons. "Abandon the notion of subject-matter as something fixed and ready-made in itself, outside the child's experience," he advised his readers in his 1902 book entitled *The Child and the Curriculum*. Begin with the child's experience and move "out from there to the organized bodies of truth that we call studies."[64] The task force that Cohen assembled in 1973 followed this Deweyan precept closely. Its members ignored the conventional disciplinary boundaries of history, literature, economics, and art, and in their place created the more general conceptual categories of Purpose, Values, Self and Others, Systems, and Skills—concepts that they believed to be *inside* the experience of the adults they would be teaching and that could provide connective threads of learning across all eight semesters.

The most obvious similarity between Dewey's vision and Cohen's model is the attempt to bring together theory and practice, to make learning meaningful by its application to action. "I believe that ideas (intellectual and rational processes) . . . result from action and devolve for the sake of the better control of action" wrote John Dewey in Article IV of his pedagogic creed.[65] Audrey Cohen's educational creed was similar: "For all of my adult life, I have struggled conceptually with the idea of blending theory and practice."[66] The curricular grid that evolved from the task force's work was essentially an effort to realize this vision. It used competencies derived from the world of practical social service and interlaced those competencies with theoretical ideas gained from the five transdisciplinary dimensions of knowledge. Most importantly, every student, every semester, must engage in extensive fieldwork involving a Constructive Action that relates to that semester's competency and makes use of the academic knowledge gained in the classroom.

A final Deweyan element that has gained significance over the years is the way that the curricular matrix organizes the student body into long-term cohorts. A new group of students enrolls in Purpose I each semester, and because there are no electives, those students generally proceed through all eight semesters as a group. An unplanned consequence of this system is that the students learn much from each other—some claim to have learned even more from their peers than they have learned from their professors. Indeed, in Purpose IV, when they are assigned to read Dewey in their Values class, many students remark on the cohort model as being an aspect of Dewey's writing that connects with their own experience at the college. "I believe that all education proceeds by the participation of the individual in the social consciousness of the race," Dewey states at the beginning of his pedagogic creed,[67] and students are quick to relate personally to these words. They recognize, and the faculty members who teach them recognize, that the college's cohort model encourages a degree of social learning that is rarely found at other undergraduate institutions of higher education.[68]

In sum, even though Dewey was focusing on the education of children, his principles are relevant to adult education as well, and these principles are clearly at work in the curricular model that Cohen's task force created in 1974. The new model's blending of academic study and field experience, its sequencing of the competencies from self-assessment to the promotion of social change, its stress on active learning through a "constructive action" were, as Sunderland observed, essentially Deweyan in theory, and in practice they actually worked. As mentioned in Chapter 2, however, neither Cohen herself nor any of the other participants in the curriculum design process ever explicitly mentioned Dewey as an influence on their thinking.

Audrey Cohen in her early twenties, about to graduate from the University of Pittsburgh, where she double majored in political science and education. *Courtesy of Wendy Cohen.*

Audrey and Mark Cohen on their way to Japan in 1953, where they lived for six months while he served as an intelligence officer with the U.S. Navy. *Courtesy of Wendy Cohen.*

While living in Japan, Cohen was able to travel throughout the country visiting elementary schools. *Courtesy of Wendy Cohen.*

From 1964 to 1966 Cohen worked day and night to establish the Women's Talent Corps, the precursor to Metropolitan College of New York. The outreach efforts took her to low-income communities where she recruited potential Corps Women and to charitable organizations where she drummed up financial support. *Courtesy of MCNY Archives and of Wendy Cohen.*

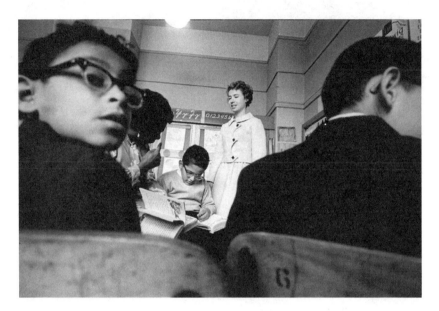

Many of the preprofessional jobs that the Women's Talent Corps created in the mid-1960s were for teacher assistants in elementary schools. In a photograph accompanying an article about the project in *Vogue* magazine, Cohen is shown visiting one of the elementary schools where a teacher assistant from the Talent Corps is helping a first grader learn to read. © Condé Nast/Patrick Litchfield/*Vogue* magazine.

Cohen visits a classroom of the fledgling College for Human Services. Although MCNY is today a fully accredited college with bachelor's and master's programs, most classes are still relatively small and consist of discussions rather than lectures. *Courtesy of Estate of David Gahr.*

In the spring of 1970 the College for Human Services received its charter from the Board of Regents of the state of New York. Laura Pires-Hester, who worked with Cohen to create the college, is standing second from the right. *Courtesy of MCNY Archives.*

On November 20, 1970, the College for Human Services held its first graduation, with 45 graduates receiving Associate of Arts degrees in Human Services. *Courtesy of MCNY Archives.*

Women with a dream. Cohen and her close associates in the 1960s and 1970s. Left to right, top row, Audrey Cohen *(Courtesy of MCNY Archives)* and Laura Pires-Hester *(Courtesy of Laura Pires-Hester)*; middle row, Barbara Walton *(Courtesy of MCNY Archives)*, Janith Jordan *(Courtesy of MCNY Archives)*, and Alida Mesrop *(Courtesy of Alida Mesrop)*; bottom row, Sylvia Hack *(Courtesy of Sylvia Hack)*, Deborah Allen *(Courtesy of Deborah Allen)*, and Millie Leet *(Courtesy of Aileen Robbins)*.

In a federal building that is presently a post office, the classroom space at 201 Varick Street was barely adequate. *Courtesy of MCNY Archives.*

Although Cohen was active in the civil rights movement in the early 1950s, her educational outreach in the 1960s and 1970s focused on income rather than race. *Courtesy of MCNY Archives.*

In January 1988, Audrey Cohen was married to Dr. Ralph Wharton. With her at the wedding were, from left to right, Laura Pires-Hester, Alida Mesrop, and Barbara Walton. *Courtesy of Wendy Cohen.*

A photograph taken at a College for Human Services graduation in the 1980s shows President Cohen flanked by Janith Jordan (on the left) and Vice President Alida Mesrop and Dean Shirley Conyard on the right. *Courtesy of MCNY Archives.*

Success in business depends on who you know.

Frederick Douglas

THE COLLEGE FOR HUMAN SERVICES
345 Hudson Street, New York, N.Y. 10014
(212) 989-2002
Audrey C. Cohen, President and Founder

In the 1980s the subway ads for the College for Human Services were bold and imaginative. *Courtesy of MCNY Archives.*

201 Varick Street CHS entrance.

Canal Street MCNY entrance. The college has always been housed in the area west of Broadway and south of Houston Street in New York City. The Women's Talent Corps was at 346 Broadway, and the College for Human Services was at 201 Varick Street and later at 345 Hudson Street. The present location of Metropolitan College of New York is at 431 Canal Street. *Courtesy of MCNY Archives.*

One of Cohen's last projects was to push for the conceptual framework of Purpose-Centered Education to be adapted throughout elementary schools across the USA. Here is a first grade classroom that used the model. Note the sign for "Constructive Actions" above the topic "Let's Be Safe." On the left is a sign for "Skills," one of the five dimensions of the curricular matrix. *Courtesy of MCNY Archives.*

The photo was taken at the Lotos Club in the last year of Audrey Cohen's life. She had just been interviewed for an article in *Education Week* entitled "The Outsider: Breaking the Mold—The Shape of Schools to Come." © Editorial Projects in Education/Benjamin Tice Smith/*Education Week*.

CHAPTER 8

THE COLLEGE FOR HUMAN SERVICES GAINS RECOGNITION (1975–1979)

To have an impact on policies, one cannot be quiescent. In a real sense, one must be 'empowered.' One must be informed, able to negotiate with or through the many systems which affect one's life, and capable of using these systems on one's own behalf. One must take control of one's own life. If there is to be social justice, citizens must act as integrating agents for their own needs.

—Cohen, 1978, p. 2

No sooner was the new design for the College of Human Services' curriculum put in place than the administration was ready to announce to the world that it had developed a new system of higher education. Cohen was eager to spread the word. As she stated at a luncheon with faculty at Northeastern Illinois University in October 1974, she was already afraid that other institutions would pick up on some of her ideas and manipulate them. "We really are quite frightened, frankly. I'm just hoping that we can get the new model out before it gets distorted too badly, and that means finding other people who care about it."[1]

"Getting the model out" was Cohen's main concern for much of the 1970s. The college's archives provide ample documentation of her work. In addition to writing the three major articles that are summarized later in this chapter, Cohen gave more than twenty-seven formal presentations and speeches in these years—in venues ranging from Tufts University, Ramapo College, Bryn Mawr, the University of Iowa, City College, Newport College, and UCLA to the U.S. House of Representatives. Her written output was also impressive. A 1979 Curriculum Vita lists eleven articles or chapters authored or co-authored during these years. As with many other highly productive people, Cohen was also a member of several different professional organizations, ranging from the American Association of Higher Education, the National Vocational Guidance Association, and the National Organization of Women to the New York Council for the Boston Symphony—and was a member of five different boards of directors.[2] She was busy.

IN THE BACKGROUND

How did Cohen's busy professional life affect her personal life? Never even hinted at in the college's archives are the challenges at home that Cohen was wrestling with at the same time as she was trying to build a college. Before launching into the college's institutional history during the 1970s, it is useful to take a brief look at her family's personal history during the same period.

In terms of the family's dynamics, Dawn was the more contentious of the Cohens' two daughters, having decided at an early age to assert her independence in terms of her religious commitments. Feisty and assertive like her mother, Dawn sometimes resented the time that Audrey devoted to her work, and in a push-me-pull-you relationship the two often argued. "It was never a true 'I totally get you and I think you're fantastic just the way you are' from her, and it was never a 'I feel completely accepted by you' from me," Dawn recalls.[3] Wendy recalls their battles also, but interestingly saw their differences in terms of Audrey's high expectations for Dawn. Audrey put a lot of pressure on Dawn "to be the best, to achieve, to stand up straight." In Wendy's view, Audrey wanted her oldest daughter to be "perfect."[4]

As is often the case with adolescent children, a source of contention at 37 East 67th Street in the girls' teenage years was Audrey's and Dawn's opposing attitudes about dress and general appearance. "I just could not *stand* Mom's vanity," Dawn remembered. Audrey would spend up to an hour every morning putting on her makeup, and because the apartment had only two bathrooms it became an issue. "I saw her as somebody who cared more about her looks than she cared about *me!*" Only later did Dawn understand that her mother's behavior was due in part to her vulnerability. "She was gorgeous, but she had acne from childhood. She had some pits, and I think she was sensitive about her skin." Dawn now understands that "you have to look a certain way in a certain world." But, she adds, not giving in, "I don't want to be in that world, so I don't put myself there." She sees that for her mother it was important to put on makeup and beautiful clothing, and even if she was only five feet tall, "sort of puff herself up" enough to have everyone in the room "listening to *her*, and not trying to knock her down every five minutes."[5] As an adolescent, however, Dawn could not see her mother's needs so clearly.

Another source of contention for Dawn, at least in retrospect, was her mother's insistence on hard work. "She refused to call herself brilliant, and it always bothered me, because I thought, 'if this is not brilliance, what is?' " Instead, Audrey always told her daughters that accomplishments come from effort. "*It's just hard work*," she would tell them. Being told that, Dawn recalled, was in some ways threatening. "I was a kid and didn't want to work that hard."[6]

Although some lessons may have been hard to hear, both daughters continue today to be grateful for their mother's strong commitment to feminism. "She raised me to be a feminist," Dawn acknowledges, and proudly recalls that when she was only seventeen she worked for a while at *Ms.* magazine as an intern for Gloria Steinem. After graduating from the Chapin School in 1975 Dawn briefly attended Kirkland, a short-lived women's college affiliated with Hamilton College in Clinton, New York. When Kirkland closed in 1976 Dawn transferred to Brown University to be with a close friend.[7] Two years later when Dawn's sister Wendy entered the University of Massachusetts in Amherst, she too took her mother's commitment to feminism seriously and spent her junior year doing an internship at an abortion rights organization in Boston.[8]

One incident that caused some consternation in the Cohen family at the time but could be laughed about later happened when Dawn was at Brown. Dawn became politically active with a group of students who were protesting the university's attempt to break the union that represented janitorial workers and cleaning personnel. After a two-day nonviolent protest, eleven of the students, including Dawn, were intentionally arrested. The next day she called her parents from jail.

"Hi Mom! Hi Dad! Gotta tell you something . . ."

"We already know," was the answer.

"How do you know?"

"Because your aunt called this morning and told us to turn to page 14 of the *New York Times*."

The paper carried not only an article about the protest but a photo of Dawn being hauled away by the police. At this point in her recollection Dawn said, "I think my mom's next words were 'We're so proud of you.'" There was a silence on the phone, and then her mother said firmly, "*But don't do it again!*"[9]

Still searching for more independence and a more temperate climate,[10] Dawn left Brown the next year (she was nineteen years old) and set out for the West Coast. She eventually settled near Oakland, where she finished school, got married, joined a closely knit synagogue, and soon began raising her own family. Wendy stayed closer to home. After graduating from UMass she was for a year the director of Zero Population Growth, an organization in Boston focusing on birth control issues, but then realizing the need to be able to earn more money, she returned to East 67th Street and enrolled in New York Law School.[11]

In the meantime Audrey and Mark's marriage had begun to fray. In 1970 the Cohens had bought a farm in the Berkshires, in Western Massachusetts, to use as a weekend and vacation getaway. For the first few years, the whole family, or sometimes just Mark and the girls, or sometimes just Mark and Audrey, would spend time at the farm as a break from the their demanding jobs. Wendy remembers that Audrey was "gung-ho" about country life at first, raking leaves in the fall and renovating the house in the winter.[12] She rigged a clipboard to the glove compartment of the car so that she could work on speeches and memos during the two-hour drive to and from the city.[13] But gradually Mark became more taken with rural life and very involved in gardening. He had spent the previous fifteen years traveling around the world working as an international tax attorney for American Express, and now he was ready for a change. He planned for an early retirement and wanted to move out of the city.[14]

Audrey would have none of it. Her life's work was in the city, and she loved the life of the metropolis. Although Mark later thought that they might have worked it out, they didn't.[15] By the end of the decade they were divorced. Friends and acquaintances were surprised at the news, since the marriage had seemed stable.[16] The two Cohens decided to go their separate ways. Audrey eventually bought the apartment on East 67th Street, and Mark moved into a new home in western Massachusetts.

To her credit, Audrey Cohen never let any of the unsettling events of her personal life interfere with her professional goals. Although her daughters sometimes resented the time she spent away from them, they came to admire her sense of purpose, her concentration, and her pluck. Their pride in their mother, and their gratitude for her example of strong womanhood, grew as they themselves developed into successful women with families and careers of their own.

THE CHANGE GAME

In the spring of 1974, Cohen's lasting legacy, including her influences on her daughters, could not have been foreseen. But Cohen and her colleagues were full of grand hopes for the new performance-based curriculum they had created in February of that year. Immediately they set to work organizing a conference to be held at Columbia University in June that would publicize the results of the previous year's planning and would provide the occasion for announcing a "new profession" of the human services. The sixty guests invited to attend included government and foundation officials, representatives from the community-based organizations where College for Human Services students worked, administrators from academic institutions, social workers, feminists, and representatives from New York City public schools.[17] Some remembered that Alvin Toffler, author of *Future Shock*, also attended the conference.[18]

In announcing a new profession of human services, Cohen was both identifying a growing movement and giving her own institution a distinctive role in that movement. By the 1970s the field of human services was in fact not entirely new. As Jean Macht and Douglas A. Whyte make clear in their overview of the field, a number of factors—ranging from the de-institutionalization of the mentally ill to an increasing demand for community agencies to care for troubled youths, substance abusers, and the aging—had led other educators besides Cohen to recognize the need for an alternative to the more specialized profession of social work.[19] The term "human services worker" had thus become widely used to refer to generalists,[20] often recruited from low-income communities and trained in a broad range of skills, who then returned to their communities to work in service agencies.[21] But most of the training programs for these generalist human services workers were located in community colleges and carried with them only an associate's degree. What was unique about Cohen's project, and what was emphasized at the June conference, was the stress on the word "profession." Her college was aiming to offer one of the few baccalaureate human services programs in the country and at that time (though not for long), the bachelor's degree was a sign of professional status.[22]

Cohen greeted the assembled guests and announced that the work of the conference would be to play the "change game." Participants were given a ten-page document explaining the rules. The game's premise was that a new profession was being created to deal with service delivery problems in schools, hospitals, counseling centers, prisons, and other agencies. This new profession was predicated on a "new standard of service delivery, new accountability to the clients, and new approach to the education of professionals." The change game consisted of each participant being assigned to a group that would come up with ways to *counter* a list of possible objections to the new profession from clients, established professionals, union officials, potential employers, or students. The challenge was to not agree with the possible objections but only to think of positive rebuttals to them. Although some participants complained of manipulation, many willingly participated with a sense of the new venture's possibilities for success.[23]

As Gerald Grant, who attended the conference, later observed, the change game was a bold and ingenious strategy that produced helpful responses and prevented the conference from turning into a "stop-the-college" event. In the afternoon there were many expressions of support for the college, ranging from graduates who as a result of their experience at the College for Human Services were now receiving a steady paycheck, to the head of the Fund for the Improvement of Postsecondary Education (FIPSE) who praised the faculty for its dedication and support of students. But there were also skeptics. Harold Lewis, dean of social work at Hunter College expressed his doubts about the rigor of the program and the ability of its students to meet the standards of the usual five-year master's in social work program.[24] The question of how to provide the credentials to meet those standards would in fact become a tough challenge for the college in the years ahead.

DOING CRYSTALS

As the Wikipedia entry for the term "crystal" makes clear, a crystal is a solid with surfaces extending in all three spatial dimensions and whose atoms form an orderly arrangement or pattern.[25] When Audrey Cohen first used the term in her keynote speech at the Sterling Forest retreat in January 1973, she had in mind a multifaceted unit, like a diamond, that was both solid and many-sided and that reflected light. In her speech she used the image of a crystal to refer to the way that a young woman she named Humanity might experience her education in an imagined future. It is important to note that in Cohen's 1973 speech and in the college's later use of the term, there was none of the 1990s New Age association of crystals with magic or healing. A crystal was simply a way to describe a specific structure or form.

The crystal imagery apparently stayed with Cohen over the next several months during the planning process that was described in Chapter 7. Deborah Allen reported that Cohen was talking about crystals well before the February 1974 curricular breakthrough. "She wanted students to be able to go into a 'crystal,' do everything they had to do in connection with a certain competency and then move on to the next one," Allen remembered. "She actually jumped from one place to another to show me what she meant."[26]

When the new curriculum was rolled out in the spring of 1974, the term *crystal* was used in place of what the planning group had referred to as competencies.[27] The eight semester-long units of study—organized sequentially from a focus on learning about oneself and developing professional relationships, through working in groups, teaching, and counseling, to community liaison, supervision, and managing change—were now termed "Crystals," each of which incorporated five "Dimensions" of learning. Because each semester's learning was gained through five dimensions, or facets, (with the purpose dimension at its center), the crystal image fit the curricular model well and was in fact used as the college's logo for decades.

As the following graphics from an article published in 1976 show, the college's unique curriculum could be represented as a prism made up of the overlay of crystal segments onto concentric circles representing the dimensions.[28] In some contexts these graphics were used as an alternative to the planning group's representation of the curriculum as a grid.

In the 1990s, partly due to the New Age pseudoscientific claims about the use of crystals for healing, the term "Crystals" was dropped and "Purposes" was used instead. (See the diagram in Chapter 7.) Today "Purpose" continues to be used to identify each semester's performance focus.

To make the college's unfamiliar model comprehensible to students, a significant decision that first year was to create handbooks for each semester's overall academic program. The policy has remained in place until the present day. At the beginning of each semester every student at the college

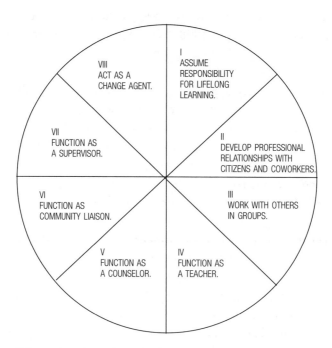

Figure 8.1. "The Eight Essential Modes for Providing Service to Empower Citizens." *Courtesy of MCNY Archives.*

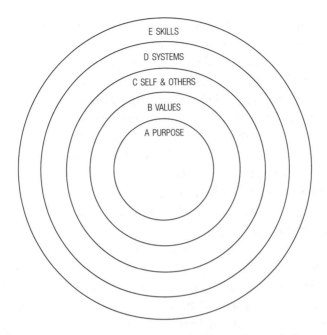

Figure 8.2. "The Five Constant Dimensions of Effective Service." *Courtesy of MCNY Archives.*

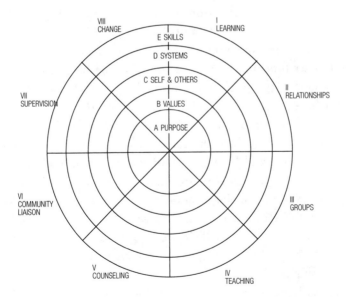

Figure 8.3. "The Interplay of Service Modes and Dimensions Creates the Performance Prism." *Courtesy of MCNY Archives.*

receives or gains online access to a forty- to ninety-page *Purpose Handbook* containing an introduction to the semester's theme or purpose, general information about policies and requirements, an academic calendar, and the syllabus for each of the five dimension courses. With the *Purpose Handbook* tucked into a handbag or knapsack (or downloaded onto their personal electronic device), students can know exactly which readings are required each week in each course, how much each paper that they write or quiz that they take will be weighed in the determination of their final grade, and on what day the makeup classes for Columbus Day will be held.[29] For students who are often on the run from home to college to an internship site, the *Purpose Handbooks* provide a compact, efficient reminder of their academic responsibilities.

In terms of the long-term policy at the college that Cohen founded, it is important to note that except for choosing between a day schedule and evening schedule, or an evening–weekend schedule, there are no choices for students to make. There are no electives, and each incoming cohort of students proceeds through the program at the same pace. Although such a prescribed curriculum might not work well for eighteen-year-olds hankering for multiple paths to self-determination, it has worked well for adults who have complex pressures from work and family and who are looking for coherence in their lives. Because the *Purpose Handbooks* all follow the same general format, the structure of the eight-semester curriculum gains familiarity over time and becomes a source of meaningful learning.

Throughout the mid-1970s the College for Human Services continued to develop its own special terminology. In a policy paper dated 1977, the college's unique terms are listed and defined. The list begins with the term *citizens*, which the college insisted that students and faculty use instead of the word "clients." "Citizens are the people human service practitioners serve," the paper states. "We call them *citizens instead of clients* to emphasize that the helping relationship is a relationship of equality and mutual respect. We call them *citizens instead of consumers*," the explanation continues, "to emphasize that there are no passive members in the helping relationship—both citizen and practitioner take an active part in making the relationship work."[30]

Empowerment is another term that the college appropriated early on. Sometimes claimed to have been invented by Cohen herself, the term continues to be used today to describe the primary aims of the college that she founded.[31] The 1977 position paper states that "Empowerment of the citizen is the ultimate goal of *every* helping relationship." It then adds, "practitioners do not empower citizens—only the citizens themselves can do that." Nevertheless, "the human service practitioner works to create a situation that permits and encourages empowerment—just as the health professional works for a situation that encourages healing."[32]

With *citizens* and *empowerment* defined, the position paper goes on to define the rest of the college's unique terms. *Crystals* are the eight areas in which "practitioners must be competent to achieve maximum success in promoting citizen empowerment," and the *Dimensions* are "the constants of effective performance."[33] A *Constructive Action* is a planned effort in the field "to help one citizen, or several, or even a community, to achieve greater empowerment." (In another context it was defined as "a meaning-ful piece of service delivery."[34]) It must be "a time-bound effort, directed to specific outcomes [and] represents a methodology of human service."[35] On a related page, are two more special terms that in recent years have been less frequently used. At the College for Human Services the students were generally referred to as *student practitioners*, that is, "professionals-in-training engaged in an intensive full-time effort to blend theory and practice," and professors were called *Coordinator-Teachers*, "who earn their title by coordinating the learning of their students in the classroom and the field."[36]

A compulsive aspect of her leadership style that later became prob-lematical was Cohen's possessiveness about the college's terminology. Tom Webber remembers her "going ballistic" when, shortly after determining that *empowerment* was the goal of every Constructive Action, a number of other colleges began using the term. "She was convinced that *we* had coined it first" and even mentioned the possibility of suing other institu-tions that used the term.[37] Eventually she moved to have many of the terms trademarked to prevent their unauthorized use by others. Cohen exerted similar proprietary control over reports and research projects that described the college's model, a practice that often distanced her from her faculty.

Although the young college's unique vocabulary might have been off-putting to new faculty members and to outsiders, its students (or "Student Practitioners") picked it up quickly used it in their daily talk. In elevators and hallways, and on the way to the subway, one could hear students saying, "For my CA in Crystal Four I was working with a whole group of Citizens but in Crystal Five I was working only with one," or "Who do you have for Self and Others? Oh, I had him for Values in Crystal One, and he was really great." Although today the term *Crystals* has changed to *Purposes*, most of the other terms have remained the same and provide an in-house lingo for those who are connected to the college.

SERVICE AS EMPOWERMENT

With its unique model in place, the college began an intensive effort to publicize its uniqueness. In the four years covered by this chapter, staff members were busily at work churning out papers explaining and lauding the college's newly discovered model. Steve Sunderland was especially prolific, writing more than fifteen reports and occasional papers, but Ruth Messinger, Laura Pires-Hester, and others also produced important work.[38]

Even more significant than the writings produced by her staff, however, were three substantial articles written in the mid-1970s by Audrey Cohen herself. In all three essays Cohen uses the concept of a "service society," or, as she sometimes names it, a "service economy," as a rationale for the then still fledgling College for Human Services' unique structure and aims. How valid is Cohen's use of the service economy as a justification for the college's unorthodox educational model? After a brief summary of the articles, I explore this question more fully, in particular regarding the relationship between service and the kinds of empowerment that Cohen wanted her college to contribute to the world.

Cohen begins her 1975 essay entitled "The Third Alternative" by identifying two structural models that have characterized most of higher education in the West over the past several centuries. The first and older model dates back to the medieval universities in Bologna and Paris and to the early modern educational systems in England, Scotland, and Germany. In this system, Cohen claims, knowledge is treated as a "commodity purchasable for so many hours of effort [and] redeemable in a degree after a sufficient amount of time has been served." In this traditional model knowledge is also divided into separate departments and disciplines that encourage research and specialization. By the 1960s, she reminds the reader with a reference to Clark Kerr's well-known dictum, American universities following this first model had added on so many different disciplines and subdisciplines that they came to be known as "multiversities."[39]

Meanwhile, another model emerged in the United States that aimed to provide an alternative to the impersonality of the large Model I universities. This second model included smaller, more experimental colleges such as St. John's, Antioch, and Sarah Lawrence. After the student rebellions of the 1960s, Cohen writes, these Model II institutions proliferated, including newer projects such as Empire State and Chicago's TV College, and later the University Without Walls and the Regents External Degree Program in New York State. These newer colleges catered to individual needs and enabled students to plan their own programs and receive credit for experience.

Cohen then makes a strategic shift. Despite the apparent differences between these two models, she says, in fact Model II programs were actually no more than extensions of the existing Model I system because they emphasized the same "academic trappings" such as credit-hour equivalents, tests, semester patterns, professional hierarchies, scholarship, and research. Moreover, neither of the first two models addresses the needs of a service society. Citing a 1974 work by Alan Gartner and Frank Riessman, Cohen points out that the service sector had already outpaced the goods producing sector and represented almost 70 percent of the nation's economic activity. Suggesting that within the service sector, those jobs that fall under the category of "human services" are also projected to grow, she argues that "We must have professionals who can offer citizens a broad range of human services, provided effectively and humanely, and a new assessment system that reflects actual job performance." Professionals in this field must be prepared to concern themselves with "all aspects of the welfare of those they help." They must be able to work with people young and old, in groups and individually. They must have the competencies "to teach, to advise and counsel, and to advocate for" the people they serve.[40]

Because neither Model I nor Model II colleges address the new service requirements, what is now required, Cohen proceeds to argue, is a third alternative that will focus not only on a student's individual needs but also on a student's education in terms of its "effect on citizens' service needs."

The necessary third educational model is a performance-based system that "integrates theory and practice." It assumes that "the professional is primarily responsible to the client rather than simply to supervisors or to a bureaucracy, and that professional competence must be redefined in broad, humanistic terms." After a brief aside in which she analyzes the failure of the New Careers movement in the 1960s, Cohen delivers her main point. Although other institutions of higher education may have made "piecemeal" attempts to change, she says, her own institution, the College for Human Services, has succeeded in creating this third alternative. Through an intensive effort of research and development, the College for Human Services provides a way of "structuring professional education to meet the needs of the emerging human service society."[41]

The final section of the article is entitled "The Spreading of Model Three." Here Cohen mentions both Alverno College and Lincoln University as other institutions that are working to develop at least a part of the third alternative into their own conceptual frameworks. But she also emphasizes the radical essence of a "true" Model III institution. To be truly a third alternative, she writes, colleges must recognize and accept the idea that the ultimate goal for human service education is "to achieve social change that will benefit the citizens who receive services." And this involves a new perception of the client. In a theme that she embraced as far back as her community outreach work in 1965 and that reappeared in all her writings, Cohen asserts that the client is no longer a passive recipient of the actions of those who would do good; "he or she is now an active participant in the planning and carrying out of the actions that will change his or her life."[42]

In these final paragraphs Cohen is putting forth a concept of client or student empowerment that is suggestive of the educational philosophy of Paolo Freire. In his 1970 book, *Pedagogy of the Oppressed*, Freire criticized what he called the "banking" method of education, which treats the student as a passive receptacle for deposits of knowledge made by an all-knowing teacher. In its place Freire argued for a more liberating "problem-solving" pedagogy that treats teachers and students as active participants in the teaching and learning process. "The teacher is no longer merely the-one-who-teaches, but one who is himself taught in dialogue with the students, who in turn while being taught also teach," Freire wrote. "The students—no longer docile listeners—are now critical co-investigators in dialogue with the teacher."[43] Despite such conceptual similarities, however, as with the question of her familiarity with the writings of John Dewey it is difficult to pin down the extent to which Cohen's thinking was influenced by seminal educational philosophies of the mid-twentieth century and the extent to which she came to similar patterns of thought on her own.

Cohen authored two other seminal articles in the 1970s that connect the college's empowerment goals to the needs of the larger service economy. "The Service Society and a Theory of Learning Linking Education, Work, Life," published in 1976, reiterates some of the main points laid out in "The Third Alternative" but adds more about the development of the college's unique curriculum and includes the graphics that are reproduced earlier in this chapter. Another article, "The Citizen as the Integrating Agent: Productivity in the Human Services," was published in the *Human Services Monograph Series* by Project SHARE in 1978 and continues to be used today to familiarize MCNY students with the college's conceptual framework.

The 1978 article begins with an extended discussion of empowerment and focuses on the needs of the citizens that a human service professional must be trained to meet. Again the service economy is the pushing-off point for a discussion of the service ethic. "Most of us were educated in an industrial model of education that glorified the entrepreneur, the captain of industry, the powerful loner," Cohen writes. "The model I suggest is different. It is based on a service ethic." This ethic implies that caring about other human beings is both important and satisfying, that most people will earn their livelihoods by working with people more than with things, and that rewards can and should come from doing a good job for others. The new model for education she proposes elevates "humane and caring values," to a primary importance and shows how such values can be integrated into educational practice.[44]

Cohen proceeds to articulate a definition of empowerment that remains in use at the college today. Empowerment, she writes, is "the ability of people to manage their lives, to recognize and meet their needs, and to fulfill their potential as creative, responsible and productive members of society to the extent compatible with the empowerment of others."[45] This, Cohen asserts, is the ultimate goal of human service, and it can be developed in five dimensions of learning. She then proceeds to define the five dimensions that later appear in the accompanying graphics for the College for Human Services curricular model.

In a footnote at the beginning of the article Cohen mentions that in 1975 the College for Human Services' name had been approved by the U.S. Commissioner of Patents and Trademarks. Later on she was accused of being overly possessive about the usage of the college's terminology and of actually limiting the college's influence by trademarking and copyrighting its vocabulary. Here, however, the note provides the context for Cohen's critique of the way that other institutions were using the concept of human services. Although the proliferation of human services programs around the country indicated a recognition of the need for reforms that would make a positive improvement in the lives of those who needed help, for the most part the institutions referring to human services used the term not to identify new approaches to service or a concern with social justice, but simply to "relabel" already established traditional programs. Only when we can institute new thinking about human service that actually leads to self-sufficiency and empowerment, she asserts, will we have "a realistic chance to achieve social justice."[46]

Much of "The Citizen as the Integrating Agent" focuses on the needs of the citizens or clients that human service professionals must be prepared to address. Included are discussions of early and current perspectives on how to think about those in need, observations on the recent phenomenon of self-help groups, and changes in assessment criteria. These sections of the article continue to be instructive to students at the college who are assigned to read her work today.

Of additional interest in the article is Cohen's explanation of why the college uses the word *citizen* rather than *client* for the people its students are aiming to help. Historically, Cohen points out, the word *client* goes back to the early French word for "to hear" or "to listen," and, according to the Oxford English Dictionary, was used to refer to "one who is at the call of a patron." In many service professions—medicine, social work, law, education—the inequality between client and professional, this "imposition of the latter's judgment upon the former," has continued. In the past few years, however, the idea of imposing service on a client has been challenged; the client is now viewed as a person with certain rights. Hence there must be a change in terminology. " 'Citizen' implies equality," Cohen asserts.

" 'Client' does not. 'Citizen' is harmonious with the concept of empowerment; 'client' is not."[47]

The final section of the article is entitled "Productivity in the Human Services." Here Cohen introduces a new assessment tool, the Citizen Empowerment Chart, an early version of the evaluation rubrics that became popular in educational assessment procedures later on. The Citizen Empowerment Chart had by 1978 become part of each student's Constructive Action document; in a systematic way it requires the student practitioners to track quantitatively the progress of their citizens across the five dimensions. Although the chart looks somewhat archaic today, it shows that Cohen was ahead of her time in thinking innovatively about ways to measure human service performance outcomes.[48]

Most of the information that Cohen included in the three articles reviewed here was later consolidated into a chapter entitled "Human Service" that she wrote for a large compendium on *The Modern American College* published by Jossey-Bass in 1981. There, too, she located the need for a new field of human services in the rise of the service economy, stressed the distinction between the "generalist" training of human service workers and the overly fragmented and "specialized" training of social work professionals, and described in-depth the novel "holistic" educational model that the College for Human Services had developed. Although covering much of the same material, the tone of Cohen's voice in the book chapter is more secure than in her earlier articles; in some passages she even sounds triumphant. Human service is not "simply social work given a new name or self-help on a large scale," she asserts. "It is not 'a' helping profession, it is *the* helping profession." A human service perspective, so critical to effective service delivery and the hallmark of a service society, has been seriously neglected in American education, Cohen concludes. "It is time to incorporate realistic human service education into American life."[49]

The review of Cohen's seminal writings of the 1970s prompts several questions, the first of which concerns her use of the expanding service economy as a rationale for human service education. Was Cohen's easy linkage of current economic trends with her own educational model simply a form of blatant opportunism? Certainly the definition that economists use for the service economy includes many more occupations than those falling under the designation of "human services."[50] Lawyers, janitors, bankers, domestic workers, and dentists are all part of the service economy, yet none of them would be considered providers of human services. The occupations included in the category of human services are those that focus more specifically on social work, education, therapy, nursing care, and community organizing.[51] A second problem is the challenge of accurately measuring how important human services are in economic terms. Although the human services clearly constitute part of the overall service economy, it is difficult to gauge how large a part of that picture they fill. In her footnote citing Gartner and Riessman's work, Cohen quotes them as admitting that "it is difficult to estimate accurately those actually engaged in human services—those occupations characterized by closeness to consumers and a 'lack of tangible product'" (p. 18).[52] And yet throughout "The Third Alternative" and other writings of the 1970s Cohen seems eager to make the human services nearly synonymous with the larger concept of a service economy.

How can one best understand Cohen's deliberate conflating of human services with the service economy? A closer look at her concept of service may give one a better understanding of the logic behind her argument. After all, the notion of service can have a pejorative connotation especially to those who are wishing to advance beyond the kind of service roles their parents may have had as maids, butlers, and janitors. I remember a discussion with a College for Human Services student who came to me for help with a paper when I was working as a tutor at the college in the 1990s. It had suddenly dawned on him that the word "service" had the same root as the word "servant," and he was perplexed. "And aren't both these words," he asked, "related to the word for slave?"

I had a hard time answering him, and it is possible that Cohen, too, was aware of the trap that the student's question implied. She needed to make clear that the College for Human Service had higher aims than creating "servants"; she needed to relate "service" to "empowerment." Fortunately the economic indicators of the mid-1970s gave Cohen a way to put her institution on the cutting edge of national growth. The service sector was now the driving force of the economy, so service could be shown as mainstream, not underground. It became easy, even compelling, to emphasize the overlap between human service competencies and the needs of the larger economy.

As her 1970s articles clearly show, however, there is another impulse at work in Cohen's preoccupation with the service society. When one looks more closely at her definitions of service one sees an insistence on the *ethic* of service that gives her prose a texture that distinguishes it from the promotional writings of many other college presidents. In the 1975 essay this is expressed as an argument for a true collaboration among the agencies delivering human service, the institutions preparing people for human service occupations, and the individuals receiving the service. A Model III institution must "bring together life and learning, encouraging and enhancing each student's ability to do for others what he or she would like done for him or herself."[53] In her Preface to the reprinting of the article in 1988, this "Golden Rule" ethic comes across even more strongly. There she refers directly to "an education built around a service ethic. . . . an ethic of helping others"[54] and points out that although there has been a growing awareness of the importance of the service economy since 1975, when she first wrote the article, the emphasis in most schools is still on "individualism and competition, *not* on working together, respecting others, acknowledging our community of interest."[55]

In musing about the source of Cohen's deep commitment to a service ethic, it is perhaps useful to recall that as a young college student she chose to spend some of her summer months working for the American Friends Service Committee. The American Friends, or Quakers, have long been known for their ethic of service. As their present website states in its very first sentence, the AFSC includes people of various faiths "who are committed to social justice, peace, and humanitarian service."[56] Also to be recognized here is Barbara Walton's possible influence on Audrey Cohen. As mentioned earlier, Walton had attended Swarthmore College and although a member of a Unitarian congregation had always admired the Quaker emphasis on service.[57] In fact, after the sentence in "The Third Alternative" quoted above where Cohen refers to the Golden Rule—"each student's ability to do for others what he or she would like done for him or herself"—there is a footnote citing a paper by Barbara Walton as the source.[58]

Nevertheless, as was suggested in Chapter 4, the idea of personal influence on Cohen or any other person is tricky. After all, it was the young Audrey Cohen herself who *chose* the AFSC as a context for her own extracurricular learning in her college years. It was she, too, who *chose* the soft-speaking, clear-thinking, Barbara Walton as her colleague, adviser, and friend. The source of Cohen's commitment to the service ethic that permeates the three key essays that she wrote in the mid-1970s remains an open question.

A final point to be made here is that for the students who have been attracted to Cohen's educational vision, there is nothing at all problematic about the alignment of service with empowerment. Many of the adults enrolled in MCNY have lived their lives in service to others, and their service provides the terms of self-validation with which they define themselves as human beings. One of the pleasures of teaching at the college is to encounter men and women who have not been given much but whose most deeply held passion is to give to others. As an early Corps Woman in the Women's Talent Corps stated in framing her own educational goals, "I have helped people as best I can. I feel that this is service that each one should give to others who can't find themselves."[59]

Cohen's intensive efforts to spread the word about the College for Human Services brought results. The archives index lists twenty-three pieces of publicity about the college in the 1970s, and the college was sometimes in the news. In November 1978 Cohen's good friend Frank Newman, with whom she had served on the Newman Commission and who had become president of the University of Rhode Island, sent her a clipping from the *Providence Sunday Journal*.[60] Entitled "New College for Human Services Gives Courses in Purposeful Living," the UPI article opens with a brief description of its founder as a "dauntless" leader, "full of galvanic drive, crusading and visionary spirits."[61] The author quotes Cohen's disparagement of traditional higher education as "going through hoops without much meaning" unless the student has a chance to try out what he or she is learning "in the real world." Some of the college's graduates had opened storefront advising centers, established neighborhood parks from scratch, and organized community centers for the elderly or daycare centers for children. The article ends with the story of a former student who had come to the college as an unemployed factory worker and had ended up as the supervisor of a family service agency earning what was then a decent salary—$15,000 a year. Another student is quoted as saying that at the college he had learned how "to care" and "to help."[62]

The most significant, though not uncritical, publicity for the college during these years was the chapter entitled "The Activist-Radical Impulse: The College for Human Services" that appeared in *Perpetual Dream: Reform and Experiment in the American College* by Gerald Grant and David Riesman referred to in Chapter 7. Although Cohen and her colleagues were unhappy about some of the errors in the article (the authors state that the Women's Talent Corps opened in 1965 rather than 1966 and that the strike occurred in 1972 rather than 1970), the analysis was thorough and thought-provoking. It ends with questions of whether the College for Human Services fully met New York standards for granting a bachelor's or master's degree. When the Grant and Riesman article went to press, that issues had not yet been decided.

Perpetual Dream received a positive review in the *New Yorker* magazine by well-known psychologist and educator Robert Coles. Although the book covered several examples of reform, the College for Human Services was the main focus of Coles's review. Making a characteristically broad assessment of the college's purposes, Coles states that the its aim was to serve the economic and social interests of students and at the same time to make the professions (medicine, law, nursing, teaching, library work) more open to hiring members of minority groups. "Men and women down on their luck but eager and street-smart are encouraged to take a chance on themselves, on their learning capacities," Coles wrote. Whereas students at conventional colleges get a degree that will earn them social position and privileges, students at the College for Human Services learn right away that higher education will give them the opportunity "to hold an interesting and remunerative" job. The review ends with a ringing endorsement: "The college is visionary, idealistic, and firmly critical, but it is also short on rhetoric and long on specific concrete programs."[63]

Robert Coles' words capture both the college's impressive achievement and its ongoing quest.

OLD STRUGGLES ON A NEW LEVEL

The title for this subsection comes from an outline for a history of the college sketched by Alida Mesrop in the late 1980s under the heading "Getting the Bachelor of Professional Studies Degree." She probably chose the subheading because, like the college's battles in the late 1960s to obtain recognition for the AA degree, the effort to obtain the bachelors degree-granting status required multiple efforts before succeeding. Mesrop's outline for this part of the college's history lists, in order, the registration of the professional program, the New York State Education Department's first visit, its report, redesigning the program, resubmitting the report, the next visit, and finally, another new heading, "the pot at the end of the rainbow"—formal registration of the Bachelor of Professional Studies degree.[64]

The college's actual history suggests a more complex and problematical process. Once again the accreditation efforts began with an eyebrow-raising effort by President Cohen. Only a few months after the creation of the new curricular grid in February 1974, Cohen set her staff to work proposing that the young college be granted the right to award not just a bachelor's degree but a joint bachelor's and master's degree. (As her friend Alida Mesrop noted, Audrey "always thought big."[65]) The credentials for professional human service employment were becoming more stringent, and a master's degree was now a common requirement even for what had earlier been known as a "new career." A complex alignment of the college's unique field placement scheduling with more traditional credit-hour allocations enabled Cohen and her colleagues to claim that each Crystal actually was the equivalent of 1¼ semesters, and thus that the college's "professional program" was the equivalent of five academic years[66]—in many universities a possible time frame for both a bachelor's and master's degree. But for a relatively new and unorthodox college, the proposed program was admittedly a stretch.

Even the college's Board of Trustees, which generally deferred to Cohen's vision, had some reservations about the proposal. David Seeley, who came on the board in 1974 and had worked at the state level on education reform, was skeptical about getting the New York State Board of Regents' approval.[67] Although he valiantly engaged in "word lobbying" with regents and commissioners, he understood the reluctance of the educational bureaucracy to allow an upstart institution to award a master's degree even before it had gained authorization to award a bachelor's. It would make people suspicious that there was "some kind of wild flimflam going on," he later said. It would be threatening to the more traditional institutions that were toeing the line. The sheer chutzpah of it would put people off. "What's this outrageous little upstart pipsqueak outfit think they're doing by saying they're worthy of giving a master's degree when they don't even have an academic faculty? They don't even have a history department! This is ridiculous!"[68]

In May 1975 an article in the education section of *New York Times* suggested the audacity of the college's reach. "Beverly Hastings, 30 years old, divorced and the mother of three children, is working for her master's degree although she has no bachelor's degree," the author of the article begins. "But then," he continues, "some of her fellow master's degree candidates at the College for Human Services never graduated from high school." Furthermore, the article continues, "the college has yet to get permission from the state to award the master's degree Mrs. Hastings hopes to earn." In most academic settings, such a situation might be cause for some alarm. But at the College for Human Services, the administration takes it in stride. "We think it will work out," the author quotes Cohen as saying.[69]

Work it out Cohen and her colleagues eventually did, though it took nearly five years of back and forth negotiations with the New York State Department of Education. A preliminary proposal was submitted to the NYSDOE in August 1974, and a task force under the chairmanship of Dr. Wilbert McKeachie, a professor of psychology at the University of Michigan, was hired to assess the curriculum. The task force gave the program an encouraging evaluation, and in March 1975, a team of consultants selected by the New York State Education department visited the college. The team made positive suggestions but also made recommendations for improvement.[70]

By October 1975 the NYSDOE was still not satisfied that the program met its requirements. Seeing the handwriting on the wall, the college withdrew its petition for a master's degree with the understanding that it would be resubmitted at a later date. After a meeting in January 1976, Cohen met with the deputy commissioner for higher and professional education and was advised in a report later on that the DOE needed to have evidence that students pursuing the master's "possess either a baccalaureate degree or its equivalent." One of the four suggested options was to alter the program "to provide for both the baccalaureate and master's degree" rather than a combined bachelor's/master's degree. The college agreed to pursue this route. But by April 1977, the college had resubmitted its curricula and other documentation to the New York State DOE, requesting authority to award both a baccalaureate degree and a combined baccalaureate/master's degree. In December 1977, a five-member team of consultants from the department visited the college, and their reports were submitted to the state. By early 1978 the college was still awaiting a draft of the state's recommendation to the regents on the degree decisions.[71]

In the meantime, thanks to Cohen's ceaseless networking and outreach, the College for Human Services had developed a positive reputation beyond the confines of New York State. In 1976 Lincoln University in Pennsylvania had instituted its first graduate program, an MA degree in human services (MHS), which it developed under the aegis of the College for Human Services.[72] Like the College for Human Services model, the Lincoln University MHS curriculum today consists of a sequence of "competency units" (totaling five, not eight), in the form of a curriculum matrix intersected by five "dimensions" that are named Values, Self/Others, Systems, Skills, and plus an "Integration and Practice" seminar.[73]

The College for Human Services itself also began to expand. Supported by another grant from the Foundation for the Improvement of Post Secondary Education (FIPSE), in 1978 the college opened a new branch in Oakland, California, and the next year it opened a branch in Fort Lauderdale, Florida. To the frustration of those in the college's New York City offices who felt they were being given a runaround by New York State, the Southeastern Association of Independent Colleges granted the authority to award a combined bachelor's/master's in professional studies degrees to the College for Human Services in Florida.[74] The news about the College for Human Services branch in Florida being able to award the master's seemed to compound the irony that Lincoln University, which had created a program based on the College for Human Services model, was also able to do so.[75]

In addition to the worry about accreditation during these years there was worry about funding. As Dellie Bloom's "Narrative Summary" of 1970 to 1980 relates, 1975 was a terrible year. Not only did the college learn that the New York State Department of Education could not yet make a favorable recommendation to the Board of Regents for the proposed joint bachelor's and master's degree, but in March of that year Cohen had to inform the Board of Trustees that the Department of Labor would no longer be funding the college.[76] "This is the lowest down-dip in what has always been roller coaster funding," was how Cohen described the looming disaster. "Real down," she said privately.[77] Given the city's own financial crisis in 1975, the news could not have come a worse time. The college now had to negotiate with the New York City Department of Labor for funds when the city itself was at this point near bankruptcy.[78]

In 1976 the college was able to get some funding from the Comprehensive Employment and Training Act (CETA) in Washington, but CETA now required that the money be funneled through the Department of Employment, a newly created offshoot of the Manpower and Development Council—the very agency that Cohen and her associates back in 1967 had staged a major demonstration to avoid (see Chapter 6). The new department insisted that the college comply with the department's criteria for unit costs per trainee, but to fit that requirement was a mind-boggling data-management challenge for an educational institution. How many students got jobs? At what salary level? How soon after training? How much did it cost to train them?[79] For a few months in 1977 to 1978 the college even set up an office in Washington to lobby for political support, but it became too costly to maintain.[80] Fortunately, the college's contract manager for the department was Flavia Sinapoli, a staunch supporter of the program who was also politically astute. She soon advised Cohen and her colleagues to look elsewhere for funds. CETA could not be relied on much longer, she thought, and in any case its rules and regulations were becoming increasingly restrictive.[81]

ALIDA MESROP BECOMES DEAN

In May 1979 the news finally came that the Board of Regents of the State of New York had given its unanimous approval to register the College for Human Services as a Bachelor of Professional Studies degree-granting institution.[82] The news was not exactly the pot at the end of the rainbow that Alida Mesrop's outline labeled it. "I made no bones about my distress at not getting the right to the Masters as well, after all we've been through," Cohen privately wrote.[83] Nevertheless the news was greeted with great relief by Cohen and her staff. On the plane back from Albany after the announcement, Cohen made an important move. She asked Alida Mesrop to become the college's dean.

The request came as a complete surprise to Mesrop. As mentioned in Chapter 1, Mesrop had worked with Cohen on projects for Part-Time

Research Associates and then worked at the Women's Talent Corps and later the College for Human Services. She increased her time commitment as her children grew older, but she had never worked more than 24 hours a week. During those years she and Cohen had developed a close but frank relationship. Mesrop could and did tell Cohen everything she felt about the college. "I was not your typical yes-person at all." In fact she was often critical of how the institution worked. She was especially concerned that the administrative functions were very haphazard. "I kept saying, why isn't this being done?" Mesrop never guessed that she would soon be the person having to address the college's many problems. But she felt ready for the job. "I had a lot of confidence. I didn't worry about that. But, wow, what a job!"[84]

One consequence of both the fiscal woes of the 1970s and the college's new status as a degree-granting institution in 1979 was the departure of Steven Sunderland. His own explanation for his need to leave referred to an "arc of hypocrisy" that the worsening job market and the college's new accreditation forced on him. In the mid-1970s, as the placement rate for graduates fell from 90 percent to 80 percent and eventually down below 50 percent,[85] he found it increasingly difficult to engage students with rosy expectations for future employment. It was emotionally painful for him to say to students, "We hope there will be jobs for you at the end." He later said that he could feel in himself, and could feel in the students, the sense of "you are playing with my life for your social ideology and it's unacceptable." When the college's state accreditation came through and the jobs didn't, he felt that Cohen should have simply closed down the college, "shut the doors," rather than to continue the wishful thinking.[86]

By this point Sunderland's personal views of Cohen had also become very mixed. While continuing to admire what he called her "genius,"[87] he also felt that she was a "ruthless" person to be with, and he accused her staff of being afraid of her. Yet he admitted that he, too, was not an easy person to work with; he recognized that he, too, was a very controlling, very center-of-attention type. "I had lot of her qualities," he acknowledged.[88] At some level he may have also been deeply jealous of Cohen. In his lengthy reminiscences about his years at the college he even refers to Cohen as a man, "one of the strongest men I know." In discussing Cohen's resiliency Sunderland says "I think she would come up way ahead of me. . . . I'm always second." To illustrate, he created the following image. "While we're being thrown out of the window, and we're falling 25 stories to the ground, just before I become *splat*, she has landed and says, 'And now we can climb back up,' not ever recognizing that we had actually been thrown down!"[89]

Sunderland later admitted that other factors were at work in his decision to leave. The Brooklyn neighborhood where he lived in during the 1970s was a center for drug trafficking, and his car had been stolen from right in front of his building several times. The last straw was when his five-year-old daughter's room was vandalized by intruders.[90] The city's problems became too much for the family, and they decided to move out to Cincinnati, Ohio, to start a new life.

When Sunderland told Cohen his reasons for leaving and tried to persuade her to give up her project, she calmly replied, "The College will survive." One development that enabled the college to survive was the decision, taken in 1979, to cease the hand-to-mouth funding relationship with federal and state agencies and to begin charging tuition. Interestingly, much of the impetus for the move came from the faculty, who could see from close range the effects that the funding uncertainties were having both on their own financial security and on the attitudes of students. Once again, a retreat was planned to deal with the issues collectively. Faculty and administrators prepared position papers on the pros and cons of charging tuition, and together with a few carefully selected students they gathered to wrestle with the decision. Soon a consensus was reached: "Whatever the risks, tuition was the way to go."[91]

The first tuition-paying students enrolled at the College for Human Services in December 1980. As Dellie Bloom later proclaimed, with a new dean who was action-oriented, decisive, and perfectionist, "a new decade, and a new era, had begun."[92]

CHAPTER 9

CONSTRUCTIVE ACTIONS (1980–1989)

As a practice methodology, the Constructive Action helps the practitioner to prepare comprehensive and realistic plans, act on them effectively, and assess what has been achieved.

—Audrey Cohen College, 1999, p. 18

"Whichever way we looked, we saw risk, risk, risk and change, change, change," Alida Mesrop recalled when reflecting on her first year as a college dean. The process of gaining accreditation from New York State and the decision to charge tuition had brought both advantages and challenges. As a consequence of becoming fully accredited, the faculty could now feel that they were teaching at a real college rather than a training institute, and the students, too, could now be more confident about the credentials that they were receiving. But the process of becoming a fiscally independent college required institutional renovation. As a student stipend program, totally funded by the Department of Labor, the college had lacked many of the systems most colleges initially have. The registrar, admissions office, and financial aid program were wholly inadequate for the institution's new identity. A supportive and efficient financial aid office became especially critical, for students were now confronted with unfamiliar paperwork of filling out applications for state (Tuition Assistance Program) and federal (Pell) grants.[1] To add to these challenges, Steve Sunderland's departure had left an "administrative shambles" in his wake. "We were an accredited college with no infrastructure to support it," Dellie Bloom observed.[2]

During Mesrop's first months on the job, the college's physical premises were also in a shambles. One consequence of its newly independent status was that the college was forced out of the old federal building at 201 Varick Street and had to find new space at 345 Hudson Street, a few blocks away. "They were knocking the walls down around us while we were trying to hold classes and there was dust everywhere!" Mesrop remembered running down to a health service on a lower floor to ask if the college could use some of its open spaces for a meeting. "It was like you were sticking your fingers in the dike, just trying to keep it from falling apart."[3]

In the larger political sphere loomed even more momentous changes that cast a shadow over Mesrop's job and added uncertainty to Cohen's long-term project. In November 1980, in a landslide victory, Ronald Reagan was elected president of the United States. The election ushered in a new era of governmental downsizing and a retrenchment of social programs. Safety nets unraveled and subsidies were cut back. Homeless men and women began appearing on the streets of Manhattan for the first time in decades, and panhandlers frequented the subways. A new anxiety gripped those working in the nonprofit sector, in community-based organizations, and in human service agencies about their ability to survive in the new era of "trickle-down" economics. Meanwhile, high up on the scaffolding of a luxury apartment building under construction on East 79th Street, the words "Affluence," "Indulgence," "Beauty," "Luxury," "Extravagance," could be seen printed in large bold letters to celebrate a new shamelessness about anything promoting material growth. "Greed is good," announced an advertisement in *Fortune* magazine.[4]

Having been a critic of some aspects of the college's administrative functioning over the years, Mesrop was acutely aware of the challenges. But with gumption she jumped right in. She had good organizational skills ("I always think that I could organize the world") and a strong belief in what the college was doing. "We used our logical common sense and tried to take the college from step A to step B." As a person who didn't like to leave things hanging, she often stayed at the college until 9 or 10 in the evening to finish a task. She was also clear about the need for others to get things done and would often walk through the college's offices, chatting with staff about how their work was going. "That way I could kind of nudge if necessary." As Dellie Bloom described her, Mesrop was "upfront and can-do, crisp and efficient, with no taste for intrigue."[5]

Although Mesrop looks and speaks like a classic WASP, she is a first-generation Italian American and is proud of her background.[6] She grew up in New York City, on Charlton Street in Greenwich Village, which in the late 1930s and early 1940s was the heart of bohemia. Her parents divorced when she was very young; she didn't even know her father until she was thirteen. Alida's mother was a literary buff and loved reading Shakespeare but had to work long hours supporting the family, and as Alida remembers, was always fighting to get a raise or a promotion. Alida's grandmother was her primary caretaker in her early years. Alida took an early interest in theater and dance and attended Hunter College High School, which she immediately loved but where she struggled to be an average student. She then went on to Hunter College, where she excelled, majoring in speech and drama and also English. Graduating with honors, she got a job right away with the National Broadcasting Company (NBC). She knew she wanted to be in broadcasting, not as a performer, but behind the scenes.[7]

At NBC Mesrop worked first on *The Today Show*. She was ambitious and soon became the public relations coordinator for *The Tonight Show*. When there were cutbacks and her position was eliminated, she went on to become the public relations and publicity director for WPIX-TV. It was there that she met Don West who, when Mesrop's first child was born and she was looking for part-time work, suggested that she contact Audrey Cohen. The story of Mesrop's and Cohen's first meeting outside their Stuyvesant Town apartments is recounted in Chapter 1.

When Mesrop began working full time as dean in 1980, the college's enrollment totaled around one-hundred students. In the next decade it grew nearly tenfold, to 959 by the fall of 1990. During that ten-year period Mesrop missed only one day of work.[8] "Audrey had the vision and I was supposed to figure out how to make it happen," Mesrop said about her years as dean of the College for Human Services.[9]

Assisting Mesrop with these changes was Sylvia Hack. Hack had been a close associate of Audrey Cohen's since the early days of the Women's Talent Corps. By taking care of administrative tasks and handling the paperwork to and from Washington, she was essential to the college's early growth. Through grant writing, statistical reports, and fund raising, she helped the college survive through its many difficult transitions. Hack also was responsible for the design and construction plans for the college's new space and for its infrastructure, including its phone system and computers.

One early hurdle during Mesrop's deanship was to prepare the college's first Self Study for accreditation by the Middle States Commission on Higher Education, an organization that accredits degree-granting colleges in the eastern United States. No sooner had the college settled into new space at 345 Hudson Street and had begun to establish the necessary infrastructure for an academic institution than it needed to begin preparing for an external review.

As is the case with many Middle States reviews, the process was fraught with tension from the start. Mesrop acknowledged that the Self Study aims to give an institution a sense of its strengths and weaknesses and an impetus to address those weaknesses. But the process also requires setting up a warren of committees and subcommittees, some of which develop their own political agendas. Mesrop was a co-chair of the Self Study, but she was also on a subcommittee that had faculty members who seemed to be pushing for more power for themselves and who tended to be suspicious of a dean who didn't have a doctorate. Preparing for the Middle States review gave those who had had little prior chance to complain, a forum in which to ventilate and to voice their concerns about the direction in which the college was moving. "This was the great ventilation," Mesrop later said. "So you learned an awful lot."[10]

Mesrop's hard work soon succeeded in overcoming the faculty's initial distrust. Her co-chair of the Self Study had been pessimistic about the college's ability to become accredited, especially because there had recently been a drop in enrollment and a number of faculty members had been dismissed. But Mesrop asserted optimism. "Of course we're going to get this accreditation. How can you even think we're not going to get it?" She was terrified, she admitted later, "but what am I going to say?" No matter what her doubts might have been, she continued to tell the naysayers, "Yes, we can! Yes, we can!"[11]

And they did. After submitting the Self Study and being visited by a team of evaluators, the college received a positive report. In granting accreditation the Middle States Commission gave special commendation to the college's devoted faculty and staff and to the leadership abilities of its "dynamic and forceful founding president." The report's introductory paragraphs noted "the special commitment the College has to social change" and, quoting the Self Study, 'to persons who might otherwise find it difficult or impossible, by reason of age, race, national origin, gender, sexual orientation, or income to obtain an education in keeping with their aspirations and abilities."[12] Thanks to Mesrop's painstaking commitment to Cohen's vision, the College for Human Services was establishing a recognized role in American higher education.

LOOKING FORWARD

In May 1984, the College celebrated its twentieth anniversary by hosting a formal dinner at the Lotos Club, a private club on the East Side of Manhattan that Cohen had access to through friends who were members. More than one-hundred guests attended, including community leaders and representatives from the fields of education and business.[13] The keynote speaker was Gordon Ambach, then commissioner of education in New York State. Ambach's speech took the form of a straightforward report on the demographics of higher education, but Cohen's introductory comments were full of the college's past accomplishments and its grand plans for the future.

Reviewing the college's accomplishments, Cohen began with the theme she had been stressing since the mid-1970s—the connections between service and work. She and her colleagues had a very real vision to guide them, she said. That vision was that "service is the future of work." What did service mean in the 1960s? It meant opening new kinds of jobs that had never existed before—the job of the legal assistant, the teacher assistant, and the mental health worker. Service also meant fighting to make these jobs become part of the employment structure of New York City and eventually the entire country. "We were successful," she went on. Today hundreds of thousands of these new jobs exist "as crucial components" of both the profit and the nonprofit sectors of the American service economy. Moreover, such jobs were being filled by those who needed jobs. The college had focused on low-income members of minority groups who, due to poverty and prejudice, had never had the opportunity to enter the professional arena. But now individuals without previous college education could enter the market and move up into the American mainstream—first as paraprofessionals and eventually as professionals.[14]

Cohen then turned her focus on the educational model that the college had developed to educate students for the new roles in the service sector. At this point she asked the assembled dinner guests to look at the bowl full of crystals that had been carefully placed on each table as a centerpiece. "They are symbols of our educational approach," she said, with reference to the crystals that throughout the 1980s still represented each semester's multifaceted or multidimensional purpose. "Crystals grow in nature in all directions simultaneously. We want our students to grow in very much the same way, to be able to think comprehensively using all parts of their brain and to see the connection between all aspects of knowledge and their own performance" in the field.[15]

The exciting news, Cohen continued, was that the college's new model overcame the age-old divide between humanistic learning and job readiness. "Delivering a comprehensive liberal arts education along with *practical preparation* for the world of work was not only *ideal,* but *possible.*"[16] To illustrate she gave the following examples.

> Our students might study Jean-Paul Sartre's *No Exit* wondering if any of the existentialist's premises about self-determination could be useful to the citizen they are serving at King's County Hospital. Is Garcin's [one of the characters in the play] refusal to leave hell when he has the chance similar to the patient's resistance to help himself when he is able to?
>
> Or, the structure of a particular agency or organization might be studied and explored in terms of Lewis Carroll's *Alice in Wonderland.* Students might ask themselves how their agency is or is not like a kind of wonderland and how changes can be made within that system.[17]

Other college presidents had often told her, Cohen proudly reported, that at the College for Human Services she was doing what educators had been dreaming of doing for decades. "You are offering a liberal arts education *and* presenting it in a way that gives true meaning to a person's life." Aiming her pitch to her well-heeled audience, Cohen added that bridging the distance between theory and practice in this new way "will make people the best possible problem solvers and go-getters that business and the traditional social service agencies could ask for."[18]

A sampling from the college's *Purpose Handbooks*—the photocopied booklets that contained each semester's syllabi and essential information for students—would have given Cohen's audience ample evidence to support her claims. Intermingled with case studies and articles of current interest related to the human services professions were the staples of liberal arts curriculums found at more traditional schools. In a fourth semester course focusing on the skills of teaching, the assigned reading included Plato's *Symposium* and George Bernard Shaw's *Pygmalion*.[19] In a second semester course where the purpose is to develop professional relationships, the required readings to be applied to the students' fieldwork included the then path-breaking study, *In a Different Voice* by Carol Gilligan, and the classic *Othello* by William Shakespeare.[20] In another course students were required to read Colin Turnbull's *The Mountain People*—a popular introductory anthropology text—together with Arthur Miller's *Death of a Salesman*.[21] Unstated but obvious to any outside observer was the fact that each of these innovative combinations was made possible by the college's use of Dimensions, rather than disciplines, in the curricular structure that had been created back in 1974.

Cohen's reference to business as well as social services in the college's twentieth-anniversary celebration speech marked an important development in the institution's identity. The previous September, with little fanfare or even preparation, the College for Human Services had added a program offering a bachelor of professional studies in business. Although some members of the college community raised questions at the time about the compatibility of human services and business (human service agencies being clearly "nonprofit" and business enterprises essentially "for profit"), the incongruities were generally overlooked. Like the administrators of other educational institutions that were adding more business courses to their offerings, the College for Human Services was pragmatically adjusting to the tenor of the times.

In addition to the new business program, Cohen in her twentieth-anniversary speech pointed to other expansionary moves that the college had already set in motion or was planning for the near future. The college now had small but fully accredited branch campuses in California and Florida and had shared its model with Lincoln College in Pennsylvania. In an experimental new venture and with funding from the Edwin Gould Foundation, it had also opened a College for Human Services Junior High School in East Harlem and was hoping to create a new high school based on the college's unique curricular model.

Toward the end of her speech Cohen could summarize her and her colleagues' bold accomplishments with pride:

- In a commodity-oriented society the college has remained true to its vision of service;

- In a materialistic society the college is value-oriented;

- In a credential-oriented society, the college emphasizes performance.[22]

And, in an uncanny perceptiveness of what the future might bring, Cohen listed among her long-range projects "to put the Crystals on video disc and computers so that we can enroll students all over the United States."[23] Cohen made this statement in 1983—nearly three decades before "distance learning" had become a clear option for educators. The woman was, as many people who knew her noted, a "visionary."

FACULTY DEVELOPMENT

Cohen's twentieth-anniversary speech made little mention of the College for Human Service's faculty, but each new step of the college's evolution into an accredited institution for higher education had required a new emphasis on the faculty's credentials. No longer could the college rely solely on the dedicated commitment of social workers with master's degrees or retired teachers and community organizers. With New York State accreditation behind them and Middle States accreditation ahead, Cohen and her colleagues in the 1980s made a focused effort to hire new faculty members who had PhDs as well as a commitment to the college's unique combination of pedagogical innovation and community engagement.

Young, idealistic, and diverse, the recently minted PhD holders who were hired by the College of Human Services in the 1980s turned out to be huge assets in terms of forging the institution's identity and assuring its future growth. Over the course of that decade they developed curricula, created new programs, and attracted an ever-growing body of eager students—even while they taught courses and made visits to human service agencies and community-based organizations to check on student performance in the field. Many of the young idealists hired in that decade continue to be veteran members of the faculty today. They are still engaged in heroic service to the college and are among its most beloved teachers. Who were they, and why did they come?

One early hire was Clyde Griffin. Griffin had grown up in Cleveland, Ohio, and attended Ohio State University where he pursued an interest in philosophy but majored in the Romance Languages (French, Italian, and Spanish).[24] He went on to the University of Iowa where he taught French as a graduate assistant for a few years, and then in 1963 he joined the Peace Corps. Stationed in Nigeria, Griffin planned curricula, prepared students for exams, put together a library and a medical dispensary, and coached basketball. Instead of returning to the United States right away he spent a year in Paris and then several months in Florence reading Dante's *Divine Comedy* in Italian. Upon his return to the United States he became the first African American to be hired by the Hillsdale School, an all-girls' private school in Cincinnati, and from there he moved on to become the chair of the foreign language department at the Cincinnati Country Day School, the most prestigious private school (all boys) in the city. He stayed for eight years teaching foreign languages, conducting seminars on Homer, Dante, and Cervantes, and preparing students for SAT exams.[25]

In 1978 Griffin's accomplishments as a teacher made him a winner of the nationally coveted Joseph Klingenstein Fellowship for Excellence in Teaching. The fellowship allows a recipient to take a full year of free courses at Teachers College, Columbia University. Once immersed in the stimulating intellectual and cultural milieu of New York City, Griffin did not look back. At Teachers College he earned a master's of arts in languages, literature, and social studies, served as a coordinator of the TESOL program, and began working on a doctorate in applied linguistics. In 1982, on the advice of his dissertation advisor at Teachers College, he applied for and was hired to lead the College for Human Services Life-Experience program, which included the recruitment and counseling of students who were coming to the college with possible credits for their previous human service experience.

"I was helping people to think about and bring meaning to their lives, helping them to validate themselves," Griffin recalled, reflecting on his early years at the college.[26] And his background in linguistics made him appreciate the deliberately "languaged" aspect of the institution. Whereas others might see the college's unique vocabulary as a barrier to communicating with the outside world, Griffin saw the *Crystals* and *Purpose-Centered* curriculum as an asset. "In developing a common language, the institution defines itself, its space."[27] He was also impressed by the administration's level of literacy. Alida Mesrop, Barbara Walton, Deborah Allen—"all the women here could *write!*"[28] In addition to teaching courses in the Values dimension, Griffin's work in the 1980s at the college included curriculum development, orientation sessions for new faculty and staff, and training teachers for the expansion of Purpose-Centered Education into elementary and secondary schools. Today Griffin continues to be a stimulating and provocative teacher who introduces students to literary works ranging from Seneca's *Moral Letters to Lucilius* and Dante's *Inferno* to Harriet Beecher Stowe's *Uncle Tom's Cabin* and Sister Souljah's *No Disrespect*.

Richard Grallo was another young academic who was drawn to Cohen's project in the early 1980s and who today is still an immensely important member of the faculty. Grallo grew up in Boston and attended Catholic schools. After high school, thinking he might want to join the priesthood, he briefly attended a seminary in the Archdiocese of Boston. He was impressed by the morality and spirituality of the brothers and priests but realized that he really wanted to be a teacher. Seeking a broader outlook, he transferred to Boston College where he studied philosophy and then went on to MIT to study philosophy and science. Philosophy provided "a bunch of interesting models," he later said, "but they weren't being put to the test!"[29] Seeking a more scientific focus he switched to psychology, finally finding his niche in the Department of Educational Psychology (now part of Applied Psychology) at New York University.

Shortly after getting his PhD at NYU, Grallo came onto the full-time faculty at the College for Human Services. Over the years he has taught and developed the Self and Others dimension, introduced students to rational models for problem solving, and provided wise and well-reasoned leadership of the Faculty Council. His background in psychological measurement and educational assessment has been a tremendous resource both to faculty and to administration, and his nurturing of students' own research skills has been exemplary. He has frequently encouraged students to polish their academic work for conference presentations and even publication.

Another key faculty member hired by Cohen in 1983 was Humphrey Crookendale. Born in Barbados, Crookendale came to New York when he was fifteen years old. As an eleven-year-old in Barbados, he had not passed the exam guaranteeing entrance to the "best" schools, and much to his parents' dismay was headed for a trade school. Once in New York, however, he entered Erasmus Hall, the oldest standing public school in the city and at that time one of the most prestigious. To be given new options, was, he says, like opening "a new page on life . . . a revelation." From Erasmus Hall Crookendale went on to Queens College where he took a wide range of courses in politics and economics. "In the morning I had a course with Michael Harrington and in the afternoon one with Andrew Hacker. You couldn't ask for anything better than that!"[30]

Crookendale's interest in political science drew him to the law school at Howard University in Washington, DC. He graduated in 1983 and, having decided that he was not quite ready for the practice of law, was looking for a "stopgap" job. He saw an ad for a teaching job at the College for Human Services and applied. At that time potential faculty members were interviewed in a group. Crookendale found himself surrounded by other applicants with PhDs, all of whom were asked to identify a piece of literature or a book that they had read recently that had had a significant influence. "All of these guys were waxing eloquently about political philosophers. Then it came my turn and I was sure I couldn't compete." But Crookendale proceeded to tell the committee that he had been very impressed by the debates between the Madisonians and the Jeffersonians in the *Federalist Papers*, which would eventually lead to the framing of the U.S. Constitution. The response landed him the job. Later on a member of the hiring committee told him, "Humphrey, you stood apart. You were the only person who took the material and applied it to things that could be translated into *teaching* in the classroom."[31]

As Crookendale frequently quips, his "stopgap" job has lasted more than thirty years. One high point was when he was asked to write course outlines for a proposed master's of science in administration program that ultimately became a master's in public administration degree. Other more senior faculty members were originally involved in the task, but they gradually fell by the wayside, and Crookendale found himself and Deborah Allen in charge of the project. "I was like a kid [he was still in his twenties] but had ideas about how it should be. And then to have New York State approve it! It was like my crowning glory to feel I was a part of all that."[32] For decades Crookendale has been a beloved teacher (his students affectionately call him "Crookie"), and he is now the dean of the master's of public administration program that he helped draft in 1988.

Today Anne Lopes has moved on from the MCNY faculty, but her contributions to the college from 1987 to 2007 were essential. Petite, efficient, and independent in her thinking, Lopes grew up in the Bronx and attended Ramapo College, a small liberal arts college that is part of the New Jersey public university system. She went on to receive a master of arts in political theory in a Goddard College program located in Cambridge, Massachusetts, and three years later completed her doctorate in Germany, earning a PhD in political science *summa cum laude* from the Freie Universitat in Berlin. When she returned to the United States she lived for a while in Philadelphia but wanted to relocate to New York when she heard about the College for Human Services.[33]

The college looked like a place where Lopes's values would fit in well. She was interested in educational models that were innovative and "outside the mold," and she had always wanted to work with students from low-income backgrounds. Her first impressions, however, were somewhat off-putting. As in Humphrey Crookendale's case, the faculty hiring process began with a group interview, with ten people applying for a job brought together in a circle with several faculty members. She almost walked out. "I found it just appalling that the administration didn't have the courtesy to hold an individual one-on-one interview."[34] But a week or so later she got a call back, and because another applicant with whom she had struck up an immediate friendship had also been offered a job, she decided to accept the offer. She remained an engaged and outstanding member of the faculty for the next twenty years, developing curricula, especially in Purpose IV;

fostering new procedures for faculty and field-supervisor communication; and serving on search committees. Among her many lasting contributions were to create assessment instruments for faculty peer evaluations, set up a mentoring program for at-risk students, and coordinate the college's first computer-integrated curriculum. In 2007 Lopes became an associate dean at Empire State College, and as of this writing she is associate provost for strategy initiatives and dean of graduate students at the John Jay College of Criminal Justice. But she still remembers her time at MCNY as among the most productive of her life and continues to see the college as a place where the faculty really cares about teaching.

As might be expected, with the newly credentialed faculty came sources of contention for Cohen and her colleagues. Ever since the strike and dismissals of 1972, the administration had governed the college with little resistance from the teaching staff. But now a new faculty with its own sense of professional standards and its own professional needs became a force to be reckoned with. Cohen's sense of personal control over the institution she had founded became more rigid as time went on, and faculty members increasingly chafed under the limits that her need for control imposed.

Cohen would often visit classes to check on what was being taught—a practice that earlier faculty members accepted as part of their job but that new faculty found disconcerting. ("It was her way of ensuring the integrity of the product," Crookendale wryly termed it.) An annual ritual that faculty members dreaded was a luncheon "retreat" arranged by Cohen at the Lotos Club where faculty members were required to share formally what they were teaching in their Dimension courses. In essence the idea may have been a good one—to showcase ways that the humanities were actually being covered in the curriculum—but the practice was bitterly resisted by the faculty and ridiculed behind Cohen's back. Richard Grallo and Humphrey Crookendale remember at one point being asked to prove to Cohen that they could teach the documentation of a Constructive Action by producing one themselves—a request at which they balked. As a compromise they agreed to create a detailed outline of a Constructive Action's essential elements—an exercise that Crookendale says was ultimately very useful and that he still uses as a guide today.[35]

Another source of contention was the periodic visits that faculty members were required to make to the field agencies where their students were working as interns or employees. Some of these agencies were located in unsafe neighborhoods, and once or twice in the 1980s and early 1990s faculty members reported that they had been threatened or mugged on their way to or from an agency. Although a number of faculty members continued to be committed to the practice,[36] gradual resistance to the field visits on the part of faculty developed over time, and eventually the faculty pushed for the visits to be replaced by phone calls. This was one battle that the faculty clearly won, but it further estranged Cohen from the faculty, and the close ties between the classroom and the field that had distinguished the college in its earlier years became weaker as a result.

THE CA DOCUMENT EVOLVES

In his most emblematic work, *Democracy and Education*, John Dewey laid out five steps of what he called "the general features of a reflective experience": (1) confronting a problem, (2) defining it, (3) researching it, (4) creating a plan of action, and (5) implementing the plan and evaluating the results.[37] Audrey Cohen never acknowledged that the college she founded was in any way inspired by Deweyan principles. In fact, she vociferously denied any suggestion of having intellectual forebears. Yet it is interesting to note the parallels between Dewey's formulation of basic reflective experience and the outlines for the Constructive Action (CA) document that the faculty developed in the mid-1980s and that continue today to be assigned at the college that Cohen founded. Notwithstanding wide variation across the college's several programs, most of the CA document outlines follow the general model of scientific thinking that Dewey suggests. First, the student explores the environment he or she has agreed to be placed in (whether it be a human services agency, a business, or a hospital or school) with the aim of zeroing in on a need that can be met or a problem that can be resolved within that semester. Second, the student then states this need in the form of a Constructive Action goal and does research on that goal (called a *Literature Review*). Third, out of the literature review the student develops a plan of action that includes goals, objectives, and strategies. Fourth, over the middle four or five weeks of the semester the student implements the plan and records that implementation in journals or logs (called *Implementation Logs*). Fifth, and finally, the student assesses the results in the final Assessment of Results section of the document.

Having a goal, implementing strategies to meet that goal, and then assessing the results with an aim of further action is a cycle of purposeful endeavor that is common to much of human life. What Dewey, in *Democracy and Education*, calls "the general features of reflective experience" could also be simply called "problem solving." Also, with regard to Cohen's background as an education major and in view of the college's future growth, it is interesting to note how closely the phases of the Constructive Action documentation process parallel the required steps that any teacher must go through as a part of lesson planning. Creating plans for instruction, implementing them, and assessing the results are the essential features of all teaching, and when Metropolitan College of New York developed a master's of science in childhood education program in 2004, the college's generic Constructive Action document outline was easily adaptable to state and national requirements for the training of teachers.

But there has always been another aspect of the CA documentation that goes beyond the step-by-step representation of a reflective experience. In "The Service Society" Cohen described how she had first come up with the concept of a Constructive Action. In the late 1960s, after a meeting of the Newman Task Force on Higher Education in San Diego, California, she and other members of the commission were driving back to their hotel and passed by the Coronado Bridge. She was immediately struck by its many qualities—its beauty, its practicality, and "respect" for the fit with its surrounding natural environment. She noted that the designer of the bridge had "brought together theory" from many specialized areas of study to produce a result that benefits people on many levels.[38]

Seeing in the bridge the embodiment of the idea that an educated person is one who knows how to use theory for "the benefit of other human beings," Cohen immediately thought about the educational aims of her own institution. The lesson of the bridge, she wrote, "helped me conceptualize a teaching methodology, the Constructive Action, which directs students in the blending of theory and practice."[39] She began to see in service projects performed in the field, in "constructive actions," that students should "bring together theory from many disciplines and focus it on practice."[40] In a speech later on describing the uniqueness of her college she emphasized the theory/practice nexus. All students must complete eight major acts of service, one each semester, to achieve their degrees. Each Constructive Action, she continued, must prove that "they can use the knowledge they gain by applying it to improving service at their agency or corporation."[41] In another context she wrote,

> Performing a *constructive action* gives the student the chance to think about and plan for goals of varying magnitudes, to develop further one's capacity to perform human services by applying theories and research discussed in the classroom to the needs of actual human beings—in short, to link theory with practice.[42]

Cohen's vision of the Constructive Action as a way to bring together theory and practice has provided the focal point for faculty engagement and creativity since the early 1970s. Having invented a curricular grid in which *Dimensions* of learning provide the content knowledge that informs each semester's *Purpose*, the challenge came to be to make the *Constructive Action* process into the "tool for social change" that it was intended to be.[43] How could the documentation of a Constructive Action in the field incorporate content knowledge gained in the more academic, dimensional courses? Could the theory-practice integration be accurately assessed? To what extent could the documentation process be used to develop students' writing skills?

Much of the academic energy of the 1980s and beyond was devoted to refining and perfecting the ways that the Constructive Action and its documentation could serve to embody and assess the theory-practice integration that Cohen saw as essential to all human progress. In the late 1970s the *Purpose Handbooks* were mimeographed pamphlets of twenty pages or so, and the Constructive Action outlines that appeared on syllabi were relatively general guidelines requiring students to come up with a plan of action, write daily logs recording their progress, and analyze their results. The integration of concepts and theories from the dimension classes was simply implied by the lists of questions that students were to keep in mind as they completed their actions in the field. By the late 1980s, however, the *Purpose Handbooks* had expanded into forty-page photocopied booklets containing four- or five-heading outlines with detailed subheadings for the theory/practice integration that Cohen and her faculty saw as essential to any Constructive Action.

As it evolved in the 1980s, the CA document came to serve theory-practice integration in many ways. In terms of formative assessment, the CA outlines asked students early on in their documentation process to do a "dimensional analysis" of the need that their CA project was aiming to meet. How does the need relate to the semester's overall Purpose? What are the Values and Ethics issues involved in meeting this need? In terms of Self and Others, what kinds of personal dynamics are at work? What Systems (e.g., health care, educational, political, even biological systems) may impinge on the prospects of this project's success? What Skills will be called on to meet the need? Thus, even before the midterm, students were asked to think about how the knowledge that they were gaining in their dimensional courses could be applied to the specific human service goal that they were addressing in their internship or place of work.

Examples of how a student might complete the dimensional analysis would depend on his or her CA goal. If a student was in Purpose IV, for example, when the focus is on empowerment through teaching and communication, and she was helping to tutor at-risk children in an after-school program, the application of the *Purpose* dimension knowledge might involve a reference to a teaching method (e.g., the use of manipulatives or direct instruction) suggested in the textbook assigned in the Purpose seminar. Her application of the *Values* dimension knowledge might include references to the competing educational philosophies of constructivism and positivism, which she had been introduced to in her Values dimension course. A student's application of the *Self and Others* dimension knowledge might include a discussion of the child development theories of Piaget or Vygotsky covered in a textbook on child development assigned in the Self and Others course. And her application of *Skills* dimension knowledge might include the skill of using elementary statistics to plot learning outcomes. What professors were looking for in grading the dimensional analysis in this early section of the CA document was what one later faculty member called "connective thinking"[44] across the various dimensions of each semester's Purpose.

Some faculty members also required that students do a dimensional analysis for every log (or journal or process recording—the term varied from one professor to the next) written during the implementation phase of the CA. They argued that a dimensional analysis could thus serve as a "heuristic" to help students look at their experience.[45] Where the theory-practice integration was most commonly required, however, was in the Citizen Empowerment Chart, a schematic representation of dimensional thinking included at the end of most CA documents.

An early version of a Citizen Empowerment Chart appeared in Cohen's 1978 essay, "The Service Society." By the end of the 1980s it had become a widely used summative evaluation instrument for assessing a student's ability to integrate theory and practice. In one of the four pages of tables to be filled out, students were required to identify the dimensional components (Purpose, Values, Self and Others, Systems, and Skills) of their CA goals; on another page they were required to identify the dimensional components of the project's results. Even more striking is that in columns to the right of each of those dimensional identifications, students were required to give a numerical rank and percentile weight to the importance of each dimension as seen by the student practitioner herself, by her supervisor, and by the client(s) or "citizen(s)" whose empowerment the Constructive Action aimed to achieve. In the last page of the chart the combination of weights and results across each dimensional row resulted in a numerical value for the CA's outcome.

Although both faculty and students increasingly grumbled about the exercise becoming too repetitive and mechanical from one semester to the next, the Citizen Empowerment Chart in fact represented a new way to think about educational outcomes. For embedded in the chart's layout was the radical principle that classroom learning is to be valued to the extent to which it helps the student to facilitate the empowerment of others.[46] At a time when the desire to measure the "Value Added" by educational experiences in schools today has baffled the expertise of statisticians and professional educators, as early as the mid-1980s the College for Human Services had invented a practical method of quantifying empowerment.[47]

Another phase in the evolution of the documentation of the Constructive Action took place in 1985, when a group of faculty members got together to discuss the ways that the Constructive Action document could be used to develop students' writing skills. An explicit assumption of the project was that through writing about their experience, students would become "increasingly self-aware practitioners."[48] Called the Constructive Action Documentation Project, the group read nearly one-hundred CA documents from the previous nine years and analyzed both the range of skills that CA documentation called for and the extent to which student writing skills developed from one semester to the next.

The group observed that in terms of the patterns of exposition required, there was not much variation from one semester to the next in the CA document outlines. Whether it was for Purpose I—Self-Assessment, Purpose IV—Communication and Teaching, or Purpose VII—Supervision, students needed to state goals, describe people and situations, narrate experience, and analyze and evaluate outcomes. The writing tasks of identification, description, narration, analysis, and evaluation were thus consistently required throughout the eight-semester curriculum and gave students opportunities to practice a wide range of expository forms.[49]

What the group found lacking was a conscious sense of the progressive *complexity* in CA writing tasks that would push students to higher levels of reflective thinking over the course of their education. Appreciation of this developmental strand led the group to view the CA documents as "stages in a process by which students became more accomplished and versatile writers as they became more perceptive and versatile practitioners." In their conclusions, the group members made some specific recommendations such as requiring that the logs for Purpose I take the form of personal journals, that in Purpose II students be required to write about some critical incident as a means of "becoming more aware of the dyads they find themselves in," and that in Purpose IV they be asked carefully to compare planned teaching interventions with actual learning outcomes. By the end of their undergraduate experience, the completion of increasingly complex writing tasks would hopefully result in CA documents that represented the derivation of theory from experience and the application of theory to experience[50] that the overall curriculum intended.

IMPROVING THE WORLD

" 'Get Out There and Make Social Change.' That's the mandate given to students at the anything-but-everyday College for Human Services." So reads the title of an article about the College for Human Services that appeared in the *Chronicle of Higher Education* in 1980. The college trains "what it calls 'human-service professionals'" to help people in need, "from alcoholics and abused wives to tenants in slum housing and older people struggling to feed themselves and pay the rent." Quoting Cohen, the article states that the college's mission is "to improve society while improving education and service delivery," and that it does so by teaching students to promote "humane and caring values" and to help their clients become self-sufficient.[51]

Despite its somewhat snide tone, the *Chronicle of Higher Education* article provides positive examples of the Constructive Actions that were accomplished by students enrolled at the college at that time. Featured in the article are D. Lee Ezell, who set up a primary health-care center in the Morris Heights area of the Bronx; Diana Kervel who convinced administrators in a legal-aid office that they could serve more clients if they ran four decentralized offices rather than the central one they had been operating; and Antonia Tamplin, who helped members of another Bronx community get a neighborhood park cleaned up.[52] A further survey of CA documents from those years shows that various other College for Human Services students:

— Tutored recovering alcoholics to prepare for the High School Equivalency Exam in mathematics.

— Compiled a directory of social service agencies for obstetrics clients at a municipal hospital.

— Counseled a developmentally delayed client to build his sense of self-esteem.

— Met with a neighborhood committee on Staten Island to improve the relationships between the community and a group home for mentally disabled adults who had recently moved to the area.

— Set up a teen counseling unit in a downtown Brooklyn hospital and got local schools to refer students there. Students who wanted birth control were referred to a place where they could get it.

— Organized a tribute to Paul Robeson at the Brooklyn Academy of Music to inform the community about its cultural history and to raise money to educate people about Robeson's work.

— Taught preschoolers the alphabet at a Head Start program in the Bronx using visuals and manpulatives that the student had created from paper and fabrics.

— Held weekly discussion groups addressing current events, attitudes, and ways in which people cope with daily life as a way to placate residents of a Queens nursing home who got angry when their relatives did not visit them.

— Organized a career fair at the college involving 20 organizations and more than 140 students.

— Developed a business plan to market computerized accounting and financial services to small businesses in Greenpoint, Brooklyn.[53]

Although College for Human Services students' efforts may not have served to "make social change" in any major way, their work did improve the world in small ways and even more importantly, perhaps, exemplified what human service is all about.

STUDENT SUCCESS STORIES OF THE 1980s

At the end of the 1980s, Dellie Bloom conducted interviews with several alumni of the College for Human Services as part of a project to write the college's history. One interview was with Myrna Willis, who had begun her college career with the Women's Talent Corps. As a Corps Woman Willis's field placement was at the Brooklyn Psychiatric Center, one of the agencies to join the Women's Talent Corps' first cooperative pilot project with the New York City Department of Mental Health to create a career ladder for what was then termed *Mental Health Technicians*. On completion of her training she was hired by the center and spent the next seventeen years in the mental health field. Along the way she earned a bachelor's degree, and in 1990 was carrying a caseload in every way identical (except for her salary) with that of other professionals on the Brooklyn Psychiatric Center staff. Now that her children were grown she was planning to go on for a master's degree. "The College's biggest contribution to my life has been to make me believe that what I know is valuable, that I can learn, that I can learn more." She started spreading the word. "After I went to school I thought that the whole world should go to school."[54]

Another success story was that of Leonard Ampy. At the age of fourteen he had dropped out of school and had spent sixteen months in a residential substance abuse center, but once clean he had worked his way up from security guard to addiction counselor at Harlem Hospital. He began to realize, however, that even though his supervisors trusted and respected him, he would never see any significant salary increases without more formal education. Also he had married his childhood sweetheart in 1976 and he and his wife wanted a large family. Little by little, he said, he got the idea that "repairing the gaps in my schooling" would be important for his future.[55]

Ampy heard about the College for Human Services, sent for the literature, liked its focus, and enrolled. Confident of his job skills, he was not at all sure he could "hack the classroom work" and at first was overwhelmed with how much he needed to catch up. But with help from the staff and faculty he began to make progress. There were many other people of his age in his cohort, and they pushed each other, "day, night, and weekends." After the first few months he knew he could handle the work because it related to his job. His professor made several visits to Harlem Hospital to help him fit the Constructive Action assignment to his employment needs.[56] His commitment paid off. After graduation he was promoted to the job of addiction program administrator at the hospital, responsible for the operation of four methadone clinics and a support staff of twenty-two that included security officers, doctors, nurses, addict and rehabilitation counselors, and clerical workers.

Ampy had gotten a bachelor's degree as a form of job security, he recalled, but there were also "secret" rewards. For the first time in his life he began to enjoy reading (though "not everything, of course"). He also acknowledged that he now wrote more effectively. "You cannot supervise by memo, but neither can you just rap one-on-one to get your ideas across. My thinking now is much sharper, more analytical."[57] Getting the bachelor's degree was a great accomplishment, he said, admitting that he had never been to a graduation before. And like Myrna Willis, he, too, couldn't wait to get started on his master's.

Another appreciative alum of the 1980s was Theresa Rodrigues. As a child she had had difficulties in school and was forced to leave at the age of fourteen to help support her mother and younger siblings. In those years, she recalled, she learned more than she wanted about surviving, and she learned it too soon. She married, had children, stayed home for five years, and then began a series of jobs as a telephone receptionist, office worker, and volunteer at her church, none of which gave her sustained satisfaction.[58]

In 1985, several years after her husband's death, Rodrigues heard about the College for Human Services from a friend and timidly agreed to go with her to the college to get additional information. The admissions officer sensed Rodrigues's shyness and low self-esteem but was impressed by her steady work history and her volunteer efforts. To Rodrigues's surprise she was accepted into the college, and once enrolled began to blossom. "Over time I did discover that I have the ability to change." As a church volunteer she had started a self-help bereavement group but had never thought she could run a group professionally. In Purpose V, which focused on counseling, Rodrigues chose to focus her Constructive Action on improving the bereavement group. "I studied the literature of loss in fiction and in medical and other professional journals, read up on group dynamic theorists, learned about criteria for starting a group, about commonalities, and outreach." Gradually she became not just a group participant but a facilitator. "I could now strike the balance between professional distancing and empathy."[59]

Rodrigues reflected that she had come to the college feeling like she was at the bottom of the ladder but midway through discovered that she had the ability to turn "something negative, my street smarts, into something positive." After graduation she got a full-time job as a case manager at the Good Shepherd Society. The other case manager had a master's degree in social work. "We share common interests, use common terminology. There is mutual respect, professionally and personally. That is important to me."[60]

Patricia Cross was already on an impressive career ladder when she first enrolled in the College for Human Service's new business program in the mid-1980s. Born in Alabama with nine siblings, Cross had been an employee at Chase Manhattan Bank for fifteen years when she began to consider going to school full time while continuing to work full time. At first her supervisor at the bank had tried to persuade her against the idea, especially because her job often required late work and overtime hours, but she persevered. It was hard. "There were many times when I was ready to quit. I not only surprised him [her supervisor], but I surprised myself by hanging in."[61]

When Cross enrolled at the college she was already beginning to supervise a small clerical unit at the bank. It was a tricky situation, because she was now overseeing many of the same people she had worked alongside of until her promotion. The decision-making aspects of the job terrified her, but one of her first courses at the college included decision-making skills. "I was forced to confront myself on the spot. I still remember my instructor's opening comment, 'A manager gets the work done through other people. If he or she is doing the work, that is *not* managing.'" Cross kept those words in mind as she worked out her new supervisory assignment, and for her Constructive Action she was able to redesign the work in her unit. Gradually she parceled out the work to others in the unit so that she would have time for her new managerial responsibilities. She had always had the knowledge of tasks to be done; "what I did not know until I got to the college was where and how to *delegate*."[62]

Cross's college experience continued to add to her career opportunities. Her supervisor at the bank noticed changes in her, and she in turn made sure that "he had a memo from me on every money-saving idea that I came up with." He began to write memos back, commenting favorably on her improved writing and how clearly she expressed herself at staff meetings. After graduation Cross was transferred from supervisor in the clerical division to a supervisory role in the corporate control division. It was a heady move. "The connection with the bank's overseas branches made it feel more glamorous." Nevertheless she took care to nurture the self-esteem of her fellow workers. Whenever the Chase Annual Report was published she would get her staff together to make sure they would see how important their contributions had been. "If you understand how your work fits into the larger picture, then you understand it is your service that enables another unit to do its job properly. By cooperating, the job gets done. Seen that way, we are all service providers."[63]

Members of the faculty during these years found it gratifying to watch students like Myrna Willis, Leonard Ampy, Theresa Rodrigues, and Patricia Cross take to the college's opportunities for learning and self-transformation. Given the college's intensive, accelerated scheduling (students could complete a bachelor's degree in two years, eight months) and the on-the-job training that was embedded in the curriculum, what the college termed *empowerment*, was often an observable learning outcome. Undeniably, many students who entered the program were not able to complete it. A child's asthma, a mother's stroke, a husband's incarceration, or a loss of a job could derail a student's prospects for educational achievement temporarily or even permanently. But working with those who managed to thrive was a source of deep satisfaction for the faculty. Anne Lopes remembers the sense of exhilaration that resulted from seeing students who had enrolled through funding from the New York State's Higher Education Opportunity Program (HEOP) succeed. "It was exciting to see the college really giving students that opportunity," she recalled.[64]

One more important success story of the 1980s is that of Bernadette Smith, who currently serves as vice-chair of the college's Board of Trustees. Smith grew up in the Bronx, graduated from Dodge Vocational High School in a program that focused on secretarial skills, and went on to enroll in the John Jay College of Criminal Justice. At John Jay she became impatient with the curriculum and dropped out to get more hands-on experience in the "real world." She became a corrections officer and began devising a therapeutic program for inmates in the New York State Department of Corrections. But she soon realized that she was not fully equipped with the skills and maturity needed to work at such a challenging task.[65]

One day in 1983 she was riding the subway and saw a sign that said "*Some students talk about changing the world. Our students are actually doing it.*" It was an ad for the College for Human Services. She was intrigued and sent in her application. At that time there was a group interview process for student applicants as well as for faculty, and she was thrilled when she was accepted. She enjoyed the small classes—a welcome contrast to the large classes she had attended at John Jay—and right away started doing her internships in the college's Student Services office. "I was never so excited to get up early on a Saturday morning to get downtown to school!"[66] In retrospect Smith now feels that the college changed her life.

"It was the warmth and the dedication and the commitment to students' growth that was so transformative—in addition to the whole exciting idea of transdisciplinary education."[67]

After graduating from MCNY, Smith enrolled in the Touro Law Center in Huntington, New York. She graduated in the top quarter of her class and joined the Bronx County District Attorney's Office where she prosecuted felony cases in the Trial Bureau. From there she went on to serve as principal court attorney to a judge in the New York State Supreme Court Criminal Term. By 2001 she had established her own law office and was practicing in the area of employment discrimination. In gratitude for her educational experiences at MCNY Smith has taught courses as an adjunct and helped coordinate the site in the Bronx. She has served as chair and as vice-chair of the college's Board of Trustees; she has also chaired the Presidential Search Committee and served on the Academic Affairs Committee.[68] She continues to care deeply about the institution that had such a lasting impact on her life.

A SECOND MARRIAGE

For Audrey Cohen personally as well as for the college, the 1980s was a period of stability and accomplishment. She and her first husband, Mark Cohen, had divorced in 1980, and their daughter Dawn had started a new life on the West Coast. From 1981 to 1983 their daughter Wendy shared the 67th Street apartment with her mother while attending law school. Wendy has fond memories of her mother's outreach and inventiveness during those years. She remembers once walking along Third Avenue with her mother and seeing a homeless man on the sidewalk holding a sign with the word "HUNGRY" hand-printed on it. Audrey Cohen went right up to the man and politely asked him what kind of sandwich he would like. After a brief conversation she went into a nearby deli, bought the sandwich, and brought it back to him. Wendy was particularly impressed that her mother had actually taken the time to have a conversation with a homeless person, to ask him what he needed. "I saw that a lot. I saw how she talked to service people or to someone helping her get a cab. I saw her being respectful to people."[69]

Wendy also saw her mother's entrepreneurial side during these years. Audrey Cohen was compulsive about cleanliness: when she went to yoga class she would put a paper towel down over the mat, and at home she would walk with paper towels on her feet to clean the kitchen floor instead of using a mop. "Mops just move the dirt around!" she complained. Determined to do something about it, she began to thinking about how to create a disposable mop. Wendy had a college friend who was a designer, and together the friend and Audrey came up with a prototype of a disposable mop that Audrey urged Wendy and her friend to patent and develop. They never did, and when Good Housekeeping came out with the Swiffer a few years later Cohen chided them for not following through with the idea. "We could have been rich!" Wendy laughs, in telling this story.[70]

In the early 1980s Cohen's entrepreneurial instincts had led her to apply to the President/Owner Management Program at the Harvard Graduate School of Business Administration, and she was accepted. The six weeks of intensive immersion in business management enabled Cohen to have a Harvard connection and to develop her skills of institutional outreach. Alida Mesrop remembers dreading hearing about the new ideas that the Harvard experience put in Cohen's head, for she knew that she, Mesrop, would be the one responsible for implementing them, and that would mean more work. "Every time she came back from someplace, she would say, *'I have a thought,'* and I thought, Oh, my God . . . now what?" On this occasion, when Cohen returned from the Harvard program she gathered her colleagues together and once again announced, *"I have a thought."* At that point, Mesrop recalls with a laugh, Cohen opened a desk drawer and pulled out a rubber chicken. It was a freebie from a Frank Perdue case study of how he had become so successful. "She was *gleaning* from that the things that we should do to advance the program. I'll never forget sitting near that damned rubber chicken!"[71]

Being a graduate of the Harvard program gave Cohen a membership in the Harvard Club, which she often made use of both for college events and for her own personal socializing. It was there that she met Dr. Ralph Wharton. By now Wendy had moved out and gotten married, and Audrey was on her own. She had dated occasionally, but until meeting Wharton, there was nothing serious.[72] Ralph Wharton was a successful psychiatrist at the Columbia-Presbyterian Medical Center and clinical professor of psychiatry at the Columbia University College of Physicians and Surgeons. He had graduated from Harvard College and had received his MD from Columbia.[73] He, too, had been married previously and divorced, and he loved to travel. For the fifty-seven-year-old Audrey Cohen, it seemed like a good match. They were married at the Lotos Club, and she wore the same wedding dress that Wendy had worn at her marriage a few years earlier. Barbara Walton, Laura Pires-Houston, and Alida Mesrop were all part of the wedding party. A photo of the four of them shows Audrey grinning like a young bride.

The minutes of the Board of Trustees meetings in the winter and spring of 1988 make no mention of President Cohen's marriage to Wharton. Documented instead is news about the Regents of New York State officially granting the college a permanent charter, the expansion of the college's program in New York City schools, and a generous gift from board member Marie Kessel of $100,000 to develop the college's library holdings through computerization.[74] Ongoing challenges were to find a permanent new building for the college, and to identify "a natural donor constituency." At one meeting Cohen reported triumphantly that James Dumpson, the Commissioner of Welfare who had originally opposed degree-granting status for the college during its early struggles, had recently congratulated her on the college's success and had apologized for his previous opposition. In fact, he had told Cohen, the existence of the field of human services, which he had been leery of when she first proposed the term in 1967, had bolstered the development of social work bachelor's degree programs.[75]

By end of the decade Cohen was clearly at the peak of her prime. In retrospect it might be said that the 1980s were the college's "golden age" of creativity and accomplishment, for the next decade would bring unforeseen challenges, especially to the health and well-being of its president. Before continuing with the story of Cohen's life, however, the uniqueness of the curriculum that she developed needs further scrutiny. This chapter has focused on how the college prepares students for responsible work in community settings. The next chapter shows that Cohen's founding vision included not just training but reflection, not just career education but humanistic learning.

CHAPTER 10

BEYOND VOCATIONAL EDUCATION

You really had to be a true believer if you were going to remain here. And because of the faculty teams I worked on, it was not hard to be a true believer. Not only could you see the integration with the faculty, but when you saw the students do so well with the integration, then you knew that there was something really right about this type of education.

In this whole empowerment model that Audrey was moving us forward with, the faculty were the ones who were very practical about how to make it operationalized. Audrey was much more the visionary, not the nuts and bolts type.

—Franklyn Rother, faculty member since 1980[1]

In January 1988 the short article that appeared in the *New York Times* announcing Audrey Cohen's marriage to Dr. Ralph Wharton stated that the bride was the founder and president of the College for Human Services, "a liberal arts college."[2] Some readers familiar with the college's early history as a training institution for low-income women may have raised their eyebrows at the use of the term. Was the college that Cohen founded a "liberal arts college"?

Certainly the curriculum provided for students at the College for Human Services bore little resemblance to the curricula offered at most liberal arts colleges. In 1989 Cohen was invited by the *McNeil/Lehrer Report* (a precursor of the PBS *News Hour*) to join Michael Sovern, then president of Columbia University, and Vartan Gregorian, the president of Brown

University, in a televised interview about the relevance of a broad-based liberal education in today's world. During the interview Cohen asserted that the way traditional liberal arts core curricula are taught at colleges like Columbia is *not* suited to present needs. Those are "ancient" attempts to solve what is a very new problem, she said. Although she agreed with Sovern and Gregorian that students should be introduced to the important concepts of the past and be familiar with the works of great thinkers, she insisted that students also need to learn how to "use" those ideas. Given the new global, high tech service economy, she said, students need "to take the great ideas—from Spinoza, or Freud, or Machiavelli—and *use* that knowledge to improve the world." When McNeil asked her directly if she would think a graduate of Columbia's famed core curriculum a failure, she turned directly to Sovern and, with a challenging smile, said "yes, a student would be a failure if he or she hadn't learned how to *apply* the learning gathered from the great books" to somehow make the world a better place.[3]

The uniqueness of the liberal arts curriculum that Cohen envisioned for her college will be the focus of this chapter. Taking a detour from the chronological path that has shaped the narrative thus far, the discussion that follows explores at close hand the extent to which the students at what is now MCNY receive what might be termed a *liberal education*. As was evident throughout her life, Cohen herself was deeply committed to the liberal arts and had always insisted on giving history, philosophy, literature, art, science, and math an essential role in the Purpose-Centered curriculum. With its unique intersection of Dimensions and Purposes, she proudly believed that her college had transcended the age-old divide between humanistic learning and job readiness. "Delivering a comprehensive liberal arts education along with practical preparation for the world of work was not only *ideal*, but *possible*," she had proclaimed at the college's twentieth-anniversary dinner in 1984.[4] But as the college evolved, to what extent did the reality fit the rhetoric? Was the college that approached the new millennium an institution that could claim to be both a liberal arts college and a college for careers in the new service economy? Borrowing Cohen's own words, is it indeed possible to deliver "a comprehensive liberal arts education along with practical preparation for the world of work"?

WASHINGTON AND DU BOIS REVISITED

In her claim to infuse practical skills with liberal learning, Cohen was bridging a conceptual divide that is as old as the history of the idea of education. In Book VIII of his treatise on *Politics* (350 BCE) the philosopher Aristotle stated that there is a kind of education in which parents should have their sons trained "not because it is necessary or because it is useful but because it is liberal and something good in itself." Aristotle proceeded to criticize an overemphasis on training in "mechanical" pursuits, especially for men engaged in the responsibilities of citizenship. For the sake of a healthy and vibrant politics, Aristotle claimed, the useful knowledge imparted to young people should not be so extensive that it makes them "mechanically minded."[5]

Cohen herself never articulated at any length a rationale for providing students with a comprehensive liberal arts education while also preparing them for useful work. After her death in 1996, however, the importance of humanistic education for civic life was the subject of a paper written by Stephen Greenwald who had recently been appointed president of what by then was named Audrey Cohen College. For a roundtable discussion at Oxford University on the challenges to traditional, not-for-profit colleges of the new vocational, for-profit colleges like the University of Phoenix and De Vry, Greenwald—in line with Aristotle before him—emphasized the civic uses of a broad-based humanistic education. One of the roles of humanistic learning is "to produce aware, informed and engaged citizens, in the broadest sense of that term, through education in civics, history, values and ethics in the public realm," Greenwald wrote. Another role of traditional higher education, he said, echoing the college's mission, is "to empower students to be leaders and agents for positive change in their lives, careers, and communities." These goals go far beyond the narrow vocational purposes of the for-profit colleges. Institutions holding onto the broader humanistic goals engage students with a basic understanding of society and culture, equipping them with the "higher order skills of creativity, critical thinking, and communication, and with the ability to link concepts and ideas from different fields and disciplines."[6] These are leadership skills that only a broad-based education can provide, Greenwald concluded, and that are lacking from the more narrow career-oriented, for-profit schools like the University of Phoenix and De Vry.[7]

In between Aristotle's seminal writings and Greenwald's Oxford paper was the celebrated debate between Booker T. Washington and W.E.B. Du Bois, which raised similar questions about higher education's ultimate aims. In the late nineteenth century, Washington founded the Tuskegee Institute (now Tuskegee University) on the conviction that the recently freed blacks were in need of marketable vocational skills in order to gain a place in the developing economy of the New South. "Our greatest danger is that in the great leap from slavery to freedom we may overlook the fact that the masses of us are to live by the productions of our hands," Washington proclaimed in his Atlanta Exposition Address of 1895. "No race can prosper till it learns that there is as much dignity in tilling a field as in writing a poem."[8] These words were soon a source of contention, especially on the part of W.E.B. Du Bois. Du Bois objected to Washington's focus on vocational education and, like Aristotle before him, made a case for liberal education based on political considerations. Essential for the political advancement of blacks, Du Bois argued, was the education of a Talented Tenth who "through their knowledge of modern culture could guide the American Negro into a higher civilization." Without a higher education in culture, history, sciences, and the arts, the Negro would have to accept white leadership, which "could not always be trusted to . . . guide this group into self-realization and to its highest cultural possibilities."[9]

To develop students' consciousness about their own educational choices, the debate between Washington and Du Bois has been an ongoing part of the MCNY's Human Services curriculum for nearly twenty years. Coming midway in the program, in the Values and Ethics Dimension of the fourth semester, short excerpts from Washington's and Du Bois's published writings raise provocative questions. For American schools in general, should the purpose of education be vocational or humanistic? Should the main aim of education be economic productivity or political responsibility? At MCNY, which of the two visions predominates—Washington's vision of training for marketable skills or Du Bois's vision of broad-based humanistic learning? Which vision *should* predominate at the college—vocational training or liberal learning?

When students discuss the general questions that the assigned readings of Washington and Du Bois raise, the volume of the debate often rises to such a pitch that the instructor needs to shut the classroom door and demand that the participants tone it down. Young people need to be taught marketable skills so that they can survive in a competitive economy, some students vociferously argue. Yes, but even more than that they need a general education so that they can fight for their rights, others heatedly respond. When the discussion turns to applying the concepts to MCNY, however, and students are asked which vision—Washington's or Du Bois's—predominates in their own curriculum, the reactions become more subdued and more equivocal. Their college includes *both* liberal learning and vocational training, students assert firmly. The need to complete a Constructive Action in their fieldwork, the close reading of case studies from the professional literature, and the emphasis on practical skills—these aspects of the curriculum give students a sense of being prepared for hands-on professional work related to human services. At the same time, getting a taste for philosophy, mastering basic algebra, reading provocative plays, learning about the digestive system, and listening to non-Western music are experiences that make the college's students, many of whom have lived their lives on the margins of American mainstream society, feel equal to more traditionally educated college students. Students report that they can hold their own in conversations with their supervisors in the field who have been educated at NYU or Fordham, and one student recalled with pride that once on the subway when he was reading Marcus Aurelius's *Meditations* he got into a discussion with a well-dressed man who said that he had read the same book at Harvard.[10] Professional training and the humanities are "kind of blended," students conclude.

GREAT BOOKS

The inclusion of humanities texts in the Purpose-Centered curriculum has rarely been questioned at Cohen's college, at least by the students. Only occasionally does one hear, "Why do we have to read this?" Students who would never consider signing up for a philosophy course in a traditional college setting willingly accept the requirement to read Dewey's "My Pedagogic Creed" in the Values dimension of the fourth semester where the focus is on teaching; they valiantly struggle to absorb selections from Aristotle's *Politics* in the Self and Others dimension of the eighth semester where the focus is on promoting social change. Part of the motivation for doing the reading is to try to apply the ideas from the texts to one's Constructive Action. Edward Albee's *Who's Afraid of Virginia Woolf?* makes more sense to adult students in a semester when they are focusing on Developing Professional Relationships in the Workplace than it might in a course called Twentieth-Century American Drama—because the lessons about how communication can break down in a family are applicable to the students' office work or field experience. And even the program-wide requirement to take statistics is less threatening when taught in the Skills dimension of the third semester, where the focus is on Working in Groups. The students often find that they can immediately use their new statistics skills in the Constructive Action document that records their field project for that semester.

Here it must be admitted that MCNY's emphasis on applying humanistic knowledge to practical problem solving in the workplace "instrumentalizes" the liberal arts in ways that graduates of more traditional liberal arts colleges might find disappointing. What many college-educated people love about liberal learning is that it is engaged in for its own sake and conveys qualities such as complexity, nuance, ambiguity—even beauty—that have no utilitarian purpose. The Harvard College Office of Admissions, for example, boldly asserts on its website that a liberal education "is an education conducted in a spirit of free inquiry undertaken *without* concern for topical relevance or vocational utility."[11]

But MCNY students are at least a decade older than most Harvard undergraduates and are squeezing a college curriculum into a life already crowded with work and family responsibilities. Over the years, several students have transferred out of another college and into MCNY primarily because the other college required that they take History of Art. These students argue that they could not afford (in terms of both time and money) to take a course that has no relevance to their future careers, and what they most appreciate about MCNY is the way the assigned materials relate to their challenges on the job. Thus despite the overemphasis on its use value, it is only by making the humanities relevant to students' professional lives that MCNY can offer a liberal education at all.

And in surprising ways, classic texts can touch adult students' personal lives as well as their professional lives. In the early 1990s a middle-aged Latina student burst into the Student Services cubicle where I was working as a writing tutor. "Do you know this story about Antigone?" she breath-lessly asked. "This is such a story!" She was eager to write a paper about the play but didn't know how to begin. Sophocles' fourth-century BCE drama about a conflict of loyalties had aroused the passion of this student more than anything she had previously read. As we worked together on how to structure the paper it became clear that the impossible dilemmas the play portrays—between respect for the law and honor to one's family, between obedience to custom and obedience to one's own conscience—were dilemmas that the student deeply understood, and wanted to write about.

In the last semester of the Human Services program, selections from the Roman Stoic philosopher Epictetus are assigned in the Self and Oth-ers dimension course. Many students are intrigued with the emphasis on balance and limitation that Epictetus' *Handbook* argues for. His advice to avoid desires that are outside one's reach serves as a guiding theme both for their work as change agents during the semester and for their own personal struggles. Students familiar with self-help groups are impressed to learn that the Serenity Prayer adopted by Alcoholics Anonymous ("God grant me the serenity to accept the things I cannot change; courage to change the things I can; and wisdom to know the difference") was adapted by Reinhold Niebuhr from Epictetus's writings.[12]

A story I like to tell involves a student who had just read Jean-Jacques Rousseau's *Emile*. One of the aspects of the text that has often interested MCNY students, many of whom are parents, is Rousseau's advice to avoid pampering children.

> Instead of keeping your child mewed up in a stuffy room, take him out into a meadow every day; let him run about, let him struggle and fall again and again, the oftener the better; he will learn all the sooner to pick himself up. The delights of liberty will make up for many bruises. My pupil will hurt himself oftener than yours, but he will always be merry; your pupils may receive fewer injuries, but they are always thwarted, constrained, and sad. I doubt whether they are any better off.[13]

A student in the class who had worked as a nanny for a wealthy Upper East Side family was invited to her former charge's birthday party in Central

Park. At one point the child fell down and bruised her knee. The mother, in a state of alarm, was about to rush over to tend to the child, but my student calmly told the child to get up off the ground and resume her play. To the assembled mothers' amazement, the child got up, brushed off her knee, and ran off to join her friends. "But she usually screams when she falls down. Where did you learn to say that to her?" they asked. "I learned it from Jean-Jacques Rousseau," the student replied.

The crucial role of the liberal arts has become harder to maintain in college curricula throughout the country in recent years. During most of MCNY's history, however, foundational texts in the humanities and the social sciences have remained staples of the curriculum. The following list includes the required texts from the 1990s to the early 2000s. It exemplifies what MCNY students have read, discussed, analyzed in writing, and, most importantly applied to their thinking and actions in the real world.

Abelard, *The Letters of Abelard and Heloise*
Chinua Achebe, *Things Fall Apart*
Edward Albee, *Who's Afraid of Virginia Woolf?*
Aristophanes, *Lysistrata*
Aristotle, *Politics and Nichomachean Ethics*
Marcus Aurelius, *Meditations*
Sissela Bok, *Lying*
E.A. Wallis Budge, ed., *The Egyptian Book of the Dead*
Dante Alighieri, selections from *The Divine Comedy*
Albert Camus, *The Plague*
James West Davidson et al., *Nation of Nations: A Concise History of the American Republic*
René Descartes, *Discourse on Method*
John Dewey, *My Pedagogic Creed*
W.E.B. Du Bois, selections from *The Souls of Black Folk*
Epictetus, selections from the *Enchiridion or Handbook*
Amitai Etzioni, *The New Golden Rule: Community and Morality in a Democratic Society*
Paolo Freire, *Pedagogy of the Oppressed*
Franz Kafka, *The Trial*
John Locke, selections from *An Essay Concerning Human Understanding*

Garcia Lorca, *Three Tragedies*
Athol Fugard, *Master Harold and the Boys*
Niccolò Machiavelli, *The Prince*
Karl Marx and Friedrich Engels, "The Communist Manifesto"
Horace Mann, "Twelfth Annual Report" on education, 1848.
Arthur Miller, *The Crucible*
Maria Montessori, selections from *The Montessori Method*
Toni Morrison, *Beloved*
Eugene O'Neill, *Long Day's Journey into Night*
Plato, *Meno* and selections from *The Republic*
Robert Putnam, *Bowling Alone: The Collapse and Revival of American Community*
Jean-Jacques Rousseau, *Emile*
Sophocles, *The Three Theban Plays*
Robert Sowell, *Ethnic America*
Harriet Beecher Stowe, *Uncle Tom's Cabin*
Booker T. Washington, selections from *Up from Slavery*
August Wilson, *Fences*

In addition to the seminal humanities and social sciences texts listed here, students have also (in some courses exclusively) been required to read, digest, and apply standard disciplinary knowledge from well-known textbooks. Among the widely used textbooks that have reappeared on syllabi over the years are Mason, *Thinking Mathematically*; Meyers, *Exploring Psychology*; McConnell and Brue, *Macroeconomics*; and Schram and Mandell, *An Introduction to Human Services: Policy and Practice*.

TEACHING

Clearly the faculty members at the college Cohen founded have successfully taught a wide range of texts. How have they managed to make elements drawn from a classical liberal arts curriculum meaningful and compelling to students whose main reason for coming to college was to get better jobs? Classes at the college have always been small, so there is ample opportunity for generating discussions as a way to engage students in questions of interpretation or analysis. In terms of vital teaching, however, at least as important as the class size has been the breadth of experience of the college's faculty. While no single selection can do justice to the infinite ways in which a faculty member's background contributes to his or her teaching style, a sampling of some of the college's veteran faculty may serve to give a sense of the teaching that MCNY students have been exposed to over the years.

Vanda Wark provides a good example of a faculty member whose early range of studies led to the successful integration of liberal learning and professional training. Wark's parents believed that a girl's education should end at high school, but in defiance of what she later termed their "class prejudice against education," she worked after school and saved enough money to pay her own way through Shepherd University in West Virginia where she majored in English, speech, and writing. After college she worked at assembly line jobs, first packing computer chips and then soldering, but the work bored her and she was fired. For several years she worked as an actress on a cruise ship, performing in one-act plays. Later as a counselor in private practice with a therapist she learned to do hypnosis on patients, and that experience motivated her to continue on to pursue a master's and later a doctorate in psychology. But the theater world still exerted a pull, and in her off time she began writing plays, using her psychological knowledge to create complex interactions between the characters.[14]

What came to be named Audrey Cohen College was Wark's first teaching job. Hired in the mid-1990s, she felt that she had found a good niche. The work allowed her to be creative, and her past experiences in the workforce enabled her to relate to students who were returning to school and who had other obligations while attending school. The transdisciplinary curriculum intrigued Wark and allowed her to teach both psychology-related courses and plays. "You learn a lot while you are teaching about how things fit together," she once stated in an interview for *The Crystallizer*, the college's student newspaper in the 1990s.[15]

In a Values dimension course of the third semester, which focuses on Working in Groups, Wark uses Eugene O'Neill's *Long Day's Journey Into Night* to supplement the assigned textbook. She begins by teaching the textbook version of the six characteristics of a primary group, using the primary group of the family as an example. She then has students read O'Neill's play to analyze how the six characteristics may be applied to a specific family. The students themselves are divided into small groups and given a sheet listing the six characteristics of primary groups (interaction, structure, size, goal, cohesion, and temporal change). The task of each group of students is to give two specific examples of how the Tyrone family does or does not exemplify each of the six characteristics. One area that generates a lot of debate is the question about the size of the primary family group in O'Neill's play. What is the size of this family? Should it be only four—the specific living biological members? Should it be five and include Eugene, the baby who died before the opening of the play? Could it be six and include Catherine, the maid who the mother of the family talks to? Some students even fight for Bridget, an off-stage cook who the audience never sees, to be considered part of the family.[16] The exercise opens students' minds to the ways that social groups influence values and norms over time, and it eventually helps them identify the implications of group influence for the human service profession.[17]

Wark's training in psychology has also prompted her to experiment with the motivational aspects of teaching. To ensure that students always come to class having done the assigned reading, Wark now includes on her syllabus scheduled quizzes on the assigned reading and includes in her lessons exercises on memorization and test-taking. To prepare for these additions to her course work she has furthered her own psychological knowledge by studying brain structure and the science of cognition, particularly the difference between short-term and long-term memory. She also teaches an introductory statistics course—which she leads her students through with care and compassion—and consistently receives glowing evaluations of her teaching. But she has never given up her love for the theater, and over the years has become a well-published playwright, at one point earning a letter of praise for her work from Edward Albee.

Another faculty member whose background has provided a potent preparation for the integration of liberal learning and professional training is Theodor Damian. A native of Romania with a PhD in theology from the University of Bucharest, Damian came to the United States in the late 1970s on a program sponsored by the Presbyterian Church. He traveled around the country visiting various religious communities in more than forty states and living with host families, an experience that he says gave him an insight into cultural diversity.[18] Eventually he earned a scholarship to study theology at Princeton University. After receiving his master's degree he went on to Fordham University for his PhD in theology. In addition to full-time teaching, Damian writes essays, articles, and poetry and has published widely in both English and Romanian.

At MCNY Damian mostly teaches Values dimension courses, in both the undergraduate Human Services program and the graduate master's in public administration program. "I like the fact that we call our philosophy classes 'Values' because it gives one a kind of flexibility," he says. Depending on the audience that is in front of you, "you can lead the course in so many ways." He sees no contradiction between theology and philosophy. "There is continuity and compatibility between the two, and I demonstrate that in the classroom."[19]

One of Damian's favorite texts to teach is E.A. Wallis Budge's translation of the *Egyptian Book of the Dead*, a staple of the first semester's Values curriculum for decades. He begins by asking students to reflect on their own concepts of death and dying, and from there to explore assumptions about their own religious affiliations and spiritual experiences. Once they have articulated what people think about God or religion today, they are able to see sources for those beliefs in the *Egyptian Book of the Dead*. Damian introduces the concepts of the vertical aspect of one's religion, that is, its theological elements, and the horizontal aspect of one's religious, that is, its ethical elements—how the religion asks the believer to connect to people. This leads to the account of the "negative confession" in the book and to lively discussions about reincarnation and transfiguration, and eventually to self-assessment and preparation for practice, the theme of Purpose I.[20]

Texts frequently assigned in Damian's Purpose VIII courses, where the focus is on structural change, include Chinua Achebe's *Things Fall Apart* and Luminitza Zava's *Chained Generations*. Both books describe traumatic social transformations from the perspectives of young people who observed them at first hand. Damian brings his own experiences of living in Romania to bear on the experiences recounted in both books—a sense of connection that enhances students' own reading of the texts.[21]

On paper, Charles Gray's background appears to be the most conducive to a teaching style focused mostly on professional development, but he too is committed to the blend of vocational and humanistic learning that Audrey Cohen insisted on while she was alive. Gray has a master's degree in social work from New York University and a doctorate in social welfare from Yeshiva University. Prior to being hired at Audrey Cohen College he worked for the Department of Social Services as a caseworker and a supervisor; from there he moved on to the New York City Department for Aging as an associate director for the Bureau of Community Programs. He has long served as an active member of the National Association of Social Workers (NASW). His hands-on knowledge of the fields that most MCNY students aim for (social work, counseling, geriatric care), makes Gray a valuable resource both inside and outside the classroom. But he also cares passionately about developing critical thinking skills in his students. He believes that students must be able to support their opinions with scholarly research and look at both sides of an issue with an open mind.[22] He insists that they go beyond the textbooks in the Literature Review that they must complete as part of their Constructive Action documents. "I don't want you to be robotic," he tells students. "Be a risk taker."[23]

"Everything is political and we should make the students understand that," Steven Cresap once asserted in an interview. Cresap earned a master's in philosophy and a PhD in history from Cornell University, and in addition to part-time teaching jobs before coming to MCNY, he worked as a researcher at the South Street Seaport in lower Manhattan. Describing his main interests as "metaphysics and entertainment,"[24] Cresap has long served to provoke students' thinking by presenting them with "contrarian" texts that stretch their thinking and challenge entrenched cultural norms—a goal that is facilitated by the college's practice of organizing content knowledge into dimensions rather than disciplines. Over the years his assigned texts have included the *Letters of Abelard and Heloise*, Nietzsche's *Genealogy of Morals*, and Max Weber's writings on charisma. He often includes works that provoke discussions about race—from the "Curse of Ham" story in Genesis and Aristotle's pronouncements on slavery, to Frederick Douglass's autobiography and the film series *Eyes on the Prize*. Cresap also enjoys teaching Plato's *Meno*, a staple of the Purpose I Values curriculum. The *Meno* is a text that has to do with abstract thinking, he says, which students have to be introduced to before they can proceed with their studies. Although many students may not have the capacity for abstract thinking in the first semester, "they at least learn that developing that particular capacity is on the agenda."[25]

THE THEORY-PRACTICE NEXUS IN
THEORY AND IN PRACTICE

The foregoing overview demonstrates that the educational experience offered at the college does manage to link together areas of knowledge that are generally separated at other institutions. Situated in an academic landscape somewhere in between a traditional liberal arts school like Barnard or Brooklyn College and vocational schools like Monroe or TCI (Technical Career Institute), MCNY can claim to provide career training at the same time that it aims to produce "aware, informed and engaged citizens, in the broadest sense of that term," as Steven Greenwald phrased it.

But does the blended curriculum also serve to foster the theory-practice integration that Cohen and her associates envisioned? Does the knowledge content that students are introduced to actually inform their practice in their internships or jobs? Adding spice to faculty members' conversations about teaching at MCNY are disagreements about whether the founders' vision of the dimensional courses providing the theoretical content for Constructive Actions actually works—either as an educational theory or in its practical application.

Much of the faculty's and administration's energy in the 1980s was devoted to fine-tuning the required structure of Constructive Action documents across all eight semesters.[26] Addressing the challenge of theory-practice integration, a significant step in that process was the inclusion of dimensional analysis exercises throughout the document. Students were required in each section of the document to state the Purpose of the action, the Values involved, how the project dealt with relationships between the Self and Others, what Systems needed to be understood, and what Skills were involved. As Deborah Allen has written, "President Cohen wanted students to practice using the five Dimensions like a mantra, applying these five lenses to the challenges they encountered in the workplace." Asking questions was a valuable habit that would lead to continuous learning, "in short, to make the students into comprehensive thinkers as they looked for opportunities for action and planned and carried out their Constructive Actions."[27]

However, is a dimensional analysis based on the students' observations and questioning the same as theory-practice integration? Lou Tietje (pronounced TJ), who came to the college in the late 1980s with a strong background in philosophy, has thought long and hard about this question. The theory of the vaunted theory-practice integration is flawed, he believes, for many reasons. First of all, Cohen and her associates never defined exactly what they meant by "theory." Is it the same as knowledge? But that question opens the doors to other questions, for there are many definitions of knowledge, as Plato suggested millennia ago. Knowledge can take the form of belief, true belief, and justified belief.[28] Which of these aspects of knowledge includes what we mean by theory?

Furthermore, even if one simply defines theory as that which is not action, Tietje continues,[29] is theorizing prior to acting something that most undergraduate students can be expected to do? Can students be expected to approach a problem in an agency or workplace with a theory self-consciously in mind so that they can test that theory?

Taking his critique a step farther, Tietje asks: Are most people really aware that in fact every action we take already presupposes a theory? For example, if we enter a dark room and go to turn on the lamp but the light doesn't go on, we will generally proceed to try changing the light bulb; if this doesn't work we check the cord and the plug; if this doesn't work we check the fuse box. All of these actions presuppose a theory of electricity that has become part of our knowledge base but of which we are generally unconscious. Few of us stop to say, "Oh, now I must apply my theory of electricity to this problem." That kind of metacognition—thinking about one's own thinking—is out of the range of most students' range of experience or even ability, Tietje argues. In sum, the college's founders were naive about what the integration of theory and practice really means. "It was not systematically developed. There was never an attempt to settle these matters in a philosophically sophisticated way."[30]

In response to Tietje's critique, a pragmatic interlocutor will posit another way of thinking about the theory-practice interface. Granted that few students can be expected to apply theory to action *prior* to an action, they *can* be expected to apply theory *after* an action. Although the ultimate aim may be to build a theoretical foundation so that the practitioner consciously thinks of taking action with a specific theory in mind, a more realistic approach is to ask students to use an acquired theory or content knowledge to *rationalize* or *justify* their actions in the field. Veteran teacher

Charles Gray has termed this the "back-door" way of connecting theory to practice.[31] Indeed, many professors at the college interpret the college's conceptual framework in this way. It asks students retroactively to make appropriate references to authors and ideas from their Dimension courses in the documentation of their Constructive Action.

Instead of anticipatory metacognition, the back-door approach involves *post de facto* justification for an action, or what may be termed *connective thinking*.[32] To encourage such thinking one might ask a student: Does the successful lesson that you delivered to fifth graders at P.S. 19 relate more to Plato's theory that knowledge is within a person and therefore just needs to be drawn out by skillful Socratic questioning? Or does it relate more to Locke's theory that the human mind is originally a blank slate that needs to be filled in by sensory experience of the material world? In other words, which worked better—asking the children questions or giving them visuals? Or both? And why? Did the learning involve social intercourse— that is, working in groups—as Dewey would envision, or individualized interactions, as recommended by Rousseau? All four of these theorists were studied in your Values dimension course. How did you apply those theories in planning and implementing your lesson? Were there other texts from your dimension courses that were useful to you? Which method from the textbook assigned in your math methods (i.e., Skills dimension) course was used in this lesson?

According to this more circumscribed approach, the main requirement for theory-practice integration is for students to make basic connections between texts and actions, between book learning and practical work. The Constructive Action document provides the occasion to write about how the semester's readings relate to what one has planned and accomplished in terms of a specific project undertaken in the field during the semester. Veteran adjunct faculty member Franklyn Rother, who is quoted in the epigraph at the beginning of this chapter, actually organizes his Purpose seminars around the material assigned in the Dimensions classes. Students bring their notes and books from their other courses to his seminar each week, and together they discuss how what they learned in their Dimension class relates to their Constructive Action goal. He then gives students time during the class to incorporate the knowledge into their Constructive Action document.[33] The philosophical underpinning for such a system is the belief that knowledge becomes meaningful when it is applied, and without the artificial boundaries that separate the disciplines at most schools, at MCNY the knowledge can be culled from a wide range of disciplines.

Scattered throughout the Constructive Action documents of the 1990s is ample evidence of the theory-practice nexus working to promote this more accessible form of connective thinking. One student included in her plan for a Constructive Action in the eighth semester (Promoting Change) a set of reflections on change that included a quote from the pre-Socratic philosopher Heraclitus and a reference to William James, both of whom she had read in her Values Dimension course.[34] For a fifth semester (Counseling) Constructive Action that involved working with a child diagnosed with ADHD, a student found useful his reading of Sissela Bok's book *Lying*, also assigned in a Values dimension course. Of particular relevance was the chapter concerning "Paternalistic Lies" that explores the validity and ethics of lying to a child.[35] Other students cite the usefulness of a book entitled *Messages*, which carefully lays out effective communication strategies and which for many years has been assigned in the Skills dimension of the Counseling semester.[36] In many of these documents the authors not only refer to authors and titles but quote relevant selections from the texts as well.

In the later semesters the connections between what is studied in the dimension courses and what is practiced in the field often becomes more specialized. One student in the seventh semester (Supervision) who was doing her fieldwork at the Bedford-Stuyvesant Family Health Center during the height of the AIDS pandemic in 1990 chose as her Constructive Action goal to ensure that the AIDS program would be funded again by the New York City Department of Health. She successfully achieved this goal by overseeing the extent to which two outreach workers were informed about the virus. In documenting her Constructive Action the student made references to the more practical works she had been introduced to by her professors in her other dimension courses. From the Skills dimension the student utilized *Financial and Accounting Guide for Non-Profit Organization* by Calvin J. Gross and William Weshoul to write a proposal for the AIDS program, which required a financial statement listing salary, rent, and other costs. In the Self and Others dimension the student read Paul R. Timm's book *Supervision* and learned the different roles of a supervisor and how the role of supervisor differs from that of a manager in terms of their relationship with the employees. "The student practitioner found that this assisted her in her Constructive Action because she had to keep her staff motivated during a time when they had to move into a smaller office. They felt they were sacrificing more than others to keep peace in the health center," the student wrote, referring to herself in the third person as was required in CA documents at that time. From the Systems dimension the student used John M. Ivancevicit's and Michael T. Matteson's *Organizational Behavior and Management* to learn about how different corporations used to solve problems between management and employees or between one employee and another. "For example when the student practitioner had to complete her program's monthly reports [in] less than three days, by studying organizational behavior the student practitioner was able to keep her anger under control and complete her task." From the Values dimension she used *Productivity Through People* by William B. Werther, William A. Ruch, and Lynne McClure to compare different values of corporations, management, and employees. "The student practitioner learned that everyone has a reason for working. She also learned how the union plays a role in the employee's values as well as the corporation's values. . . . The Values dimension assisted the student practitioner in understanding management values of serving the citizen and understanding the values of her team serving the citizen. It was interesting to her to see that management and her team both wanted to serve the citizen the best way possible. The student practitioner feels she is more in tune with the management and the team by understanding their values and goals."[37] Clearly the professional work accomplished by this student was enhanced by her academic studies, which was the main purpose for her decision to enroll in college in the first place, and in turn, her job responsibilities gave her academic studies a depth of meaning that they would not have had without the direct application to her work.

Not all Constructive Action documents exhibit the articulated connective thinking that is evident in the documents cited above. Actual evidence of the theory-practice integration envisioned by the founders has always varied widely from one professor to the next and even, within each professor's seminars, from one student to the next. The range of student learning outcomes in this area suggests that sophisticated theory-practice integration is still a challenge for both faculty and students.

Although faculty members may complain about the usability of the theories that they teach, students themselves are generally grateful for the chance to practice what they learn. "At MCNY the whole curriculum relates to practice," one student recently summed up. "As we move from purpose to purpose, we are supplementing our learning by doing." Making references to Dewey's writings, the student continued, "we are making school fit the society's needs and making it relevant to community learning."[38] These words were written nearly twenty years after Cohen's death, but they reflect Cohen's own understanding of how the theory-practice nexus ideally works.

CHAPTER 11

THE TRIUMPHS AND CHALLENGES OF LEADERSHIP (1990–1999)

I was once asked to list those qualities I thought were most crucial to my success as an administrator. When I completed my list, I realized that some of the items could describe the classic entrepreneur. . . . Independence, persistence, lots of energy, being stubborn, being a work-a-holic—these characteristics describe a *tycoon* as much as they do a leader in the new service society.

—Cohen, 1980, p. 15[1]

In their pathbreaking 2002 book, *Founding Mothers and Others: Women Educational Leaders During the Progressive Era*, Alan R. Sadovnik and Susan F. Semel co-edited a series of reflections on women educators who, in the early decades of the twentieth century, took bold initiatives to promote educational reform. Some of the women, like Margaret Naumburg, Caroline Pratt, and Helen Parkhurst, were the founders of child-centered progressive schools (Walden, City and Country, and Dalton, respectively), while others were leaders of educational organizations, including public school districts and teachers unions. Although the book's focus is on educational reform in elementary and secondary schools rather than colleges, there are useful comparisons to be drawn between the founding mothers included in Sadovnik and Semel's book and Audrey Cohen.

What are some of the similarities between the founding mothers of the early twentieth century and Cohen's work? Obviously the historical settings for their proposed innovations were similar. The educational visions of Cohen and of her early-twentieth-century precursors were enlarged in part due to the luminous optimism of their times. The Progressive Era and the 1960s were both periods when experimentation and imagination were highly valued and when hopes for social transformation were high. A related similarity is that both Cohen and the educators who Sadovnik and Semel showcase were proponents of hands-on learning. Setting themselves and the educational institutions they founded in explicit contrast to traditional schooling that emphasized formal academic instruction, both the Progressive Era's innovative classrooms and Cohen's college were deliberately enlivened by fieldwork, collaboration, and the project method of learning. Although the child-centered progressive schools were different in structure and demographics from Cohen's College for Human Services, and although each can be seen to emphasize a different side of John Dewey's aim to fuse individual and social needs, both were informed by assumptions about learning that stemmed from Dewey's educational philosophy.

More important at this point than similarities in historical background or educational assumptions are similarities in the leadership styles of Cohen and the founding mothers of the Progressive Era. In a concluding chapter, Sadovnik and Semel list some of the attributes shared by the female educational leaders described in their book. "All of the women leaders portrayed here were strong, driven, intense, tenacious, visionary and charismatic and possessed a strong sense of social mission."[2] Those words could be used to describe Cohen. She was strong, intense, and tenacious. Again and again she was described as a visionary, and her sense of social mission was apparent ever since, in early 1964, her "fork in the road presented itself" and she decided to turn away from lucrative job-contracting for well-to-do women and to devote her energies to creating meaningful work and training for disadvantaged women.

In probing further their analysis of the progressive schools' *Founding Mothers'* leadership styles, Sadovnik and Semel make use of recent work in feminist theory. As they point out, feminist theories of leadership have often stressed the ways that women's leadership styles differ from men's. With her seminal work *In a Different Voice*, Carol Gilligan set the tone in 1982 by arguing that women think more relationally than men and that they thus emphasize collaboration and contextualization in their interactions with others. Nell Noddings's work *Caring: A Feminist Approach to Ethics and Moral Education* (1992) made similar points in terms of women's roles in schools. In general, the editors note, many feminist theories and research studies suggest that "women are more democratic, less hierarchical, and more relational" in their approach to leadership than men.[3]

Sadovnik and Semel contend, however, that the female educational leaders of the Progressive Era suggest a caveat to this theory. Many of the founding mothers were difficult to work with, and many were "far more autocratic than democratic." (The same can be said of Maria Montessori, the founding mother of the Montessori schools somewhat later in the century.) The challenges of starting a radically new educational institution with a particular mission and philosophy made collective decision making difficult, and for some of the founders, even undesirable.[4] Indeed the conclusion of an earlier study by Semel suggests that the women leaders of the early twentieth century created a "progressive paradox": they represented "democratic education autocratically delivered."[5]

Audrey Cohen's own leadership style is the focus of this chapter. An underlying theme is the extent to which Cohen's work, particularly in the last years of her life, represents the progressive paradox that Semel identified. Did Cohen's college, like the progressive schools of the early twentieth century, become a form of "democratic education autocratically delivered"? Was her leadership style overcontrolling? This chapter also touches on what Sadovnik and Semel term the "double-edged sword" of the founder's charisma and that has been identified as the "founder's syndrome" in an evolving institution."[6] On the one hand charisma is essential to a school's or college's founding, funding, and development. On the other hand, when the charismatic founder retires or dies, the institution may have a difficult time maintaining its original identity.[7]

SUPPORT SYSTEMS

As *Founding Mothers* makes clear, those who embark on creating a tuition-driven private institution need loyal supporters who can help the founders realize their dreams.[8] In Cohen's case, the loyal commitment of her founding "sisters"—Alida Mesrop, Laura Pires-Hester, Barbara Walton, Deborah

Allen, Sylvia Hack, and Janith Jordan—was essential to the birth and growth of her project. Also, in the background was the important moral and financial support of Millie Leet.

The late Mildred Robbins Leet (born Mildred Elowsky) was best known in New York philanthropy circles as the co-founder of Trickle Up, an organization that supports projects for eliminating poverty around the world. In her younger years she was an early supporter of international peacekeeping, women's rights, and civil rights. In the late 1950s she served as a United Nations representative for the National Council of Women, and in 1963—defying her own family's biases—she proudly stood on the speaker's platform for Martin Luther King's "I Have a Dream" speech.[9] Leet and Cohen first met through real estate connections, not initially through any of the political and social networks that they shared an interest in. Millie Leet's first husband, Louis J. Robbins, owned the East 67th Street building that the Cohens rented, and so for a number of years he was their landlord.[10]

Cohen asked Leet to join the board of the College for Human Services shortly after its founding. Leet was a significant player in the early 1970s during the confrontation with Preston Wilcox, and she often hosted board meetings in her Riverside Drive penthouse apartment. Leet stayed on to serve the college both as a source of wise advice for Cohen and as a loyal source of financial support, becoming Chair of the Board from 1986 to 1999 and Chair Emerita until her death in 2011. As a board chairperson she was actively engaged in the daily life of the college. One staff member remembers her warmth and involvement. "Millie came to every event we had and always remembered my name. She would talk, hug, kiss and be friendly with everyone. She would always be around, walking the halls."[11]

Humphrey Crookendale and Millie Leet once discovered that they had both attended the same high school, and Crookendale continues today to sing her praises. It was Millie, he says, who could stand up to Audrey and keep her focused on what was in the college's best interest. He remembers one specific instance in the early years when Cohen contemplated telling the faculty that they could not be paid for two weeks because of financial constraints. But Millie objected. "No—under no circumstances. If you do that, the integrity of this institution is compromised." Millie was one person on the board who was not overwhelmed by Audrey, Crookendale says. She would not just let Audrey "go any way she wanted to."[12]

That could not be said of most members of the college's Board of Trustees. Over the years Cohen's board constituted an important support group that in general deferred to her wishes.[13] One long-term member, John Stookey, when asked about his memories of serving on the board in the 1970s and early 1980s, joked that there was a spectator quality in the experience: "You pay the price of admission and get the privilege of watching Audrey!" Nevertheless he highly respected Cohen's leadership skills and was especially impressed with her resilience. He recalled one period of internal turmoil when he thought that she should simply "take a powder and go on to another effort." Six months later, however, she emerged from the seemingly impossible situation "virtually unscathed."[14]

Stookey had become acquainted with the Cohens largely through the friendship that his daughter and Wendy Cohen had developed at the Chapin School, and with a background in international business and engineering he brought to the board a sound business sense and long experience on the boards of other charitable institutions. His general assessment of the way Cohen's Board of Trustees worked was echoed in comments made by fellow board member David Seeley, who in 1974 brought into Cohen's circle a different source of expertise. Seeley was a graduate of the Yale Law School and the Harvard School of Education. He had worked since 1956 on school reform issues on the federal, state, and local levels and, since 1969, as a professor of education at the College of Staten Island.[15]

"We always deferred to Audrey," Seeley remembered. "She was not the kind of president who would take orders from the board." But Seeley quickly qualified this statement with the reasons why such a diverse group usually let her have her way. The board members' deference stemmed from their confidence in her and their realization that they were really just an advisory group. "It was her college. She had created it. Audrey was basically in charge." Sometimes new ideas appear in books and articles, he continued, but here was an institution that was actually trying to carry out these ideas, so it was exciting. "It was a revolutionary experiment that we felt we were a part of—and it was one that seemed to be succeeding!"[16]

Cohen took care to make the institution's successes evident to the board. In addition to reports on institutional growth and expansion, board members heard about the Constructive Actions performed by students in the field. In a report about the master's degree program, members were presented with the work of Sister Catherine Howard, a student who had set up a shelter for homeless mothers that became a model for other such shelters in the city. At another meeting the trustees heard about the Constructive Action of Yvonne Tyson, a student who had developed an AIDS awareness training program that she had been hired to implement throughout the state of New York. Other examples of successful work included a student who introduced a new vocational training program in the agency where she was interning, a student who created a support group for mothers who did not want their children to be placed in foster homes, and a student who arranged for homeless persons to find help at a nearby Salvation Army center.[17] Board members could see that good work was being done.

The general support for Cohen's project cannot be attributed to the board's passivity. Both Stookey and Seeley commented on the group's breadth of personalities and viewpoints. Israel Laster, a national consultant for the American Jewish Committee and an early member of the board, had had experience in a wide range of organizations and always spoke his mind. He certainly was not passive or retiring, Seeley remembered, nor was another board member, Ruth Atkins. Perhaps the most dynamic member of the board in those early years was Bill Tatum, chief executive officer of the *Amsterdam News*. He had strong views, and he didn't hesitate to express them. Unlike some leaders, Cohen "wasn't looking for stooges and yes people." There was little dissent mainly because of the individual members' confidence in Cohen's vision.[18]

Both Stookey and Seeley also referred to the nonbureaucratic and personal feeling that they enjoyed at the college itself and at board meetings. They appreciated that student representatives were invited to share their experiences, that meetings were hosted at different members' homes, and that food was always served. "I don't think I've ever been fed as well as I have on the Board of the College for Human Services," Seeley recalled, and wondered out loud if that was a conscious strategy on the part of Audrey or whether Millie Leet helped to set that standard. "There are those who say that first breaking bread together is a very good way to create a sense of collegiality that you don't otherwise have with boards."[19]

Motivating the board's loyal support for Cohen was also the sense of being a part of a beleaguered institution. Seeley compared the experience to being aboard an imperiled ship. "We were like the crew of a ship that's going through storms. You better damn well work together, and hang together, because the ship might sink. Not because it's a leaky vessel, but because there are a lot of storms. And this was a very little ship in a big stormy sea."[20]

Although Seeley admired the visionary and what he later called the *heroic* aspect of Cohen's leadership, he did see some dark clouds on the horizon. The expansion of the college into Florida and California was risky, he felt. Because the New York branch could barely manage to stay afloat itself, by taking on these other obligations he feared that they would create a bigger set of problems with which they couldn't cope. And at this point he hinted at some aspects of Cohen's style that he found disconcerting. She went through some phases, he says, when she moved from being a person whose talent was serving a cause to one who aimed at "conquering the world."[21] Here he is touching on an aspect of Cohen's leadership style that would become increasingly problematical as she approached her final years.

COLLABORATION OR CONTROL?

Millie Leet and the rest of the College for Human Services Board of Trustees served as an effective support system for Audrey Cohen over the years, but the same was not always true of the faculty. Cohen's relationships with her faculty were mixed, and here Sadovnik and Semel's discussion of how founding mothers may present a progressive paradox of "democratic education autocratically delivered" is especially relevant.[22] On the one hand the faculty, like the board, respected Cohen's leadership abilities and generally supported the educational model that she had institutionalized. Indeed, in terms of service to the college, the College for Human Services faculty demonstrated an unusually high level of commitment to making Cohen's project work. Many faculty members also saw in their president a deep well of basic human kindness and generosity. Humphrey Crookendale remembers Cohen's excitement when he announced that he was getting married, her pleasure at being invited to the wedding, and later, when their first baby was born, her gift of a substantial savings bond to support the child's future education.[23] Richard Grallo remembers Cohen renting a restaurant for end-of-the-year parties for faculty and staff, where there would be food and dancing and even a faculty show. Unlike other faculty members Grallo also still appreciates that Cohen cared enough about what individual faculty members were doing in their classrooms to organize the annual luncheons at the Lotos Club where they could share their own ideas about the curriculum.[24]

At the same time, many faculty members were critical of what Grallo called Cohen's "authoritarian" style of leadership. For Grallo and other members of the faculty this took the form of a stricture against doing research that in any way involved the college. Grallo had been trained as a researcher, and he was keen to explore systematically the extent to which the College for Human Services' unique model actually worked in terms of learning outcomes. But when he proposed the idea to Cohen, she resisted. Grallo also felt that the college should have collaborated more closely with Lincoln University, which had borrowed elements from the College for Human Services model, and with Alverno College in Milwaukee, which independently had developed a similar curricular structure. But that idea "didn't fly" when he presented it to Cohen.[25]

Other faculty members similarly remember Cohen's sense of control as being at times counterproductive. Anne Lopes recalls one Lotos Club meeting when she tried to present a critique of the word *citizen* in Cohen's article, "The Citizen as the Integrating Agent." As a political theorist Lopes had studied closely the history of the idea of citizenship—what the word *citizen* has meant historically over time and what it means in contemporary political discourse across different cultures. Using the word *citizen* to refer to the people who College for Human Services students were helping—a relationship that the college agreed was a give and take relationship of empowerment that went both ways—was, Lopes wanted to argue, some-what problematical. But Cohen's response to Lopes's critique was dismissive. For Cohen the idea of an "integrating agent" was what was important, and she made clear that Lopes' attempt to problematize the college's use of terms was not welcome. For Lopes the experience was "like talking to the wall."[26] Cohen, Lopes said, didn't want to hear any criticism of the model or of what didn't work.[27]

Lopes was also bothered by Cohen's failure to locate the College for Human Services' genesis in the history of education. Clearly there was a Deweyan influence on her thinking, Lopes says, and also a whole history around workforce participation programs that Cohen might have profitably claimed being a part of. "It's always good to acknowledge that you are standing on the shoulders of giants, to situate yourself in a discourse so as to be able to see what your actual contributions are to a field," Lopes points out. Instead Cohen only wanted to publicize the extent to which she was *outside* of the mold. The desire to be unique, Lopes argued, was isolating for the college and a barrier to conversation with faculty. There was no way to contribute because she was "only open to *her* conversation and *her* ideas."[28]

Lopes recalled that faculty members in the 1990s saw Cohen as constantly needing to be in control of the image, in control of the language. She scolded faculty members who referred to the college by an acronym—CHS—rather than spelling out the full name, the College for Human Services. Even Cohen's manner of dressing made her come across as someone who was stiff and cold: the shoulder-padded business suits and patent-leather high heeled shoes that Cohen wore in the 1990s made her seem "exquisitely remote." When reminded that Cohen had been active in the civil rights movement and had demonstrated and marched to gain support for the college, Lopes said, incredulously, "I never saw the activist in her."[29]

At one point Lopes pondered a question that connects with Sadovnik and Semel's observations in *Founding Mothers*. Did Cohen *need* to wield power the way she did in order to be successful? Could she have acted another way and still succeed in founding a completely novel educational institution? Admitting that there was a "heroic" element to Cohen's story, did she have to dig in her heels so much? Was her leadership style only tactical? Or did it have to do with who she was?[30]

Underlying Lopes's questions is a debate at the heart of the feminist theory referred to at the beginning of this chapter. Can women bring a "different voice" to leadership positions, or must they adopt, as Cohen's quote in the epigraph to this chapter suggests, the qualities of a "tycoon" in order to be effective? Interestingly, Cohen herself, at least in the early 1980s, was acutely aware of this perennial question. In a speech entitled "Leadership and the New Service Ethic" that she prepared for delivery at the Higher Education Resource Services (HERS) conference in Denver in 1980, Cohen openly discussed the values inherent in her own leadership role. Her talk would focus on a path to success and achievement that "emphasizes caring values and a commitment to cooperation and service," she began. She herself did not become a college president by abandoning her concern for people in order to make it to the top. Instead, it was her vision of social justice and human service that determined her career goals.

In her speech Cohen proceeded to point out that the caring values implicit in the service ethic are the very traits that have always been labeled "female." It would indeed be ironic, she asserted, if women were to lose sight of these values—such as compassion, empathy, and sensitivity—in an attempt to mimic their male competition and advance to top leadership posts.[31] She conceded in the very next sentence, however, that it is also necessary for a leader to be tough and aggressive and to show that you can hold your own in the political battlefield in ways that are traditionally associated with "male" behavior. Given this necessity, she herself had always tried to keep in mind that hard-headedness "was merely a means to an end, not an end in itself."[32]

HERS, the organization hosting the conference that Cohen spoke at in 1980, is a networking and support group specifically organized for and by women presidents and chancellors in the field of higher education. When she referred to hardheadedness as a means rather than an end, Cohen undoubtedly knew that her audience could relate to the distinction she was trying to make. In practice, however, means and ends often get blurred, and the distinction can be tricky. Was Cohen's hardheaded response to Grallo's research proposals or to Lopes' critique of the word *citizen* a justified means to protect the college's hard-won identity? Or was it an unjustified end of authoritarian control for its own sake?

What others perceived as Cohen's hardheadedness appeared to become more arbitrary as she approached her final years. At this point, however, a summary reflection on Cohen's leadership style may be in order. What board member David Seeley saw as good interrelation skills, he said, probably infuriated some people. He then made a telling observation:

> Visionaries often are so intent on their vision that anybody who gets in the way is dealt with harshly—psychologically if not in other ways. And Audrey may not have come across as a positive person to such persons. The vision was the most important thing. So she'll do whatever is necessary to accomplish that vision.[33]

THE SCHOOLS PROJECT

When David Seeley referred to Cohen going through phases of wanting to conquer the world,[34] the comment was made in the context of her plans to expand the College for Human Services' curricular model into other educational arenas—an effort that became a single-minded drive in the 1990s. Education had always been Cohen's primary focus. Recall that she had majored in education at the University of Pittsburgh (with a dual major in political science), worked as a student teacher at George Westinghouse High School, studied elementary schools in Japan, and taught briefly at an American school in Morocco. When she set up the Women's Talent Corps in 1966, the first "assist" jobs that the Corps created and that Corps Women moved into were teacher assistant jobs in New York City public schools. The Women's Talent Corps soon evolved into the College of Human Services, and once Cohen's Purpose-Centered system of education had been invented and implemented in 1974, she immediately began to push for the proliferation of the new curricular model. By 1976 Lincoln University in Pennsylvania had adopted the model for its master's degree in human service, and in the next two years branches of the College of Human Services were opened in Florida and California.

Eager to make the college's distinctive educational system available to more adult students around New York City, Cohen and her colleagues in the late 1980s and early 1990s opened branches of Audrey Cohen College in the South Bronx, Queens, and Staten Island.[35] Housed in clean, functional, and unprepossessing buildings, the college's extension campuses offered "no-frills" versions of Audrey Cohen College's Purpose-Centered curriculum. The Bronx site grew quickly: having opened in 1986 with 30 to 45 students, by 1991 it had grown to 120 students, and it continued to grow in the next decade.[36] The Staten Island site began in a Masonic temple but by 1992 had moved to two floors of an impressive and convenient space on New York Harbor, next to the Staten Island Ferry terminal, and thanks to a donation from a local bank, could boast of having a well-equipped computer lab.[37]

In the meantime, Cohen's ambitious educational vision was expanding vertically as well as horizontally. Not only did she see opportunities for spreading Purpose-Centered Education geographically, but she began to think about how its curricular grid could be adopted at all levels of education—in elementary and secondary schools as well as in colleges and graduate schools. As she had reported in her twentieth-anniversary speech, the college had opened a Human Services Junior High School in East Harlem, and Cohen was planning to open a high school as well. Her sights soon stretched even farther. "She was out to change the educational world," Sylvia Hack, a long-term associate, asserted.[38]

The East Harlem junior high school provides in microcosm a suggestion of both the promises and the difficulties inherent in Cohen's educational aims. David Seeley's experience with educational reform made him a source of information about the possibility of establishing the Purpose-Centered model in a public elementary or secondary school, and during his early years on the board he and Cohen began talking about the idea. He recommended that the school be located in District 4, in East Harlem, because that district had already had some experience with parental choice in their children's schooling and because there were teachers in the district who were open to curricular experimentation. Seeley introduced Cohen to the New York City school chancellor, Anthony Alvarado, and the project got under way.[39] The initial plan anticipated a minimum of reorientation for the schools' teachers. For a week in the summer teachers and administrators would come down to the college for an orientation on how to start thinking in terms of Purpose-Centered Education,[40] and during the school year staff from the college would visit the East Harlem school providing advice on how to implement it.

Unfortunately Seeley himself was not able to stay involved in the school, and he later noted that it had run into problems. Unlike other District 4 schools, which were started by individual teachers, the College for Human Services Junior High School was run by an outside agency, the college. This was helpful in terms of technical assistance and training, but to adopt a completely new curricular model also meant huge adjustments in thinking on the part of administrators, teachers, and especially parents. When Seeley visited the school several years after it opened, his impression was that in spite of all the theory and ideology from the College for Human Services, much of the teaching was still being done by public school teachers in the same way they had been doing it previously. "It's not easy to change people's habits and ideas," he noted. To do so one would need more power than either the college, "or for that matter, Alvarado had," to shift old staff out and hire new people who were committed to and conversant with the new educational model.[41]

Undaunted by the lackluster success of the East Harlem junior high school, Cohen persevered in her effort to create College for Human Services high schools in New York City. In 1985 Tom Webber had run for the city council but had lost and was looking for employment. Cohen invited him to the Harvard Club for lunch and asked him to become a dean of special programs in charge of efforts in New York City to have the College for Human Services model adopted by high schools.[42] Some progress was made in getting the project started, but the job was only part time, and when Webber was recruited to become the head of the Edwin Gould Academy, he had to move on.

Cohen's hopes did not fade. Before Webber left she pulled Clyde Griffin out of his teaching roles and asked him to work on developing the human services model in New York City schools. One positive outcome of the ongoing local effort was the recognition that a Constructive Action could be performed by groups as well as individually. The teenagers at the junior high school and later at the two high schools affiliated with the college were able to contribute constructively in their communities by working with the elderly or helping out in daycare centers, police precincts, hospitals, libraries, and small businesses.[43] But doing the Constructive Action and its documentation proved to be too challenging for the children to undertake alone. The College for Human Services team then experimented with having the students work on a Constructive Action as a group. At first Cohen herself was skeptical of the idea, but when Griffin invited her to attend one of the schools' Group Constructive Action Days, she was persuaded. Perhaps with children you *had* to have them work in groups.[44]

The concept of a Constructive Action as a group project opened up new possibilities for adapting the model to elementary and secondary schools. Although some members of the faculty were skeptical of a plan that would divert resources and attention away from the college's Manhattan campus, Cohen pushed forward.[45] By now Janith Jordan had become vice president, and her background as a high school teacher in Michigan made her a useful ally in promoting the idea. She began developing curricula based on the model that could be used throughout a system—from kindergarten through 12th grade. In 1989 the college secured a $1,000,000 grant from the Hasbro Children's Foundation that enabled the college to collaborate with schools in San Diego, California; Phoenix, Arizona; Hollandale, Mississippi; and Pensacola, Florida. For the next fifteen years Jordan was the member of the college's staff who was most closely involved with what was loosely referred to as the Schools Project.

Jordan had been a part of Cohen's team since its early years. She had been hired to join the Women's Talent Corps in 1968, had helped draft the application to the New York State department of education for AA degree–granting authority in 1970, and was an active participant in the development of the college's unique curricular grid in 1973 to 1974.[46] Her graduate training and her teaching experience in the early 1960s had given her a solid foundation in elementary and secondary education, and when the college began reaching out to adapt its model to classrooms and schools across the city and nation, she became Cohen's main organizer and spokesperson for the effort.

The schools project in Mississippi was particularly successful. When the College for Human Services first became involved with the Mississippi Delta school, it had been one of the lowest performing schools in the state; after five years of working with the college's model it had become the top school in Mississippi. A story soon circulated around the college that when Senator Trent Lott was giving Jan Jordan an award on behalf of the college's achievements, his remark was, "It's a very wonderful program; it's just a shame that the Yankees had to bring it!"[47]

From 1987 to 1989 Clyde Griffin was put in charge of implementing the College for Human Services model in an elementary school in Pensacola, Florida. Although the college hoped to involve whole schools, Griffin was at first only able to work with the sixth-grade classroom teachers. Using what he had learned from his work in the East Harlem school and collaborating with administrators and parents as well as teachers, he was able to make progress. In those years Florida was one of the first states to start implementing more rigorous state standards for education, and when the standards came in, Griffin remembers, "those teachers just froze,"[48] but eventually they learned how to work well with the standards.

Soon after Griffin had set up the program and classes were proceeding as planned, there was talk of expanding from the sixth grade into a whole school. At this point the superintendent wanted to meet with Cohen herself, so she traveled down to Pensacola to visit the new educational venture. After meeting with Cohen, the teachers told Griffin that they were surprised that she was so small, for "her ideas are so big!"[49] In Pensacola they had also expected a firebrand, but that wasn't Cohen's style at all. Cohen was a quiet presence physically, Griffin noted, and he made the same comment that John Rodgers made on meeting her in Morocco more than thirty years previously. "She was soft-spoken. Her ardent vision and passion came from within."[50]

Griffin came to know Cohen well in those years as they frequently traveled together. On their first plane trip to Florida he was about to follow his usual habit of dozing off during the flight, but she gave him a nudge. "No, no, Clyde. We can't sleep. We've got work to do." Early on she told him that there was one thing she would insist on, "and that is absolute loyalty." At first he was shocked by the request ("Oh my God, is this the Mafia or something?"), but ended up always giving her that loyalty. He also came to understand some of her more compulsive habits. Often she was a little late in meeting him in the hotel lobby, and he later learned from her husband that she was obsessive about germs. She traveled with a small bottle of Clorox and would scrub down the bathroom of hotel rooms before using them, which, added Clyde (demonstrating his loyalty) "is a very good idea, you know, if you do that much traveling."[51] Cohen's strong work ethic, her need for loyalty, and her compulsiveness were qualities that Griffin respected.

Griffin also believed that there were reasons behind Cohen's controlling style of leadership. Cohen felt that she had gotten burned in the past, he said, and that people had taken her ideas and not given her credit for them. She once had told him that in education, particularly, "people steal." She felt that she had not received adequate recognition for her work, especially the work she had done with the paraprofessional movement in the 1960s. In dicussing Cohen's need to control both the vocabulary and the conceptual framework for the college, Griffin defended her. "She had her reasons for working that way." Griffin later suggested that Cohen's possessiveness may have been justified, for in recent years some of the terms that the college invented, like Purpose-Centered Education, have been appropriated by other institutions with no attribution or acknowledgement.[52]

Griffin's understanding of the source of Cohen's need for control did not prevent occasional frustrations. One night around 10 P.M. he was alone in a hotel room in Florida about to go to sleep when he received a phone call from Janith Jordan in New York. Jordan was calling to ask him about a word change on the contract that he was scheduled to get teachers to sign the next day, laying out the conditions for working with the college. "Clyde, on page 13 it says 'only.' You have got to change that to 'solely,' *now*. So I want you to get some White-Out and make the change."

"No, I'm not going to do that," Clyde sleepily replied. "That's ridiculous. 'Only' is the same as 'solely.' I won't do it," and he turned out the light and tried to go to sleep.

But around midnight the phone rang again. "Clyde . . ." (and here Griffin imitated a soft, female, singsong voice). This time it was Audrey calling to ask him to change the wording. "Oh my God, it's the president, so I've got to do this," thought Griffin, and got out of bed. He ended up walking around the darkened city of Pensacola until he found some correction fluid—all for the purpose of changing the word "only" to the word "solely" on a document that would be signed by a few sixth-grade school teachers the next day.[53]

Like Tom Webber before him, Griffin's involvement in the schools project was short lived, and he, too, was temporarily drawn away from the College for Human Services to work at the Edwin Gould Academy. Today he admits that he doesn't know what eventually happened to the Pensacola school.[54] But Jordan and Cohen persisted in bringing the schools project to fruition. At a March 19, 1991, meeting of the Board of Trustees Jordan reported that the college was working in eleven public elementary schools around the city and that she and Cohen were reaching out to more schools in San Diego, Chicago, and Phoenix.[55]

In 1991 a friend of Ralph Wharton, Cohen's second husband, had been planning to attend an announcement by President George H.W. Bush about a new education initiative. At the last minute the friend was unable to attend the White House event and, at Wharton's suggestion, arranged to have Cohen take his place.[56] The announcement was about the creation of the New American Schools Development Corporation (NASDC, later shortened to New American Schools, or NAS), a nonprofit organization funded by the Annenberg Foundation to support the design and dissemination of school reform models. According to President Bush, NASDC was a major step toward an education revolution that would seek nothing less than "a new generation of schools."[57]

Cohen leaped at the chance to be part of the NAS initiative, and she and her colleagues set to work writing up a proposal for the multi-million dollar grant. They knew that the odds for getting the grant were slim—more than 600 proposals were submitted and only eleven would be selected—but they summoned their energies for the cause. Alida Mesrop recalled the moment when, on Wednesday, July 8, 1992, Cohen received the news that she had received the grant:

> Audrey and I were talking. It was quite late in the afternoon and there was still no phone call from Washington, and Audrey was steeling herself for a major disappointment. It was a little past five, and if a call was coming it was reasonable to assume that it would already have come.
>
> Audrey was more pessimistic than I was. It was unusual enough that she was at all pessimistic, or maybe I was just whistling in the dark. Perhaps I felt a little more confident because I knew how absolutely and meticulously I had attended to and overseen every discussion that followed the proposal writing workshops sponsored by NASDC. . . . After all, it was based on ideas we have been thinking about and trying out for more than twenty five years. . . .
>
> Although we were bracing ourselves for disappointment, it is not either Audrey's way or mine to do much brooding. So we both got back to more mundane details, since we had not touched base with each other for a few days, and after a few minutes I trotted back to my office. I no sooner settled down when Sarah Jo telephoned. "Audrey would like you to come to her office." I was a little miffed. I had gone over my agenda. What had *she* forgotten to discuss that couldn't wait?
>
> But back I went. It was now a little past five. Jan was already there, signaling madly and mouthing, "She's talking to Washington." Deborah was summoned from her office. Sylvia Hack passed by and joined the gang. And we were all openly eavesdropping, picking up whatever clues we could from the one-sided conversation. Audrey was formal and business-like, asking questions that could have been reconstructed as

responses to almost any kind of information, and taking notes. "Three? . . . How many others? . . . Oh, I see. Yes. Thank you that is exciting news."

Down went the receiver and up went a joyous whoop. "We've got it!" And that was the end of the cool dead-panning. Sarah Jo produced a bottle of champagne . . . warm.

As Dellie Bloom summarizes, "This was a rare assemblage: a victory team of women, pulled together by a woman with a vision, that had been working together for nearly twenty-five years."[58]

The New American Schools grant was for $4.65 million to be used through June 1996. With the grant the college was able to collaborate with two additional schools in San Diego and five schools in Miami, so that by 1995 thirteen schools in five states were using the Purpose-Centered model.[59] In *Bold Plans for School Restructuring: The New American Schools Designs* Cohen and Jordan wrote a chapter describing how the college's unique model of Purposes, Dimensions, and Constructive Actions was being implemented in selected schools. The chapter is a longer version of an article that Cohen wrote for the June 1993 issue of *Phi Delta Kappan* entitled "A New Educational Paradigm."[60]

Like Cohen's earlier articles on the college's curricular model, the chapter begins with a reference to the economic context that made a new educational paradigm necessary and then launches into a description of the curriculum and examples of the kinds of learning that the structure promotes. The essay documents fourth and fifth graders busily engaged in collective Constructive Actions in their communities. In a fourth-grade classroom, for example, where the fall semester's Purpose was *We Work for Better Health*, the children studied and mapped out the structure of their own bodies, learned about nutrition, explored nutrition and health care in different cultures and historical periods and invited community health care professionals to visit their classroom. They learned how to use stethoscopes, visited local health facilities, and explored the history of health care. They wrote poems and songs about health issues, and surveyed visitors on their health. The description of active learning experiences is extensive and ends with the main point that the children were learning a great deal of knowledge and developing oral and writing abilities, "all in the process of doing something beneficial for the community."[61] Although there is no mention of John Dewey in the report, the activities-based curriculum that Cohen and Jordan describe reads as an updated version of the curriculum that Dewey helped develop at the Laboratory School of the University of Chicago in the 1890s and that has since become a paradigmatic example of progressive education.[62]

AUDREY COHEN COLLEGE

In the final section of their chapter in *Bold Plans for School Restructuring* Cohen and Jordan summarized the schools project's substantial achievements. Nearly 20,000 children nationwide were being educated in schools using the college's Purpose-Centered system of education, they reported, and they predicted that given its success and the ongoing support of the NAS initiative, the use of its system would continue to grow in an "exponential" manner. In terms of their own college's expansion, the authors state that they are planning to establish a school of education that will prepare prospective teachers for its Purpose-Centered system and that will support a further proliferation of the model. As the college looks toward the future, the authors conclude, its pledge to contribute to the transformation of elementary and secondary education is shaped by "its past experience and the wisdom that past experience offers."[63]

The College for Human Services' long-term experience with educational innovation was lauded in the final chapter of *Bold Plans*, which contained an objective assessment of the NAS curricular designs. Written at the end of the grant period by a RAND corporation researcher, the report calculated the extent to which the NAS projects met several criteria of effectiveness. Across almost all of the categories of the evaluation, Audrey Cohen's project merited first or second place. (The college's project is referred to as "AC" in the report, an abbreviation for "The Audrey Cohen College System of Education: Purpose-Centered Education"—the name it was given on the design plan.) In terms of the team's readiness to interact effectively with existing school organizations, to take responsibility for further curricular development, to begin with a fully worked-out design, to make progress toward goals indicated by the design—in almost every category, the project initiated by Cohen and her staff is mentioned as being among those that had the most positive outcomes. Later on in the report the college is singled out as one of the two teams that provided the greatest amount of "team specification and development" and therefore that showed the most "substantial progress toward demonstration."[64]

Audrey Cohen may have never seen the RAND Corporation's assessment of her college's success with the New American Schools project. Early in 1992 she had been diagnosed with ovarian cancer, and throughout the early- to mid-1990s she secretly struggled to conquer her illness. The RAND report was published in 1996; by March 10, 1996, Cohen had succumbed to the disease. Tragically she may never have known the extent to which her dreams for spreading the word about Purpose-Centered Education had won the respect even of RAND corporation assessors.

Cohen's final illness is the focus of the next section. A source of satisfaction prior to her death was that the college she had founded came to bear her name. As with much else that she accomplished, however, the change of name from the College for Human Services to Audrey Cohen College was fraught with controversy, and once again she was accused of heavy-handedness and over-control.

In the spring of 1992 Cohen approached selected members of the college's Board of Trustees about renaming the College for Human Services.[65] By this point she knew that she had cancer, but she had not revealed the news to anyone except her daughters.[66] Cohen gave several persuasive arguments for changing the college's name. The term "human services" was by now being used by other institutions that focused solely on vocational training, which made fund-raising in the private sector difficult. In addition, the college's outreach into elementary and secondary schools made the term too narrow for the institution's full scope. After only minimal opposition, the board voted to rename the institution after its founder.

On May 8, 1992, the staff and faculty were summoned for a special announcement by Cohen herself. After reviewing the reasons for the name change, she told them that the Board of Trustees had unanimously recommended that the college be renamed Audrey Cohen College. There was an audible gasp of surprise from the audience, and an enthusiastic round of applause.[67] Cohen's speech then continued with a review of the college's past twenty-seven-year history, its struggles and achievements. The board had looked at the work that she had done, she said, starting in 1964 and for the next two years working "pretty much alone," to get people to listen to her original ideas about opening up new kinds of jobs and designing an education that prepared people for those jobs. "It pays to persevere and fight for what you believe in. That is what the board is now honoring—some of that long struggle." She then reminded the audience of their own roles in creating the college's novel curriculum. Many of those in this room, she said, were part of the process of rethinking what would be a truly unique educational experience, where students could focus on a purpose, relate knowledge to that purpose, and then help people do constructive actions in the world outside the classroom. Returning to the college's change of name, she ended her speech with a rousing appeal to the women in the audience. "There are so few women's names on colleges today. We need to see women take leadership positions, be CEOs, and build really good institutions, as we have here at the college."[68] There was another round of applause, followed by a gracious endorsement by Kalu Kalu, now distinguished as the most senior member of the faculty.

Although the meeting had an air of spontaneity, it was clear that it had been carefully orchestrated. "No one who was familiar with the way that Audrey worked would be surprised at the careful groundwork, the sounding out, the lining up of support," Dellie Bloom observed. The public affairs officer, undoubtedly informed of the news beforehand, had been the first to lead the applause, and Kalu's remarks were too smooth to be spontaneous. Notwithstanding the careful preparation, there was grumbling both about the choice of the name and about the lack of discussion of it with faculty and students beforehand. A few members of the faculty saw the name change as the epitome of Cohen's quest for self-promotion. In general, however, most of those in the audience that day admired the fact that she could manage what could have been an embarrassment—the awkwardness of the recipient of honor being the one to announce the honor being bestowed—with charm and grace and a few tears, which were clearly unrehearsed.[69]

By the following Monday morning, the greeting on the computer screens read "Welcome to Audrey Cohen College." Within a few weeks telephone greetings were recorded; news releases were ready for the press; letters to agencies, government offices, and alumni were sent out; and advertisements for Audrey Cohen College began appearing in subway stations and bus stops throughout the city. Cohen finally knew that no matter what happened to her physically, her life's work would live on, with her name attached to it.

HER FINAL BATTLE

The archives of the college that Cohen founded contain no record of the battle with the cancer that led to her death at the relatively early age of sixty-four. Interviews with friends and family members provide conflicting information about when exactly she was first diagnosed. Her close friend since childhood, Elaine Azen-Lampl, remembers that at one point Cohen had a hysterectomy but chose to have only one ovary removed; this, Azen-Lampl speculates, was a factor in the growth of the cancer in the other ovary.[70] Ralph Wharton remembers the diagnosis coming only six months after their marriage in 1988 and Cohen being very secretive about it.[71] Cohen's two daughters are certain that their mother found out about the cancer in February 1992, Wendy remembering specifically that the diagnosis came a week before her own second child was born.[72]

Although those close to Cohen disagree about when she was diagnosed with the disease, all those who knew her during her illness concur in remembering the dauntless courage with which she fought it. Alida Mesrop remembers Cohen sailing through her first round of chemotherapy, but then having a relapse a few years later. Mesrop herself gave blood several times to support Cohen's needed transfusions.[73] Ralph Wharton, himself a doctor, marveled at the persistence with which she pursued alternative treatments, even at one point traveling to Texas for a procedure that he believed was useless. Despite her illness, Ralph's and Audrey's life was not without its light moments. They both loved to travel and managed to fit in trips to Spain, Canada, Mexico, and Haiti.[74] Throughout these years she kept news of the illness even from her closest associates. Laura Pires-Hester remembers sharing a cab with Cohen and noticing that she was wearing a wig but never being told what she was going through.[75]

Cohen's difficulties in relating to her daughter Dawn continued up until Cohen's death. Dawn remembers one hurtful visit shortly after the birth of her third child, Epi, in late May 1993. Cohen was traveling to the West Coast to check on progress at the college's Oakland campus and called Dawn to suggest that they meet at a spa. Dawn was in no mood for a spa. "I've just given birth, Mom. I'm one day postpartum." Cohen and Wharton, who was traveling with her, agreed to meet Dawn at a restaurant instead. At one point Dawn disappeared into a bathroom to take care of the newborn baby and herself ("you know what postpartum mothers are like—every part of you is oozing something"). After a few minutes Cohen stomped into the bathroom. "Where are you? Our meal is getting cold!" Dawn's response was, 'Mom, I just had a baby. Look at your grandchild. Get all excited, please." She could be incredibly warm, Dawn continued, "and the grandma that you yourself wish you had," but Dawn felt that the feeling didn't last. "She always had larger goals." Dawn is grateful for her mother's message to keep her eyes on large goals, but another implicit message came along with it: "The other message that I got from watching my mother was, 'Remember who you're leaving in your wake as you go pursue those goals.' "[76]

As had been the pattern for many years, Wendy, who continued to live in New York and by now also had children of her own, remained close to her mother during this time. Wendy and her daughter Sarah, who had been born the same week that Audrey Cohen had had her first surgery, visited regularly, often joining her for lunch. Even though Audrey was often quite ill on these occasions, Wendy's memories are upbeat. She remembers that only a day after one chemotherapy treatment her mother went roller-blading in Central Park. Another time her mother was very weak, could hardly walk, and needed a transfusion but wanted to do some shopping first. So Wendy carefully escorted her to Bloomingdales, walking very slowly. Once inside the store they were looking around, and suddenly Wendy noticed that her mother had disappeared. She finally spotted her walking energetically toward the other side of the floor. When Wendy caught up with her she told her mom, "You don't need blood, you need Bloomingdales!"[77]

Another bittersweet incident again involved Sarah, who by now was three or four years old. Whenever Sarah came to visit she loved playing with her grandmother's jewelry. On one visit, when she went over to the dressing table to find her favorite necklaces, she saw a wig that Audrey had been wearing to hide the fact that she had lost her hair as a result of the chemotherapy. Later at lunch Sarah turned to her grandmother and, tugging at her own pigtails, said, "You know, Grandma Audrey, my hair doesn't come off." Cohen was nonplussed. "That's good, Sarah. Mine does."[78]

With her awareness of her own mortality, Cohen seems to have tried to hold on ever more tightly to the detailed operations of the college. Her trademarking of the college's special terminology, her close oversight of curriculum, and her grandiose hopes for institutional growth were aspects of her leadership style that some people found difficult even in the college's early years. But from 1992 until her death in 1996, the need for control often escalated to the point of becoming counterproductive.

An example of Cohen's growing possessiveness was evident in one exchange at a Board of Trustees meeting in August 1994. Marie Kessel, who had been a loyal member of the board for many years and had contributed major funding to develop the library's computer system, asked if Bill Gates, of the then relatively new Microsoft Corporation, had been approached for money. In response Cohen explained that the college had "applied for a patent and until it is granted we should not share our ideas with any corporations." She went on to say that "all the college's words and phrases are trademarked and/or copyrighted, and that these protections shield us from plagiarism." Kessel then pointed to the irony that the college was both proselytizing its ideas and also protecting its ideas from being disseminated. At this point in the discussion Janith Jordan interceded to support Cohen in what might have become an embarrassing argument. The New American Schools Corporation is supporting the college's need to protect its ideas, Jordan claimed, but then she, too, made a troubling assertion: "We will probably charge a licensing fee as new schools adapt our designs."[79] Here both Cohen and Jordan were exhibiting an overprotectiveness with regard to the college's curricular model that in the long run did not serve the institution well.

Cohen's increasing need for control during these years was also evident in her micromanaging of the college's development office. Three different directors of development were hired in the early 1990s, and none of them could tolerate Cohen's or Jordan's leadership style. Betty Leffert, the first development officer who was hired, criticized the poor communication, roadblocks, and "tethered" quality of the job and resigned after a few months. Mark Wille, who also lasted less than a year, was similarly critical of the way he was treated. Cohen, he said, was "totally inaccessible." Meetings with her, when they could be arranged were hasty and inconclusive, and yet even a routine thank you note needed Cohen's approval. He felt stymied: the way he was treated, he commented, seemed calculated to make a professional feel "like a three-year-old." He was thwarted in his attempts to cultivate the personal contacts that would lead to a useful fundraising network. "There is no point in a development officer if you're going to keep him or her attached to your apron strings," he concluded.[80]

Leffert's and Wille's accounts are echoed by Annie LaRock, another professional fundraiser who was hired in 1995. Like Wille, LaRock felt stymied by the hurdles that Cohen and Jordan set up. As part of what she assumed to be her job she made appointments with members of the Board of Trustees to talk about their views of the college and suggestions for fundraising. But Cohen interceded. "You don't need to be going out to talk to board members. You are to stay in your office and raise money." "You don't sit in an office and raise money, Audrey!" LaRock countered.[81] Her protests had little effect. The atmosphere became difficult, she said, and she immediately began looking for another job.

An article about Cohen that appeared in the popular journal *Education Week* in the winter of 1995 also gives hints of Cohen's increasing need to hang on. Entitled "The Outsider: Breaking the Mold," the article gives credit to Cohen for creating a curricular structure that worked well both at the college level and also in the larger realm of elementary and secondary schools across the country. Cohen's design for Purpose-Centered Education, the author suggests, may just well be "the shape of schools to come," and he devotes much of the article to positive comments made by administrators, parents, and teachers in two of the schools that for a while adopted the model. On the final page, however, the author states that Cohen was fiercely territorial—"some observers would say paranoid"—about her project, and that she almost forfeited the grant because of copyright issues concerning the college's terminology. The author notes that during the interview Cohen even seemed wary of the media, turning down the reporter's request to use a tape recorder. "She's got a winner," the author concludes, but "can she delegate? Can she let go? Or will she be like Gepetto [the creator of Pinocchio], having to have control?"[82] Accompanying the article is a photo of Cohen standing alone in a wood-paneled hallway of the Lotos Club. Her face is gaunt and drawn, and her pearls hang straight down her thin, frail frame. It is one of the last photos taken of her.

As Cohen's cancer spread and her futile attempts to treat it increased, she spent less and less time at the college and relied on Mesrop and Jordan to take her place. Crookendale remembers noting that her dynamic presence suddenly "wasn't there."[83] In January of 1996 the college moved from 345 Hudson Street into its present quarters at 75 Varick Street. Cohen attended a Board of Trustees meeting in the new surroundings but did not have her usual energy. Although a president's office with a sweeping view of lower Manhattan had been planned for her, she only was in it for one day. In the early months of 1996 her health rapidly declined.

Cohen died at home on March 10, 1996. A memorial service was held at the Temple Emanu-El on Fifth Avenue, and students, faculty, trustees, staff, agency supervisors, friends, and family members filled the huge, impressive space. Close associates spoke passionately of her vision, family members recalled fond adventures, and students quietly wept. Bill Tatum, publisher of the *Amsterdam News* and a friend of Cohen's for many years, spoke about how women of color had been lifted from one status to another as a consequence of the educational model that Cohen's work had provided.[84] Alida Mesrop recalled the years when she and Audrey had met near the fountain in Stuyvesant Town, where they both lived at the time. "Life with Audrey was never dull," Mesrop summed up. Cohen's work to make the world a better place through public policy and educational leadership grew out of her civil rights experiences, her deep interest in feminism, and a lifelong passion to change education so that it worked. "And she did it."[85]

Letters and condolences poured in to Alida Mesrop, who the board had designated as the new interim president. Dodie Younger, who had been a coordinator trainer for the Women's Talent Corps, wrote that she had heard the news about Audrey's illness from Laura Pires-Hester but had not known that the ending was so near. She expressed faith in Alida Mesrop's ability to "pick up the reins" of the institution in Cohen's absence. Dellie Bloom, who herself would die of cancer in the next decade, wrote about missing Cohen's "spunk, her vision, and her chutzpah," but also expressed confidence in the team that Cohen had built over the years, ever since those "early lavender-kitchen meetings" in the 1960s. Another lifelong associate and loyal friend, Jane Addams Caulfield, wrote that she had always had "boundless regard" for Cohen's energy and visions. On letterhead from the City of New York Office of the President of the Borough of Manhattan came a letter from Ruth Messinger, who would be soon running for mayor. "I trust you will let the staff and board know how much I treasure the years I worked for the college and the impact which Audrey had on me," Messinger wrote, and included a personal check for the college's scholarship fund.[86]

A powerful source of educational vision and empowerment was gone. "Despite her diminutive and seemingly frail stature," the *New York Times* obituary stated, Ms. Cohen was "a powerhouse of energy when scorning the rigidity and failures of the contemporary educational system and proposing how to reform it." Her central idea, the obituary continued, was that education must never be abstract but must be linked to clearly understood purposes. This idea attracted wide interest, "especially to institutions serving members of minority groups, immigrants, and the disadvantaged seeking access to the mainstream of American society."[87] Audrey Cohen's lifelong purpose had been fulfilled.

In the years since Audrey Cohen's death, Dawn Cohen Margolin has become reconciled with her mother's shortcomings as a parent. "I get it now, what it feels like to be torn between loving your work and wanting to be with your kids." Dawn also recognizes how much of her own strengths come from her mother. As a leader in her community and as the founder of a neighborhood exercise program called Kindergym that brings together mothers and their toddlers from a wide circle of families, Dawn now sees that many of her most positive qualities come from her mother. It is a pity, Dawn admits "that we did not figure this out in her lifetime, because we had so much in common." But, like many other strong-willed children, she knows that she had to take a circuitous route to discover what her mother had to teach her. Although it was a struggle to be the daughter of someone who was always so determined to make a difference in the world, Dawn, like Wendy, now has "nothing but pride" for her mother.[88]

CHAPTER 12

MCNY IN THE NEW MILLENNIUM (2000–2014)

Empowerment is the ability of people to manage their lives, to recognize and meet their needs, and to fulfill their potential as creative, responsible, and productive members of society.

—Cohen, 1981, p. 514

Like a predicted blizzard that fails to materialize, the much-heralded third millennium came and went without any significant effect on American daily life. By the morning of January 1, 2000, the nation's computerized databases had been carefully resynchronized, spreadsheets were updated, and the New York City subway system, which had always operated on a paper-and-pencil system anyway, ran on time with no interruptions. What had been anxiously dubbed "Y2K" and anticipated with trepidation for several years, turned out to be just a typical New Year's Day, followed by business as usual.

The event that more traumatically marked the beginning of a new era in United States history occurred over a year and a half later, on the calm morning of September 11, 2001, when nineteen terrorists hijacked four aircraft and aimed them at the two towers of the World Trade Center, the Pentagon, and in a failed attempt, the U.S. Capitol. What followed was a world-changing moment that most people alive on that day remember with acute clarity, even if its long-term import was not immediately apparent. Steven Cresap remembers coming up out of the Canal Street subway station on his way to teach a class at MCNY and seeing one of the World

Trade Center towers, just ten blocks away, in flames. Recalling an earlier attempt to bomb the building, his first thought was, "That thing hasn't had any luck at all!" When he arrived in the south-facing classroom on the twelfth floor of 431 Canal Street, students were standing by the window, watching in horror as the second plane hit the other tower. Cresap told the students to move away from the window. An announcement to evacuate the building came over the loud speaker, but the students first insisted on signing the attendance sheet for that day's class.[1]

Over all of lower Manhattan the smell of smoke lingered in the air for many days, and, like most other businesses in the area, the college was closed for a week. MCNY's president at the time, Stephen Greenwald, predicted that the fear generated by the terrorist attack would keep students away from the Manhattan campus, and that the branch campuses in the Bronx, Queens, and Staten Island would increase their enrollments, at least for the foreseeable future. This prediction, though logical at the time, failed to materialize. Although one student who worked in the World Trade Center was killed in the attack and many others were deeply affected by it, the Manhattan site's premises were soon bustling with students once again.

Over the next decade, threats to the college's survival would come more from internal errors in leadership than from deliberate external attacks. In piecing together the history of the college in the first years of the twenty-first century, however, due recognition must be given to the economic and political forces that the college's leadership was faced with. Unprecedented competition for adult students was now appearing from for-profit, vocationally oriented schools like Monroe, TCI, the University of Phoenix, and De Vry. In a parallel development, the colleges that had previously emphasized humanistic learning began losing ground to those emphasizing business and technology. President George W. Bush's advice to Americans to "go shopping" after the 9/11 attacks marked a heightened preoccupation with consumerism that dominated both discourse and daily life. As a consequence of these and other trends, the link between empowerment and service on which Audrey Cohen had staked her college's future became, for many young people, less compelling than the link between the media and marketing. How the college survived these and other challenges during the first decade of the new millennium is the focus of what follows.

TRANSITION

One faculty member has referred to the years between 1996 and 1999 as the college's "quiet years."[2] Alida Mesrop was appointed interim president just prior to Cohen's death in 1996, and under her leadership enrollment continued to grow, the budget was carefully monitored, and the college hummed along smoothly and efficiently.[3] Although the elementary and secondary public schools project that Cohen and Jordan so carefully developed soon gradually faded into the background when the NAS grant ran out, the college's institutional outreach to welfare centers and to a wide range of human service agencies brought a steady flow of new students to the college's New York campuses and provided ongoing internships for those already enrolled. One of Mesrop's most fruitful initiatives was to establish a welfare-to-work program (later retitled welfare-to-careers) in conjunction with Pace University and Medgar Evers College. Initially funded by the New York Community Trust, the program served the college and its students for the next two decades.[4] Ads for the college in city subway trains showing white-on-black quotes from George Eliot's *Middlemarch* ("It is never too late to be what you might have been") attracted adult learners seeking a new purpose for their lives.[5] A student newsletter, *The Crystallizer*, appeared regularly and was edited by the Student Services Office under the direction of Dona Sosa, an alumna of the college. The newsletter contained news of college events and profiles of faculty, and, most importantly, became a forum for budding writers. A survey of *The Crystallizer* during these years gives ample evidence of adult students who never expected to attend college finding an educational niche in which they could study and thrive.

For the faculty, too, the late 1990s were years of relative stability. A new dean, Shirley Conyard, had a background in both teaching and social work and provided guidance for the Purpose seminars but otherwise let the faculty implement the college's curricular model with little interference from the administration. Most of the academic maintenance work was undertaken by faculty teams (headed by a team leader) that met once a month to update assigned texts, discuss individual students, and coordinate course offerings. Team meetings enabled the full-time faculty to learn what their students were being exposed to longitudinally (i.e., from one semester to the next) as well as latitudinally (across the different dimensions of each semester). Faculty members were expected to teach all three semesters each year, but because each semester was only fourteen weeks long, everyone was off for most of August. There were no expectations for faculty to publish or do research, although a few faculty did request, and receive, an occasional sabbatical leave for special projects. Nor was there any ranking of the faculty. It had been Cohen's dictum that everyone teaching at the college was a "professor," and under Mesrop that title was maintained.

The quiet years came to an end when Stephen Greenwald became president of Audrey Cohen College in the summer of 1999. At first the faculty welcomed the change. A loyal member of Cohen's Board of Trustees for many years, Greenwald had graduated at the top of his class from NYU Law School, worked as a lawyer in the film business, successfully represented defendants facing the death penalty, and was interested in expanding the college to include cutting-edge programs such as media management and health advocacy.[6] He had even taught a few courses as an adjunct in the master's of public administration program. Those who were acquainted with Greenwald found him smart, friendly, and well intended. The fact that he himself had been a member of the presidential search committee that recommended him raised some eyebrows, but in general the faculty was glad to have a president who was familiar with the college and who had an advanced degree.

At his first meeting with the faculty in the fall of 1999, Greenwald made clear that his leadership style would be quite different from his predecessors'. To distinguish himself from Cohen's notoriously autocratic stance, Greenwald encouraged the faculty to constitute itself as self-governing body with officers, committees, and advisory powers relating to curriculum and teaching. He also announced that although he was a firm believer in the college's Purpose-Centered curricular model, he did not assume the model to be "written in stone" and felt that it might be adjusted to meet new needs or new circumstances.[7] Although both of these policy announcements were initially welcomed, over the next seven years Greenwald's attempt to make both the faculty and the college's curriculum conform to more conventional academic practices caused growing discord.

A decision that soon became problematic was the hiring of a new provost and a new dean who had little understanding of the college's curricular model or its grounding in human services. The provost's background was in engineering, and the dean's background was in the liberal arts and business. With the somewhat reluctant approval of the newly formed Faculty Council, the new provost instituted a system of faculty tracking and ranking. Faculty members who opted for the scholarship track were granted a leave every third semester to pursue scholarly work, but they had to maintain a solid record of publishing to maintain that status. Faculty who were not interested in pursuing a scholarship agenda could remain on the teaching track, which, because the semesters were now extended to fifteen weeks, meant having only a two-week break between the summer and fall semesters. Eventually all but one full-time faculty member opted for the scholarship track.

The provost's push to institute faculty ranking involved another major shift in the college's academic culture.[8] Along with the new system came the need to determine the qualifications needed for each rank and a Faculty Status Committee to review applications for changes in rank. The implementation of both the tracking and the ranking systems required that the faculty submit to the dean detailed annual faculty development plans and self-assessment reports, all of which soon became sources of disgruntlement and contention. For faculty members with a multidisciplinary background like Vanda Wark and Theo Damian, the system became particularly onerous. The requirement to fit academic credentials and scholarly output within the same narrow box made what had previously been a source of strength in their credentials (given the unorthodox structure of the college's curriculum) a liability. Several faculty members who had been popular with students but who felt that the new emphasis on research betrayed the college's original mission resigned from the college at this time.

With the new faculty status arrangements resembling those at traditional research universities came other structural changes. The team structure that had provided curricular coherence under Cohen's and Mesrop's presidencies was eliminated, and in its place two administrative co-chairs were appointed to oversee the Human Services program. The staff of the office that had coordinated field placements for students in human service agencies was also drastically reduced, the office itself moving "from a large, fully staffed office to a closet," as one long-term associate of the college described the change.[9] The Schools Project, which had already begun to shrink when the funding ended in the late 1990s, was relegated to a small office at the end of a hallway, where Jan Jordan continued to work without any support from the new leadership. When Jan Jordan died in 2005, the office was discontinued and the whole project disappeared from the college's purview. Within the next few years, very little evidence of the project could be found in any of the schools in which it was piloted, except for one large high school in Miami Lakes, Florida, whose website continues to state that the school emphasizes "the importance of each individual's ability to take constructive action to benefit their community and society and make the world a better place"[10]—wording clearly borrowed from the lexicon of Audrey Cohen's educational vision.

Another administrative decision that was unsettling for many faculty members and students was the closing of the college's extension sites in the Bronx, Queens, and Staten Island. President Greenwald's decision was based on a number of factors. His visits to the centers made clear to him that they lacked essential services (no registrar, no student services office, no fully staffed libraries). Furthermore, most of the courses were taught by part-time faculty, and at the Queens and Staten Island sites the college rarely attracted the needed "critical mass" of students. The Bronx site was growing and was making money for the institution as a whole, but for Greenwald that was the problem. He told the board, "We're only making money in the Bronx because we're underserving the students in the Bronx," and that seemed to him untenable.[11] Some faculty members resented the phasing out of the extension sites and tried to convince the provost that the sites provided an important supplement to student enrollment. But these arguments were overruled.[12]

Even more momentous than the structural changes instituted by the new administration was the decision to change the college's name. Although many faculty members, students, and friends of the college believed that the college should be named after its founder and admired the fact that its founder had been a Jewish woman, some members of the board and President Greenwald felt differently. A firm hired by the college reported that from a marketing point of view the name was confusing: by just hearing the name on a survey people thought that Audrey Cohen College was a college for women only, for Jews only, or was a secretarial school of some sort.[13] After a year of focus groups led by a consulting firm, the name was changed to Metropolitan College of New York, easily shortened to the acronym MCNY—a blatant contrast to Cohen's aversion to acronyms.[14] As a concession to those still loyal to Cohen's legacy, the human services program was officially named the Audrey Cohen School of Human Services and Education, and the MCNY letterhead still includes, in small upper-case print, "FOUNDED BY AUDREY COHEN IN 1964."

Along with the unsettling changes came some new programs and initiatives that were of great benefit to the college and that have survived the test of time. Foremost among these was the creation of a master's of science in Childhood Education (MSED) program in 2004. Cohen and Jordan had begun thinking about such a program in the 1990s, and they had drafted a proposal to the New York State Department of Education (NYSED) for a teacher-training curriculum that would prepare professionals to implement a wider dissemination of the college's Purpose-Centered Education model in public elementary schools. Although Cohen and Jordan's vision of a completely new curricular structure for public education nationwide never materialized, the conceptual framework of the MSED program that was approved by the NYSED retains the progressive substance of Cohen's transformative educational vision. Each of the three semesters of the accelerated program has a *Purpose*, and all of its courses are developed as *Dimensions* of that Purpose. Teacher candidates begin working in the field on a *Constructive Action* (involving lesson planning, implementation, and assessment) as early as their second week in the program. Under the careful shepherding of Dr. Patrick Ianniello, a retired principal, the program has graduated nearly two hundred well-trained, state-certified teachers, many of whom have gone on to gain successful full-time employment in New York City's high needs elementary schools. In 2010 the program gained full accreditation by the highly respected National Council for Accreditation of Teacher Education (NCATE).

TROUBLES AT THE TOP

Other important programmatic innovations from the Greenwald years include the master's in business administration program (MBA), a master's in emergency and disaster management, and a bachelor of science in American urban studies (BAUS) program. In recognition of its unique integration of the humanities into its performance-based curriculum, MCNY became part of a "Greater Expectations" project sponsored by the American Association of Colleges and Universities (AAC&U), a national organization promoting liberal education for all. For the first five years of Greenwald's presidency the college's enrollment grew significantly, young PhDs with a wide range of research agendas joined the faculty, and the college offered an eclectic mix of educational programs.[15]

The college began to cultivate an international outreach as well. Supported by a Fulbright Fellowship, the college hosted for a year a prominent professor of educational psychology from the University of the Transkei in South Africa. As a capstone experience in the media management program, students traveled to Cannes, France, for the celebrated film festival. And early in 2002 members of the faculty and Board of Trustees made a trip to Malawi to sound out possibilities for an educational exchange—a venture that, due to political changes in Malawi, never led to further collaboration but that gave the college some publicity.

By 2005, however, troubling fissures began to appear among members of the Board of Trustees and between the administration and the faculty. As is often the case, the precipitating cause was financial. Enrollment started to shrink, possibly because of the eroding relationships with human services agencies but also because of the elimination of the extension sites and the departure of some of the more charismatic members of the faculty. At the same time, the board agreed to a major renovation effort to improve the college's first floor entrance and other areas. Paying for the renovation required a loan, which soon incurred a large debt, the first in the college's history. (Both Cohen and Mesrop had always been wary of incurring debt.[16]) As one member of the board remembers, "the ship started to sink because no one was really paying attention to the ever-increasing expenses and the shrinking enrollment. And when those two things meet, there's a recipe for disaster."[17]

One disaster was a proposal to sell the college to a for-profit educational enterprise. Concerned about the college's shaky financial situation, several members of the Board of Trustees in 2006 began making overtures to the Educational Management Corporation—a large operator of for-profit educational institutions based in Pittsburgh, Pennsylvania. (The company has since 2011 been the target of federal investigations and lawsuits alleging overzealous and inappropriate recruitment practices.[18]) The Cohens' old friend from Morocco days, John Rodgers, had become chair of the board and was against the sale, as was Bernadette Smith, an alumna of the College for Human Services who had gone to law school and had become a successful attorney and had joined the board in 1996. According to Smith, she and Rodgers found themselves on the defensive, at some points with nearly half the members of the board favoring the sale.[19]

Disputes also arose among board members about the more immediate handling of the college's finances. One board member accused Greenwald of failing to watch expenses and to carry through on his promises of increased enrollment. Heated back-and-forth communications ensued between college administrators and board members charging each other with lies, gratuitous statements, and "reckless allegations."[20] "These were very volatile board meetings," Smith recalled, fraught with angry attacks and accusations.[21]

The troubles multiplied. Although faculty members had no idea of what was transpiring on the board, they, too, were becoming extremely critical of Greenwald's leadership, particularly his apparent capitulation to the provost. Citing Middle States standards as his justification, the provost had begun to press the faculty to replace the college's integrated liberal arts/vocational curriculum with a traditional front-loaded liberal arts core curriculum. Declining enrollment and rumors of financial irresponsibility added to the faculty's growing sense that the president was not committed to the college's founding vision.

The faculty's mounting dissatisfaction culminated in a vote of no confidence in early 2007. Bill Birnbaum, a member of the board who had a strong background in education, came to speak to the Faculty Council to try to mediate. But the faculty dug in its heels. When Birnbaum saw that the situation had become untenable, he resigned from the board. "It was a dramatic resignation," Smith recalled. "He stood up at the end of the table, made an announcement in his deep baritone voice, shook his head, and walked out."[22]

With Birnbaum's resignation came the resignation of other trustees, and shortly after the faculty's vote of no confidence, Greenwald himself announced that he would resign. "So things were looking pretty bad," Smith says, "with the board shrinking, the president resigning, and rumors of a for-profit group lurking in the background."[23] By now Smith had been elected vice chair of the board, and she and Rodgers began having regular phone conversations about how to deal with the crisis. It became evident that the time had come to engage a search firm to seek an interim president who could take over the college until a full search for a new president had been completed.

The interim president from 2007 to 2008 was Joan Straumanis, whose savvy, down-to-earth leadership style brought the college back from the brink. "She cleaned house and she reorganized," and after consulting with an enrollment expert, hired a new director of enrollment. Soon the numbers of full-time students began climbing again and the college regained its financial balance. Some members of the board continued to argue for selling the college to a for-profit entity, however, and to counter those proposals required Rodgers' and Smith's ongoing efforts for several more years.[24]

Straumanis' contract stipulated that she could not be considered a candidate for the ongoing presidency of the college, so another search was set in motion. In 2008 the Board of Trustees selected Vinton Thompson as the college's fourth president. As a teacher and academic from the fields of evolution and entomology and an experienced administrator from Roosevelt University in Chicago and Kean University in New Jersey, Thompson was a good fit for the job. A new era for the college had begun.

PURPOSE-CENTERED EDUCATION IN THE LIVES OF RECENT STUDENTS

The welcome on MCNY's automatic telephone messaging system states that the college has been "transforming lives, one at a time, since 1964." In fact, colleges do not transform lives. Colleges provide the contexts for personal transformation, but the energy for such changes must come from within the individual. Nevertheless many of the students who have attended MCNY credit the college with transformative powers and claim that they would never have gotten a college education or a meaningful career without the institution that Audrey Cohen created. Even during the period of the college's administrative troubles in the early years of the twenty-first century, students continued to make effective use of the unique educational setting that the college provided. Many were the first in their families to graduate from college, many went on to graduate school, and many now are responsible for guiding others to pursue higher education and find meaningful work.

One student who credits MCNY with her own self-transformation is Loretta Robinson. Robinson dropped out of high school when she became pregnant in the eleventh grade, was a victim of domestic violence, and from her teen years into early adulthood was addicted to drugs and alcohol. By December 7, 2000, at the age of forty, she managed to break free of her addictions. She was living with her mother at the time, "sleeping on my mom's couch," and although she had held various clerical jobs, didn't know what she wanted to do with the rest of her life. Two of her children were living in a group home; the other two were adults living on their own.[25]

On the A train one day she saw an ad for what was then Audrey Cohen College. "A Fast Track to Your Future," read the ad. Robinson knew that she wanted to work in the human service field, so she took the admissions test, passed, and enrolled for evening classes. At that time, to be recovering from drug addiction counted as a disability, and she was paid to work in a state outpatient rehabilitation program during the day. She used her place of employment as her field placement and each semester completed Constructive Actions (e.g., setting up a new filing system for the agency, teaching basic math skills to teenagers) that gradually earned her a promotion. By her fifth semester she had gotten a job at Phoenix House that allowed her to focus on housing case management. Soon she was getting As in all of her courses. The college, "ignited a fire in me," she recalls.[26] She was chosen to be the speaker for her graduating class; on that day her mother, sister, children, and grandchildren were all in the audience to applaud her.

Robinson went on to earn a master's in public administration from MCNY, and she is now in the process of completing a PhD through Capella University, an online doctoral program. During the day she works as a supervisor of the housing program at Phoenix House. In the evenings she teaches as an adjunct at MCNY and is known to be a fair and competent instructor. She has recently married and owns a house New Jersey. She has fond memories of the courses she took with Steven Cresap, Anne Lopes ("I loved her!"), Clyde Griffin, Richard Grallo, Fentonie Cela (another alum of the college who became an adjunct), and Shirley Conyard. Because of Robinson's example (and nudging), her sister, children, and grandchildren have all attended or are attending college, several of them at MCNY. She attributes much of her success to what she learned through completing and documenting a Constructive Action each semester. "The CA has taught me how to look at problems strategically," she says.[27]

Daniel Gregoire's story is very different, but he, too, attributes the curve of his life's trajectory to the Purpose-Centered Education he received at MCNY. He grew up in a mostly Haitian community in Brooklyn, but when he was a teenager his parents divorced, and he shuttled back and forth between Brooklyn, where his father lived, and Brockton, Massachusetts, where his mother had moved. He enrolled in an architecture school in Boston for two years but became disillusioned with the profession and found himself drawn more to his church and community work. In the fall of 2003 he happened to see an ad for MCNY online and, thinking that it might be a good stepping-stone to law school, decided to apply.

His first semester was an eye opener. He was the youngest member of his cohort, and seeing his peers struggle with raising families while they were attending school was humbling. The theme of Purpose I is Self-Assessment and Preparation for Practice, and students are required to reflect on their past life and to assess their strengths and weaknesses as students and practitioners. Out of that self-assessment they develop a plan of action to improve an aspect of their behavior that will be useful for their future work. Gregoire remembers that in writing about his past he needed to describe his father, and when he and his classmates began talking about their families, the notion of *forgiveness* became the main topic of discussion. That semester's Purpose seminar and other courses nurtured habits of reflection that he continued to develop over the years.

Gregoire found the fieldwork required each semester at MCNY both interesting and gratifying. Over the years he worked in a range of internships—the Haitian-American Alliance, Safe Horizons Hotline, an Afro-centric after-school program for boys, the Coalition for Concerned Legal Professionals, the Administration for Children's Services, and, in his last semester, the United Nations Association of New York City (UNA-NYC). His CA goal that semester was to increase the interest and participation of young people in the UNA-NYC, and after graduating he continued to work for another year at the organization. When subsequently employed as a caseworker for the Administration for Children's Services he found that writing reports on children at risk drew on the same skills he had acquired at MCNY by writing CA documents. "Pieces of that process survive even today," he says, "especially when thinking about goals. The process is a part of who I am."[28]

In 2009 Gregoire decided that his true calling was with the Unitarian Universalist Church that he had been involved with on and off since his teenage years in Brockton. He enrolled in Union Theological Seminary where he found some of the same emotional pulls that he had felt at MCNY. "There, too, we looked at our social location and how that influences how we are in the world." He graduated in 2012 and completed his first year internship with a Unitarian Universalist Church in Maryland. Today he is on his way to leading his own congregation in Philadelphia and is optimistic about his future. "I'm a better person because of MCNY," he says firmly. He is grateful for its fostering of the "compassionate empowerment" that as a fledgling minister he is aiming to promote in his future work.[29]

In contrast to Gregoire's multidirectional search, Ethel Perez always knew that she wanted to be a social worker. She grew up in the South Bronx and did well in high school where she also played the saxophone in the school band. She went to work in the Southeast Bronx Neighborhood Center and was doing well but could not advance without a college degree. A case manager at her agency recommended MCNY, and in 2007 she enrolled. She enjoyed every Purpose, she claims, except Purpose V, which focuses on counseling. She found it very challenging at the time but now is grateful for the skills she learned.[30]

After graduating with a bachelor of professional services degree from MCNY, Perez was accepted into a master's of social work program at Hunter College. There, too, she excelled in her coursework, but in her last semester she was hit by a car and fractured her left leg in several places. She was in a cast for four months and had to complete her master's thesis at home, which her professor allowed because he trusted her honesty. At her Hunter graduation she marched down the aisle using a walker, and she still needed a cane when she returned to work the following fall. She passed the test to become a Licensed Clinical Social Worker (LCSW) and has been promoted at her agency. She hopes someday to come back to teach evening classes as an adjunct at MCNY.

Loretta Robinson, Daniel Gregoire, and Ethel Perez are among MCNY's more impressive recent graduates, but there are hundreds more.

Vesta Washington came from Saint Lucia to New York on someone else's passport to escape an abusive relationship. She worked in factories and later as a nanny to support her children. After enrolling in MCNY she made the dean's list every semester, completed her bachelor's degree in the human services program, and then went on to get her master's degree. Mutiya Vision was born with one foreshortened arm, wrote books about children with disabilities, has seven children of her own, and after completing the master's of science in childhood education program at MCNY opened her own private school in Brooklyn. Maria Martin began her college career at Boston University but missed her closely knit family and returned to New York. After doing clerical work at Mount Sinai Hospital for fourteen years, she enrolled in MCNY, and after graduating with a BPS went on to get a master's in social work from Fordham University. "The professors at MCNY intuited in me something that I didn't know I had," she says, and at Fordham she was able to outshine her peers in the research projects that she had been well prepared for by completing a CA every semester.[31] For Millie Arroyo, whose mother died of AIDS when she was sixteen and who had to drop out of school to raise her brothers and sisters, the best part of her MCNY experience was the strong support she received from her cohort of peers. Without that core group, she says, she never would have made it. But she is also grateful for the college's unique curriculum. "We were equipped to look outside of the box," she says in retrospect.[32] Although many of these alumni would have thrived at any school, many others would not have attended college at all without the unique educational option of MCNY.

CONTINUITY AND CHANGE

In early December 2009 a gala celebration was held to mark Vinton Thompson's installation as fourth president of MCNY. Among the honored guests were several of Cohen's early associates who had helped create the college—Alida Mesrop, Laura Pires-Hester, Sylvia Hack, and Deborah Allen. Others, like Millie Leet, who was unable to attend, and Barbara Walton, who had died, were represented by family members.

At the ceremony Wendy Cohen spoke movingly about her mother's educational vision. Audrey Cohen wanted to make education relevant to students' lives and to make sure that it had a purpose, she said. That purpose was to "link learning with action to improve the world." She wanted "to empower individuals so that they could make positive changes in themselves in order to improve their workplaces and their communities." In summarizing MCNY's achievements Wendy reminded the audience that more than 70 percent of the college's students are adult women and men of color, and that almost all of them receive financial aid. Purpose-Centered Education is based on the premise that students learn best when they use their knowledge and skills to achieve a purpose that makes a positive difference both in their own lives and in the lives of others. "We link learning with action to improve the world," she reiterated.[33]

In his inaugural speech, President Thompson spoke eloquently about the college's origins, locating Cohen's vision squarely in the history of the 1960s. He spoke about the college's progressive roots, about its accomplishments, and about his hopes to continue Cohen's legacy. As an entomologist Thompson ended his speech with a reference to the college's unique evolutionary niche. American society is too large and too complex to be served well by only a few educational models, he said. Just as we recognize the value of biodiversity, "we must also treasure and support diversity in institutions of higher education, and we must turn that diversity into an instrument of national progress." Emphasizing the college's distinctness, he asserted that "We will not copy; we will not mimic other higher education institutions." We can work with them and learn from them "as we continue to perfect our own approach."[34] To those in attendance it was clear that the new president was committed to Cohen's vision and determined to counter some of the mission drift that had been evident in recent years.

"To insure a long existence to religious sects or republics, it is necessary frequently to bring them back to their original principles," wrote Niccolò Machiavelli in 1517.[35] The words come not from Machiavelli's cynical advice in *The Prince* but in his more civic-minded *Discourses*, and they are relevant to the leadership of MCNY as the college celebrates the fiftieth anniversary of its founding and looks to the future. President Thompson is keenly aware of the history of the college that he now leads, and he is firmly committed to the "original principles" of Cohen's vision. He has worked hard to bring the college back from its near disaster in 2006.

One immediate step was to invite Cohen's early associate Deborah Allen onto the Board of Trustees where she provided ongoing reminders of the logic of the curricular model created in 1973. Other current members of the board who have links to the college's early history are Bernadette Smith, who is a graduate of the college; Tom Webber, who was a member of the faculty in the 1970s; Frances Walton, who is Barbara Walton's daughter; and Wendy Cohen, the founder's daughter. Although their shared ties to the institution in no way indicate unanimity in terms of their stands on policy, their presence is crucial for providing a sense of continuity and direction.

Another step Thompson took in his first four years in office was to counter some of the entropy that was evident in teaching the Constructive Action and its documentation. Especially with new or adjunct faculty, the theory-practice integration required in earlier CA documents was often neglected, and some professors had reverted to research paper formats they themselves had been taught in graduate school. Thompson created a committee to discuss and then draft a set of guidelines for the process. "At Metropolitan College of New York the Constructive Action (CA), a planned effort to use knowledge in effective action, is a major component of the student's educational experience and the primary focus of assessment," the guidelines assert. Although acknowledging that there may be some differences in the CA requirements for different programs, the authors of the guidelines state that they should apply to most programs in most circumstances. In circumstances where they cannot be fully implemented, "students, faculty and staff will make every effort to achieve them as fully as is practically possible."[36]

Under Thompson's watch the faculty has also addressed concerns about the liberal arts and general education that were raised in an early Middle States report. Rejecting the front-loaded core curriculum that the Greenwald administration was moving toward in the mid-2000s, the faculty has tweaked the traditional curricular grid to intersperse some general education courses throughout the curriculum and has added credit weights to those courses. Included are new courses in public speaking and the art of persuasion, American government, and human biology and the life sciences. These have become common courses that students in all the undergraduate programs now take.

Another important initiative undertaken by Thompson is to re-establish the college's presence in the South Bronx. The Bronx extension site was always one of the more successful projects undertaken while Cohen was alive, and its reopening provides a much-needed educational resource for a neighborhood that has a long history of urban blight and political neglect.

In 2013 the college purchased space for its South Bronx campus in a new building being constructed on 149th Street near 3rd Avenue. For the first time the college will actually own the real estate that it uses.

In a move that faculty has not appreciated, Thompson has adopted some of Cohen's policies related to the workload balance between teaching and scholarship and has moved away from the emphasis on scholarship that was instituted under Greenwald's administration. Faculty on the scholarship track are no longer granted a semester off from teaching each year to devote to research. The new policy requires that faculty members teach five out of six semesters, which has raised the ire of many faculty members, including those who were hired under Cohen's leadership but who had recently found both success and satisfaction as productive scholars in their fields. It remains to be seen whether this policy will affect future hiring of qualified faculty with PhDs.

What are the challenges that lie ahead? As with most small, tuition-based, independent colleges, the high-priority challenges are to attract students, raise money, and find suitable space. These are concerns that every college administration and board of trustees must wrestle with, in meeting after meeting, year after year. More current common challenges are to find ways to respond to recent cuts in federal student aid, address changing standards in institutional assessment, and meet the new threats to traditional educational formats posed by MOOCs (Massive Open Online Courses). Those challenges to small independent colleges everywhere have been frequently covered in the press and will not be hashed over here.

The challenges that are specific to MCNY relate to its unique Purpose-Centered Education model. Making the theory covered in the Dimension courses consistently relevant to the practice of the Constructive Action and its documentation is always a focus of concern. In recent years, veteran faculty members who were teaching in the 1990s have bemoaned the lack of team structure that once provided a forum for developing curricular coherence. The way that the courses fit together and make possible constructive actions in the field has always been the college's main strength. But when faculty members have little sense of what their colleagues are doing, that sense of coherence is difficult to sustain. Both the faculty and the administration need to find institutional supports for maintaining the clarity and integrity of the model.

A second challenge is to maintain the vitality and quality of the field-work component of the curriculum, which has been traditionally required of every student, every semester. The most serious challenge in this regard is in the undergraduate and graduate business programs, where it is often difficult for students to find field placements. Stephen Greenwald saw this as a problem early on. "The business program was never really consistent with the model. The supervisor/student relationship simply didn't exist because the business world operates on a different model from the human services program." A person in a supervisory position in a business enterprise, he continued, "is not going to . . . spend a lot of time supervising a student as part of his or her education."[37] As a result, most of the Constructive Action documents in the business programs now require students only to *plan* an action related to that semester's purpose but not actually to implement the plan. Students may still learn a lot about business, but the experiential component of Purpose-Centered Education is lost. To make the business programs more consistent with Cohen's vision is an ongoing challenge that all the constituencies—faculty, staff, and administration—are very aware of.

A third challenge is to attract younger faculty members who are both qualified for and committed to teaching within MCNY's uniquely holistic curricular model. Given the disciplinary specialization that exists at most undergraduate and graduate educational institutions, MCNY's transdisciplinary structure of "dimensional" learning that cuts across a sequence of semester-long "purposes" can at first seem confusing to prospective faculty members. An ongoing effort for the college is thus to follow Audrey Cohen's example of ceaseless institutional outreach with the aim of communicating the model's underlying coherence. "Spread the word" has been one of the pieces of advice from accreditation visits in recent years,[38] and this advice needs to be heeded as much in attracting new faculty as in attracting new students.

AUDREY COHEN'S LEGACY

At a Board of Trustees meeting six months after Cohen had been diagnosed with ovarian cancer, she introduced a visitor to the meeting, Dellie Bloom. Dellie had taught at the college in its early years, Cohen said, and now was organizing the vast amount of material available for writing an institutional history. "She is also interviewing staff, students, and others connected with the college, and keeping track of current developments of potential historical interest."[39] Cohen announced that the administration was also planning to hire a professional archivist to assist in this project.

It was not the first time that Cohen had taken steps to record the history of the college. In the late 1970s she had taped her own memories of the college's genesis in conversations with her daughter Dawn, and during the 1980s she periodically met with Alida Mesrop and others to record memories for a book to be entitled *From Dream to Reality: The Biography of a College*.[40] At various points both Barbara Walton and Deborah Allen were asked to try their hand at producing a history. But none of their efforts met Cohen's full approval. The decision in 1992 to bring Dellie Bloom back to the college to organize materials for an official history thus marked a new urgency in a process that had been in the works for many years.

Like the previous attempts to write the college's history, Bloom's project was never completed. Although the archives contain typed memos about the process, dozens of files of transcribed interviews, and pages of carefully annotated notes, Bloom's planned history was for unknown reasons abandoned in the mid-1990s. Perhaps Cohen herself became too ill to supervise the project, or perhaps Bloom found the process too daunting, or perhaps tensions developed between them.[41] Until the writing of this book, the assembled materials have remained hidden away in file cabinets in the college's archives.

What do the drafted histories tell us about Cohen's own sense of her contributions to the world? What did she want her legacy to be? The documents reveal three aspects of her life's work for which Cohen wanted to be remembered. The first was her tireless effort in the mid-1960s to establish new lines of preprofessional employment for low-income women. Cohen's energetic lobbying, as early as 1964, for "assist" jobs in a wide range of human service agencies—schools, hospitals, welfare agencies, employment centers, rehabilitation programs, even law offices—eventually led to the creation of what are now referred to as *paraprofessional* career paths. As she repeatedly noted in interviews with family and friends, this was an accomplishment for which she felt that she had never received adequate recognition. Clearly she would have wanted her legacy to include the Women's Talent Corps' successes at creating new paraprofessional careers.[42]

A second key achievement was the unique conceptual framework of the College of Human Services. As her midlife speeches and writings indicate, she was justifiably proud of the 1973 task force's conception of semester *Purposes* that are interlaced by *Dimensions* of learning and tied together by the documentation of a *Constructive Action* in the field. The new curricular model provided a way for adult higher education to become meaningful and relevant to employment needs. Her invention of Purpose-Centered Education was clearly a key aspect of the legacy that Cohen envisioned for herself; indeed in her later years she often used the term *social inventor* to describe herself in her resumes and proposals.

In Cohen's own view, her third and most impressive contribution was her ambition to make Purpose-Centered Education the predominant conceptual framework throughout the American educational system, including elementary schools. What she referred to as the Schools Project became her driving interest toward the end of her life. "The Schools Project is our destiny," she announced shortly before her death.[43]

As with everything she did, when reflecting her own legacy Cohen thought big. Her life's work included institutions ranging from elementary schools through college and graduate schools to the job market, and thus Cohen's sense of her own legacy encompassed an individual's entire life span. The perspective that the passage of time provides, however, may suggest a more modest and more realistic assessment of her accomplishments than she was able to give in her final years. What can we today make of Cohen's record of accomplishment? What was her most lasting legacy?

Cohen rightly saw that her contributions to paraprofessionalism were significant and that she deserved to be credited for the work she did to persuade the educational and social services establishments to open up assistant positions in city schools and agencies. But from a historical perspective it is clear that Cohen herself was not the only force responsible for those changes. From 1970 to the present, the paraprofessional movement has taken on a life of its own, evolving into very different forms in the legal profession and in the education profession. As Frank Riessman's work on the rise and fall of the New Careers movement at the national level demonstrates,[44] there were larger economic forces at work during those years that

Cohen's project was a part of but that she did not single-handedly initiate. She was riding the waves of demographic and economic changes, not setting them in motion. She merits recognition for her pioneering contribution to paraprofessionalism, but she alone cannot be credited with its creation.

As for her anticipated legacy regarding public elementary schools, here Cohen's expectations have been dashed by recent changes in educational policy. In stark antithesis to the progressive educational designs that were celebrated by the first President Bush in announcing the New American Schools initiative, the No Child Left Behind legislation backed by the second President Bush and the Race to the Top policy undertaken by President Obama have effectively displaced the kinds of project-based, community-oriented curriculums that Cohen was trying to implement.[45] The emphasis on high-stakes testing, discrete academic skills, and direct instruction has, for the moment at least, superseded the mid-twentieth-century experimental educational models that earlier reformers worked to promote. For those regretting such change, a small consolation is to know that if the current "reform" models prove ineffective in lowering dropout rates and raising student achievement scores, the carefully elaborated curriculum designs worked out by Cohen and Jordan two decades ago are readily available for a new educational synthesis.

Of the three aspects of her legacy envisioned by Cohen herself, clearly the most lasting is the college that she founded and whose Human Services and Education programs bear her name. Although her progressive educational vision may not fit well with current policy concerning the schooling of children, her particular appropriation of Deweyan methods is especially well suited to the education of adults. The model's tight structure, its emphasis on personal and professional empowerment, and its linkage of humanistic learning with practical action provide a compelling educational context for adults seeking a better life. At a time when the income gaps between those with college degrees and those without are widening, and when students are seeking a quick, practical return on their educational investment, the Purpose-Centered Education model that Cohen and her colleagues invented merits close attention.

Every June hundreds of black-robed students enter a large space at the Javits Center in Manhattan to receive academic degrees and celebrate their graduation. They have been introduced to a wide range of thinkers from Socrates to Stiglitz. As part of their curriculum they have engaged in constructive actions at human service agencies and community-based organizations. They have analyzed businesses and taught in schools. They all are a testament to Cohen's wish to "link learning with action to improve the world," as her daughter phrases it. Having thrived for more than fifty years as an educational setting where students can empower themselves by learning to empower others, the college that Cohen created is likely to thrive for at least fifty more.

THE KEY PLAYERS

Audrey Cohen: (d) As a college student at the University of Pittsburgh in the early 1950s, Audrey Cohen spent summer months working with the YWCA, the AFSC (American Friends Service Committee), and CORE (the Congress for Racial Equality). As a young mother in the late 1950s she established Part-Time Research Associates—a business designed to place well-educated women in part-time consulting work. In 1964, at the height of the Civil Rights and antipoverty movements, Cohen founded the Women's Talent Corps to create new paraprofessional jobs in city agencies and to train low-income women for those jobs. The Talent Corps soon developed into the College for Human Services, which by the mid-1970s offered a Bachelor of Professional Studies degree based on a unique curricular structure that the college termed Purpose-Centered Education. Prior to Cohen's death in 1996 the college was renamed Audrey Cohen College, and in 2002 the name was changed again to Metropolitan College of New York.

Alida Mesrop: A native New Yorker and a graduate of Hunter High School and Hunter College, Mesrop was one of Cohen's long-term associates and took on key roles as special assistant to the president. She became dean, and when Cohen died in 1996 she became president, overseeing a period of consolidation and stability.

Laura Pires-Hester: Dr. Laura Pires-Hester joined Audrey Cohen in 1966, first to develop field placements for the Women's Talent Corps, then as field director, deputy director, and the college's first vice president. She left the college in 1982, after serving as mental health project consultant. An anthropologist, she is now vice president at New York Theological Seminary.

Barbara Walton: (d) Before becoming Audrey Cohen's close associate in the 1960s, Walton worked for the State Department on the De-Nazification of Germany after World War II and later was active in the civil rights movement. At MCNY Walton provided Cohen with the intellectual underpinning of what came to be called Purpose-Centered Education and was secretary of the Board of Trustees. Barbara Walton died in January 2008.

Janith Jordan: (d) After receiving a master's in education at Michigan State Jordan taught high school in Detroit. She moved to New York City and became the college's academic director. By the 1990s she was vice president and director of the Schools Program, helping elementary and secondary schools adopt MCNY's Purpose-Centered Education model. When she died in 2004 her personal library was donated to the Educational Resources room in the MCNY library.

Sylvia Hack: An instinctively caring and generous administrator, Hack was essential to MCNY's early growth. Through grant writing, statistical reports, and fundraising, she enabled the college in its early years to survive without charging tuition. She also was responsible for the design and construction of MCNY's space and for its infrastructure, including its phone system and computers.

Deborah Allen: (d) A graduate of Smith College, Allen worked as an editor and an educational reformer in her local community before coming to the college as a member of the administrative staff in 1971. She helped Cohen articulate her educational ideas and develop them into MCNY's unique educational model and wrote the document that won New York State approval. She worked with faculty on the first master's program and the Schools Program and helped create the *Purpose Handbooks*. After thirty years of service she retired in 2001, but returned to join MCNY's Board of Trustees in 2008. She passed away in July 2014.

Mildred Robbins Leet: (d) A committed activist and philanthropist in the promotion of women's rights, civil rights, and the economic uplift of poor people around the world, Millie Leet was a staunch supporter of Audrey Cohen's project from the early 1970s on. As a long-term member of the college's Board of Trustees, she provided generous financial and moral support at crucial moments in the institution's evolution. She died in May 2011.

SOURCES AND
ACKNOWLEDGMENTS

When I first began to think about writing the story of Audrey Cohen's founding of MCNY, I was not aware that several of the women I wanted to include in the story had had the same idea. In the college's well-kept archives rooms at 431 Canal Street are files and boxes labeled "History," and in those files and boxes can be found first drafts of multiple attempts to record the extraordinary events and characters that would combine to create MCNY's unique model of higher education.

Among the previous attempts to write a history of MCNY I am particularly indebted to the work of Sydelle ("Dellie") Bloom who in the late 1980s and early 1990s conducted interviews with dozens of key actors from the college's early years, including a long interview with Audrey Cohen herself. Bloom had taught part time at the college in the 1960s and then returned in the 1980s to tape-record the interviews, transcribe the tapes (or have them transcribed), type up summaries of key points, and in some cases make cross-references to other interviews. In file after file, carefully alphabetized by the last name of the interviewee, the transcriptions (some of which include margin notes in Bloom's small script) provide evidence of a keen mind and a compassionate disposition. As an interviewer, Bloom's questions are probing but gentle; she listens well, makes smart connections, and often adds a note of humor. In June 2011, when I uncovered her work while browsing through the archives, my first impulse was to try to contact Bloom about co-authoring a book. After several inquiries I learned that she had died in 2006, never able to complete her project. Without her long hours of labor this book could not have been written.

I hope that the preceding pages at least partially realize her intention to record for posterity the story of an extraordinary educational enterprise.

In terms of its care and comprehensiveness, another crucial source for the writing of this book has been five volumes of an "Historical Reconstruction" of the college's early years that were drafted in the fall of 1978 by Laura Pires-Hester (then Laura Pires Houston), an early participant in Audrey Cohen's project. Pires-Hester kindly lent me her own copies of the work shortly after my June 2011 interview with her, and they have been an extraordinary resource. In part reminiscences about her own role in the college's genesis and in part analyses of the community-based organizations with which she worked, the volumes (each of which has an appendix as long as the text itself) contain records of meetings, outlines of syllabi, reflections on theories, and wise commentary. I am extremely grateful to Pires-Hester for sharing her impressive reporting and reflections with me.

Dellie Bloom's "History" and Laura Pires-Hester's "Historical Reconstruction" were perhaps the most comprehensive attempts to record the college's beginnings, but there were several other attempts that have also served as indispensable sources for this book. Alida Mesrop, who was Audrey Cohen's closest associate at the college and who succeeded her as president (and with whom I begin the story in Chapter 1), also drafted the beginnings of a history of MCNY. An efficient and lucid writer, Mesrop served as Cohen's *alter ego* for many of her public speeches and written work. For her history of the college, which was to be entitled *From Dream to Reality: The Biography of a College*,[1] Mesrop wrote a compelling opening chapter in the first person as if Cohen herself were writing her own narrative. Entitled "In the Beginning," Mesrop's chapter provided me with essential information about Cohen's childhood and early education and gave me important insights into the life of a woman whom I never had the chance to meet in person.

In the mid-1980s, in a process perhaps related to Mesrop's draft of "In the Beginning," various other members of the college's administrative team met every few months to discuss "the book"—presumably an attempt to complete a history of the college. As Cohen herself said at one of these meetings, "there are so many tapes because I was very conscious of trying to record the history." These meetings were recorded and alternative outlines were discussed. "This is a kind of a book which relies on a human interaction. It's not a book of philosophy," Cohen says at one point, adding, however, that philosophy is "woven into" the struggle to create a new kind of college.[2] At about the same time, Barbara Walton, another Cohen associate, tried her hand at drafting a history; and later in 1992 the then director of special projects, Deborah Allen, also wrote a proposal for a book about the college. There are even three undated chapters of a "History of the College for Human Services" purportedly written by Audrey Cohen herself (but probably drafted by someone else) for a series in a journal entitled *Forum*. But no final definitive text resulted from those long conversations and tentative drafts.

Finding all of this work carefully filed in the archives at 431 Canal Street has been both humbling and inspiring. Many of Cohen's associates were excellent writers who might under different circumstances have completed their projects and made my work unnecessary. On the other hand, their versions of the story have given me the double advantage of hearing about the college's formation from a wide range of voices and providing a historical perspective that can only be gained with the passage of time.

Besides the early Cohen associates on whose shoulders I stood to write this book, many students, colleagues, administrators, new acquaintances, old friends, and family members deserve acknowledgment here. Of particular note are those who agreed to be interviewed either in person or over the telephone. Alumni of the college who contributed their time and memories include Melvina Goodman, Daniel Gregoire, Maria Martin, Millie Arroyo, Ethel Perez, and Loretta Robinson. Faculty members who wholeheartedly participated in the project include Humphrey Crookendale, Theodor Damian, Richard Grallo, Charles Gray, Clyde Griffin, Anne Lopes, Franklyn Rother, Dona Sosa, Lou Tietje, and Vanda Wark. Past and present members of the Board of Trustees who graciously agreed to be interviewed were Deborah Allen, Steven Greenwald, John Rodgers, Bernadette Smith, John Stookey, and Tom Webber.

I am also deeply indebted to Audrey Cohen's family members, who, since its inception in the spring of 2011, have been supportive of the project. Mark Cohen, Wendy Cohen, and Dawn Cohen Margolin have been a delight to get to know. Their intelligence, vivacity, and large-heartedness have given me a clear sense of the woman whom I never had the chance to meet in person. I am especially grateful to Wendy Cohen for the permission to use family photos of her mother in the book. Audrey Cohen's second husband, Ralph Wharton, was also generous with his time and memories.

In addition to Cohen's family, her close friends and colleagues have been very willing to share what they remember about her dynamism and sense of purpose. Foremost on this list are Deborah Allen, Sylvia Hack, Alida Mesrop, and Laura Pires-Hester—all of them dedicated colleagues whose intelligence, loyalty, and hard work made possible the realization of Audrey Cohen's dreams. They—along with Janith Jordan, Millie Leet, and Barbara Walton, who passed away before the writing of this book—are the "founding sisters" of MCNY. Other close associates who I interviewed to fill out the picture of the college's early years were Elaine Azen-Lampl, Dinni Gordon, Judy Hozore, Annie La Rock, Lorraine Montenegro, Frankie Pelzman (since deceased), and Dodie Younger.

Essential to the book project from the beginning was the support of MCNY president, Vinton Thompson. On the first day that I announced to him my idea of writing about Audrey Cohen and the founding of MCNY, he gave me access to the college's archives, which, thanks to Cohen's foresight and the excellent work of Bill Morgan, the archivist she hired, are beautifully organized up until her death in 1996. MCNY's research librarian, Kate Adler, has been helpful in tracking down out-of-print copies of Audrey Cohen's writings, and the chief development officer, Beth Dunphe, has been helpful in tracking down photographs. Thanks also go to Nick Juravich, a Columbia University doctoral student whose research for a PhD dissertation on the paraprofessional movement has occasionally overlapped with mine and who has provided good leads to important historical materials.

Helpful critics of the early chapters of the book were Megan Laverty, Caroline Mayher, Maxine McClintock, Robbie McClintock, Sara Suleri Goodyear, Frank Roosevelt, and the late Diane Wolkstein, at that time my closest friend and most perceptive reader. Other friends and colleagues who read drafts of the completed manuscript include Beth Dunphe, John Greene, Anne Lopes, Lou Miele, and Gary Roth—all of whom made detailed comments and helpful suggestions, at several points saving me from embarrassing gaffes and misstatements. I am also extremely grateful to the anonymous readers selected by the State University of New York Press for their attentive and useful commentary on the manuscript. Any remaining errors or omissions in the book are my own responsibility.

I also wish to acknowledge my students' helpful responses to the book. Particular recognition goes to the Purpose VIII Self and Others students who were assigned a reading of two chapters as part of their study of the role of change agents in the human services professions. Jade Blount, Tawanda Burts, Shanelee Galloway, Walter D. Jones, Sherika Lee, Kayra Martinez, Hasani Powell, and Fallon Watson made helpful comments on the text.

In addition to the moral and intellectual support provided by colleagues, friends, and family members, a small grant from the Spencer Foundation provided the material support for the transcription of the interviews I conducted. A freelance webmaster, Philip David Morgan, undertook the painstaking work of transcribing the interviews. Not only did he produce impeccable prose renditions of each interview but included in each transcription the web address for obscure historical or biographical information. I remain deeply grateful for his patient, careful, work.

For their expert advice in selecting and arranging the photographs for the book I was lucky to get the help of long-term friends, Adrian and Elizabeth Kitzinger. Thanks go to Sunay Tamashev for suggestions for cover design and to Scott Gillam for his careful help reading the galley proofs. For early advice on proposal-writing, I am grateful to Ann Edelstein and Judy Gitenstein. At the State University of New York Press I am especially thankful to Amanda Lanne-Camilli and Jenn Bennett for their clarity, efficiency, and professionalism. They were a pleasure to work with throughout the publishing process.

Throughout the writing process I have received kind inquiries and helpful advice from colleagues in the MSED program at MCNY. The director of the program, Dr. Patrick Ianniello, and his remarkable assistant, Vanessa Cruz, have always provided encouraging support, as have the veteran members of the program including Lynne Dolle, Eric Fuchs, Dana Gathers, Leonard Golubchick, Lynda Kennedy, and Daryle Young.

My closest supporters have been members of my immediate family. Phoebe, Nick, and Amie have encouraged the project from the start, and my husband Frank has paid the ultimate tribute to Cohen's vision by joining MCNY's adjunct faculty. I could not have completed the work without his patient listening, deep intelligence, and steadfast love.

Thanks are due to the following institutions and publications for permission to use copyrighted materials:

Metropolitan College of New York for charts that appeared in Audrey C. Cohen, "The Service Society and a Theory of Learning Linking Education, Work, Life," published by Audrey Cohen College, 1976, 1989.

Condé Nast Publications for a photograph of Audrey Cohen that appeared in *Vogue* magazine, October 15, 1968.

Education Week, for a photograph of Audrey Cohen taken by Benjamin Tice Smith in an article by Mark Pitsch entitled "The Outsider. Breaking the Mold: The Shape of Schools to Come" that appeared January 25, 1995, vol. XIV, issue 18, p. 23.

NOTES

CHAPTER 1. INTRODUCTION

1. I am grateful to Louis Tietje for assembling the "Quotations on Purpose-Centered Education" from which this and following chapter epigraphs have been selected.

2. GR interview with Alida Mesrop June 15, 2011, Morgan transcript, 3.

3. Dionne A. Spence, MCNY Purpose 1 Constructive Action Document, "Statement of Purpose," MSEd program, Spring 2013, 4.

4. Hanover Research, "2010–2011 Annual Graduation Survey Analysis Prepared for Metropolitan College of New York," March 2012, pp. 34, 36, 41, and 43.

5. See, for example, Sabrina Tavernise, "Education Gap Grows Between Rich and Poor, Studies Say," *New York Times*, February 9, 2012. http://www.nytimes.com/2012/02/10/education/education-gap-grows-between-rich-and-poor-studies-show.html?_r=1&pagewanted=print and Thomas B. Edsall, "The Reproduction of Privilege," *New York Times*, March 12, 2012. http://campaignstops.blogs.nytimes.com/2012/03/12/the-reproduction-of-privilege/?pagemode=print.

6. U.S. Department of Education, National Center for Education Statistics, 2012 IPEDS Data Feedback Report on Metropolitan College of New York, 3 and 5.

7. See, for example, Ellen Schrecker, *The Lost Soul of Higher Education: Corporatization, the Assault on Academic Freedom, and the End of the American University* (New York: New Press, 2010); also Grace Roosevelt, "The Triumph of the Market and the Decline of Liberal Education: Implications for Civic Life," *Teachers College Record*, Vol. 108, No. 7 (July 2006).

8. See Gerald Grant and David Riesman, *The Perpetual Dream: Reform and Experiment in the American College* (Chicago: University of Chicago Press, 1978). In Chapter 5, the College for Human Services is described as an example of "The Activist-Radical Impulse" in higher education at that time.

9. See, for example, Al Baker, "In One School, Students are Divided by Gifted Label–and Race," *New York Times*, January 12, 2013. http://www.nytimes.com/2013/01/13/education/in-one-school-students-are-divided-by-gifted-label-and-race.html?pagewanted=1&_r=0.

10. GR interview with Alida Mesrop, June 15, 2011, Morgan transcript, 3.

11. Ibid., 3.

12. See HERS speech #3, 2/14/80, Archive Folder #000098, 3.

13. Dawn Cohen interview of Audrey Cohen, undated, Archive Folder #000091, 8.

14. GR interview with Wendy Cohen, June 28, 2012, Morgan transcript, 7.

15. See Archive Folder #00098, "Audrey Cohen Profile Pitch Letter," Draft, 2.

16. See Laura Pires-Houston, "The Women's Talent Corps → The College for Human Services: Historical Reconstruction," Vol. I, August 16, 1978, 4.

17. See GR interview with Mark Cohen, June 3, 2011, Morgan transcript, 11–12.

18. "HERS [Higher Education Resource Services] final draft–CH–2/21/80, 'Reflections on my Career' by Audrey C. Cohen" from Archive File #000098, 1.

CHAPTER 2. THE EDUCATION OF AN ACTIVIST (1931–1963)

1. Alida Mesrop, "In the Beginning," found in a box labeled with Barbara Walton's name. It is written in the first person as if it was written by Audrey Cohen, but actually it was written by Mesrop, 1–3.

2. Ibid., 1.

3. GR interview with Alida Mesrop, June 15, 2011, Morgan transcript, 8.

4. GR interview with Wendy Cohen, June 28, 2012, Morgan transcript, 17.

5. Mesrop, "In the Beginning," 1–3.

6. Norvelt: [Great Depression] Historical Marker. http://explorepahistory.com/hmarker.php?marketd=1-A-345.

7. In 1937 the Westmoreland Homestead community renamed itself Norvelt, in honor of Eleanor Roosevelt, who had taken a particular interest in the experiment.

8. http://en.wikipedia.org/wiki/Squirrel_Hill_(Pittsburgh).

9. Annie Dillard, *An American Childhood* (New York: Harper, 1988).

10. Dellie Bloom's interview of Audrey Cohen, labeled "ACC/DB taped 3/12/91; transcribed 3/13/91," Archive Folder #000099, 1.

11. Ibid., 1–2.

12. Ibid., 2.

13. http://en.wikipedia.org/wiki/Taylor_Allderdice_High_School.

14. GR interview with Mark Cohen, June 3, 2011, Morgan transcript, 13.

15. ACC/DB, 2.

16. Wendy Cohen, "A Purpose-Centered Life," speech to the graduating class of 2008, Metropolitan College of New York, June 2008, 1.

17. ACC/DB, 3.

18. Ibid., 4.

19. Ibid., 2 and 4.

20. Ibid., 1.

21. Ibid., 3.

22. See GR interview with Mark Cohen, 12, and GR interview with Alida Mesrop, 17.

23. See GR interview with Alida Mesrop, 3; the unpaginated interview from Barbara Walton's file drawer labeled "History," 89–92; and the transcription of a taped interview between Steve Sunderland and Dellie Bloom 8/24/91, 2 ff.

24. Dawn Cohen interview with Audrey Cohen, 11.

25. Mesrop, "In the Beginning," 3.

26. Ibid., 3–4.

27. Dawn Cohen interview with Audrey Cohen, 13.

28. Mesrop, "In the Beginning," 2.

29. See the history of CORE at http://www.core-online.org/History/history.htm, 1.

30. Dawn Cohen interview with Audrey Cohen, 13.

31. Mesrop, "In the Beginning," 2.

32. Ibid., 2.

33. "Audrey Cohen Profile Pitch Letter: Draft for Approval," Archive Folder #000098.

34. Mesrop, "In the Beginning," 3.

35. In a taped conversation with Alida Mesrop on August 4, 1986, Cohen states that her internship work with the YWCA program was "much more [potent] than let's say going to the University of Pittsburgh and taking courses," Archive File #000094, 10.

36. http://www.tour.pitt.edu/tour-080.html.

37. College transcript for Audrey Cohen, Office of the Registrar, the University of Pittsburgh, Pennsylvania.

38. University of Pittsburgh, *Bulletin* for the college. Announcements for 1949–1950, Vol. 45, No. 2, pp. 118 and 139.

39. Dellie Bloom interview with Steven Sunderland, 8/24/91, in Barbara Walton's file drawer labeled "History," 16, on an unpaged transcript of a tape recording. As Gary Roth has pointed out, however,

[I]n Dewey's model, the classroom replicates the real world or else students have limited experiences in the real world, such as internships. Either way, he holds fast to a sharp distinction between education and the world, with the former serving as preparation for the latter. Audrey's model focuses on individuals who are thrust into a highly-competitive job world that requires little in terms of skills and knowledge, and she makes education an adjunct of the students' real life experiences. The causality is the reverse of the Deweyian model, the latter predicated as it is on the middle classes. In this sense, she did go way beyond Dewey. Personal correspondence from Gary Roth, July 28, 2012.

40. Brief conversation with Professor Faye Ran, April 20, 2012.

41. Alternatively, as Gary Roth observes, her experiences with a traditional teacher-prep program provided the background from which she could reconceptualize quite concretely the educational experience and make it relevant to the specific needs of a formerly ignored group. Personal correspondence from Gary Roth, July 28, 2012.

42. "Conversation [sic] with ACC/DB: 9/15/91," Archive Folder # 000098.

43. Audrey Cohen College, History II Meeting, January 20, 1994, Archive Folder #000072, 3. Other than this 1994 summary of the episode by Dellie Bloom, there are no other references to Cohen having been threatened by a knife in her early years of practice teaching. When questioned about the story's veracity, however, several family members and associates have stated firmly that, knowing Audrey, it is probably true.

44. GR interview with Mark Cohen, 7.

45. Mesrop, "In the Beginning," 4.

46. GR interview with Mark Cohen, 2.

47. GR interview with Elaine Azen-Lampl, March 23, 2012, Morgan transcript, 1–2. Interestingly, the bonds formed at that New Year's Eve party proved to be lasting. After Audrey had married Mark and Elaine had married Alan the two couples stayed in close touch for decades.

48. GR interview with Mark Cohen, June 3, 2011, Morgan transcript, 2.

49. GR interview with Elaine Azen-Lampl, March 23, 2012, Morgan transcript, 2 and 3.

50. GR interviews with Dawn Margolin, January 18, 2012, 17, and with Tom Webber, June 18, 2012, 15.

51. GR interview with Mark Cohen, 5 and 12.

52. Ibid., 3.

53. Dellie Bloom's notes on an interview with Audrey Cohen, labeled "ACC/DB taped 3/12/91, transcribed 3/13/91," Archive Folder #000099, 4.

54. GR interview with Mark Cohen, 12.

55. Ibid., 5.

56. Ibid.

57. Eugene Burdick and William J. Lederer, *The Ugly American* (New York: Norton, 1999).

58. GR interview with Mark Cohen, 1–2.

59. Mesrop, "In the Beginning," 5.

60. Ibid., 6.

61. GR interview with Elaine Azen-Lample, March 23, 2013, Morgan transcript, 3.

62. GR interview with Mark Cohen, 7–8.

63. Mesrop, "In the Beginning," 6.

64. GR interview with John Rodgers, June 29, 2011, Morgan transcript, 6.

65. Mesrop, "In the Beginning," 7.

66. GR interview with John Rodgers, June 29, 2011, Morgan transcript, 9.

67. Mark I. Cohen and Lorna Hahn, *Morocco: Old Land, New Nation* (New York: Praeger, 1966). GR interview with John Rodgers, 8.

68. Ibid., 10 and 14.

69. Ibid., 16.

70. GR interview with Mark Cohen, 6.

71. GR interview with John Rodgers, 8.

72. GR interview with Mark Cohen, 8.

73. GR interview with Frances Pelzman, June 25, 2012, Morgan transcript, 19.

74. Dawn Cohen interview with Audrey Cohen, 4.

75. Ibid., 4.

76. See copies of Curriculum Vita and Resume in Archive Folder #000749.

77. Mesrop, "In the Beginning," 67–68.

78. Outreach Letter from Part-Time Research Associates, Archive Folder #001120, 1.

79. GR interview with Frances Pelzman, 6.

80. Ibid., 12–13.

81. Personal phone conversation with Fred Pelzman, June 2013. (Frances Pelzman died September 17, 2012.)

82. GR interview with Frances Pelzman, 12.

83. Ibid.

84. GR interview with Mark Cohen, 2.

85. See Curriculum Vitae and Resumes in Archive Folder #000749.

86. Taped and transcribed interview with Dawn Cohen, undated, Archive Folder #000091, 7.

87. Marylin Bender, "Meeting of 2 Housewives Was Start of a Business," *New York Times*, August 29, 1960, section on food, fashions, family, furnishings, 10.

88. Dawn Cohen interview with Audrey Cohen, 5–6.

89. Letter from Audrey Cohen to Carol Phillips, managing editor of *Vogue*, April 9, 1962, 2, Archive Folder #001120.

90. Dawn Cohen interview with Audrey Cohen, 7.

91. Mesrop, "In the Beginning," 67–68.

CHAPTER 3. "MY FORK IN THE ROAD PRESENTED ITSELF" (1964–1965)

1. Mesrop, "In the Beginning," 12.

2. Marilyn Hoffman, "Spare Time Made Profitable," *Christian Science Monitor*, January 15, 1964.

3. Mesrop, "In the Beginning," 9–10.

4. See the draft of a long article to be published in a periodical entitled *Forum* under Audrey Cohen's name entitled "The History of the College for Human Services," Archive Folder #000093, Chapter 1, 5.

5. See HERS speech #3, 2/14/80, Archive Folder #000098, 7–8.

6. Draft of *The History of the College*, Chapter 2, 3.

7. It is interesting to compare Cohen's drive to bring together women of different backgrounds with the more recent feminist focus on the advancement of individual women in corporate America. See Sheryl Sandberg, *Lean In: Women, Work, and the Will to Lead* (New York: Knopf, 2013) and Debora Spar, *Wonder Women: Sex, Power, and the Quest for Perfection* (New York: Farrar, Straus & Giroux, 2013). See also a critique of their approach by Susan Faludi, "Facebook Feminism, Like It or Not" from *The Baffler* No. 23, 2013. http://thebaffler.com/past/facebook_feminism_like_it_or_not. I am indebted to Maxine McClintock for this observation and reference.

8. Dawn Cohen interview with Audrey Cohen, 8–9. In this same interview Audrey Cohen describes her decision as bringing together "the need of the educated woman to do something significant with her life and the need of the low income woman to have a chance to prove that she had talent and worth and deserved a place in this society" (18).

In Mesrop's drafted chapter "In the Beginning," Mesrop in Cohen's words states the problem as follows: "I spent a summer going through resumes, and learned something that in retrospect, perhaps, is very obvious. Corporations needed women with, for example, writing, organisational and marketing skills. Yet it was rare to see a resume showing experience outside of teaching, social work, and nursing. Women were concentrated in these fields" (9).

9. Dawn Cohen interview with Audrey Cohen, 10.

10. See, for example, Caleb E. Finch and Thomas B.L. Kirkwood, *Chance, Development, and Aging* (New York: Oxford University Press, 2000), 4–7, and Robert McClintock, *Enough: A Pedagogic Speculation* (New York: Collaboratory for Liberal Learning, 2012).

11. Mesrop, "In the Beginning," 9–10.

12. http://www.americanrhetoric.com/speeches/mlkihaveadream.htm.

13. GR interview with Frances Pelzman, 2.

14. Dawn Cohen interview with Audrey Cohen, 16.

15. Donna K. Ramer, "Wendy Cohen and her mother, Audrey Cohen, founder of Metropolitan College of New York," *HBAdvantage*, Winter 2011, www.hbanet.org.

16. Dawn Cohen interview with Audrey Cohen, 16.

17. Ibid., 17–18. Punctuation adjusted for clarity.

18. Ibid.

19. However, neither the Women's Talent Corps nor later the College for Human Services used the term *paraprofessional* and instead referred to the jobs as *preprofessional* or *new professional*. See Dawn Cohen interview with Audrey Cohen, 17.

20. Dawn Cohen interview with Audrey Cohen, 18.

21. Mesrop, "In the Beginning," 12.

22. See Chapter 1.

23. From Barbara Walton's file drawer, a folder labeled "ALIDA's INTRO 10/89" but titled on upper right of document, "draft suggestions: for tone/style 3/8/91 DB," 2–3.

24. "ALIDA's INTRO 10/89," 1.

25. Ibid., 5.

26. Dellie Bloom includes this on page 5 from Barbara Walton's file drawer, file ALIDA'S INTRO 19/89" and labeled "draft suggestions: for tone/style 3/8/91 DB" and also in her typed notes on her interview with Hope Leichter, 5/17/90, from Barbara Walton's file drawer, "History 89–92" file.

27. "ALIDA's INTRO 10/89," 4–5.

28. Transcription of August 4, 1986, tape of Alida Mesrop and Audrey Cohen for "Book on the History of the College," Archive Folder #000094, 13.

29. I am indebted to Gary Roth for this observation.

30. Notes labeled "Hope Leichter 5/17/90 DB BW Teacher's College" from Barbara Walton's Folder drawer, file "History 89–92," first page. About her doctoral work at Harvard Leichter told an anecdote revealing the tenor of the times: "When I was doing doctoral work at Harvard in the late '50s, Harvard had no computers, but they did have an arrangement with John Hancock (Bank) to use their computers at night. But it violated the company's sense of propriety, and fear of God knows what, to have women working with men at night, so I had to dress like my male colleagues in order to get in and get my work done." Notes labeled "Hope Leichter 5/17/90 DB BW Teacher's College" from Barbara Walton's file drawer, file "HISTORY 89–92."

31. Notes labeled "Hope Leichter 5/17/90 DB BW Teacher's College" from Barbara Walton's file drawer, file "History 89–92."

32. Transcription of August 4, 1986, tape of Alida Mesrop and Audrey Cohen for "Book on the History of the College," Archive Folder #000094, 14.

33. Ibid., 14 and 1.

34. Wendy Cohen, "A Purpose-Centered Life," speech to graduating class, Metropolitan College of New York, June 2008, third unnumbered page.

35. Dawn Cohen interview with Audrey Cohen, 19. One early source of contacts was Israel Laster, a national consultant for the American Jewish Committee. According to Laster, he provided Cohen with names of several important contacts, including Jim Scheuer, Percy Sutton, and Bruce Wright. See Dellie Bloom's interview with Israel Laster, December 16, 1975, Archive Folder #000128.

36. Dawn Cohen interview with Audrey Cohen, 19 and 20.

37. Ibid., 20. Cohen's description of these meetings aligns closely with Laura Pires-Houston's written account. "In our conversations, Audrey had, as I remember . . . indicated that she had asked at every such meeting: 'What are the most serious service problems in your community? If you had the chance, what kinds of agency service roles do you think you would like to be able to function in? And would you like to be in such a position?'" See Laura Pires-Houston, "The Women's Talent Corps → The College for Human Services: An Historical Reconstruction," Vol. 1: Phase I: Building and Transition (1966–1968), August 16, 1978, 16.

38. See the Wikipedia entry on Alinsky at http:/en.wikipedia.org/wiki/Saul_Alinsky.

39. See, for example, http://blogs.suntimes.com/ebert/politics/saul-alinsky-comes-to-the-tea.html.

40. "The first step in community organization is community disorganization. . . . The organizer dedicated to changing the life of a particular community

must first rub raw the resentments of the people of the community; fan the latent hostilities of many of the people to the point of overt expression." Saul Alinsky, *Rules for Radicals: A Pragmatic Primer for Realistic Radicals* (New York: Vintage Books, 1989), 116.

41. Dawn Cohen interview with Audrey Cohen, 20.

42. Ibid., 20–21. See also Archive File #000094, a taped conversation between Audrey Cohen and Alida Mesrop: "The way I ran the meetings was . . . [by telling them that] I'm trying to get money to open up new jobs. What should these jobs look like? . . . I need to know what you want to do, what you think you can do. [Also] What kind of education I can structure to help you do it . . . [I'd] get started then people would all sign. Those were the first students. These people were the first students at the Women's Talent Corps . . . they were thrilled at the concept. Of course, they always accused me of never coming back and just taking out ideas. I brought someone like Hope [Leichter] with me reassuring them [that] I was [not] using them. They were very supportive. I needed to come back [with] lots of money. Because clearly they were helping figure out the ideas. Now, I used those ideas in the proposal, in the job descriptions that we then ultimately designed that were attached" (14).

43. I am indebted to Gary Roth for this observation.

44. Dawn Cohen interview with Audrey Cohen, 21.

45. GR interview with Lorraine Montenegro, January 10, 2014.

46. Dawn Cohen interview with Audrey Cohen, 21.

47. Ibid., 21–22. In an interview that Dellie Bloom did in 1975 with Israel Laster, a national consultant for the American Jewish Committee and an early member of the Women's Talent Corps Board of Directors, it was mentioned that he was the one who advised Cohen to be sure to go back to the communities in which she had canvassed. And sure enough, "She followed through." See Dellie Bloom interview with Israel Laster, December 16, 1975, Archive Folder #000128.

48. Dawn Cohen interview with Audrey Cohen, 22. In the final draft of the HERS (Archive File #000098) speech (CH–2–21–80) "Reflections on my Career" this story is reduced to the following:

> In the early 60s I was running a successful corporation called Part Time Research Associates. . . . To my knowledge, it was the first consultant firm exclusively employing college-educated women on a flexible schedule basis. Every day I dealt with women who were denied meaningful careers because family obligations prevented them from working a full 40 hour week.
>
> In 1964 I combined my concern about the wasted talents of those middle class women with concern for a different group—poor

minority women in our urban ghettoes. In my college days I had marched with CORE and became acutely aware of these women who had been left behind by our affluent society. I was convinced [that] they too had valuable potential talents to offer society if only they were able to master necessary skills. I put the two groups together and the Women's Talent Corps, the precursor of the College for Human services, was born. (3)

Also See HERS (Archive File #000098) speech, #3 / CH/2–14–80 /:

When I began my efforts to gain community support in the 60s I spent many nights in minority neighborhoods meeting residents in churches and school halls. These sessions occurred after I had made important individual contacts with people in the area. It was through this long and sometimes tedious chain of meetings with those who might be most directly affected by our original program and eventually the College for Human Services—that these institutions were shaped. (17)

49. GR interview with Laura Pires-Hester, June 21, 2011, Morgan transcript, 4.

50. See the Wikipedia entry on Robert Wagner Jr. at http://en.wikipedia.org/wiki/Robert_F._Wagner,_Jr.

51. Dawn Cohen interview with Audrey Cohen, 23.

52. Ibid.

53. "ALIDA's INTRO 10/89," 6.

54. Ibid., 7. The administration's attitude toward women's empowerment was also reflected in its policy toward gays. In preparation for the 1964 World's Fair Mayor Wagner revoked the liquor licenses of gay bars in the city, and undercover police officers worked to entrap homosexual men. See David Carter, *Stonewall: The Riots that Sparked the Gay Revolution* (New York: St. Martin's Press, 2001), 29–37. Cited online at http://en.wikipedia.org/wiki/Robert_F._Wagner,_Jr.

55. "ALIDA's INTRO 10/89," 7.

56. Dawn Cohen interview with Audrey Cohen, 15.

CHAPTER 4. SHE WOULDN'T TAKE NO FOR AN ANSWER

1. Dawn Cohen interview with Audrey Cohen, 23 and 18–19.

2. Allen J. Matusow, *The Unraveling of America: A History of Liberalism in the 1960s* (Atlanta: University of Georgia Press, 1984), 119–122, cited in James T. Patterson, *Grand Expectations: The United States, 1945–1971* (New York: Oxford University Press, 1996), 533.

3. Patterson, *Grand Expectations*, 539.

4. GR interview with Diana Gordon, October 13, 2011, Morgan transcript, 1.

5. G. David Garson, Economic Opportunity Act of 1964. http://wps.prenhall.com/wps/media/objects/751/769950/Documents_Library/eoa1964.htm.

6. "Directions from New York City Council Vs. Poverty (Antipoverty Operations Board) and the Office of Economic Opportunity (OEO), Wash. & NY," Archive Folder #000058, 1–2.

7. GR interview with Sylvia Hack, June 15, 2011, Morgan transcript 11.

8. Alida Mesrop and Audrey Cohen—August 4, 1986—Book on the History of the College," Archive File #000094, 15 and10.

9. "Brother Preston Wilcox," in *AframSouth Inc.* http://www.aframsouth.net/legacy.htm, 1.

10. Cassandra Zenz, "Wilcox, Preston (1923–2006)." http://www.blackpast.org/?q=aah/wilcox-preston-1923–2006, 2.

11. A draft of a report probably by Audrey Cohen, with Dellie Bloom's handwritten corrections, Archive Folder #000058, second page.

12. Undated memo dictated by Preston Wilcox, Archive Folder #000171, 3 and 2. Wilcox's suggestion may have been somewhat radical for its time, anticipating as it does Paolo Freire's concept of education as dialogic rather than simply narrative. See Paolo Freire, *Pedagogy of the Oppressed* (New York: Seabury Press, 1974), Chapter 2. Also interesting in the document with regard to today's educational debates is the section where Wilcox speculates about how Women's Talent Corps efforts might be evaluated. "Would it be fair to expect that there would be an increase in the level of functioning as it relates to education on behalf of those students who have to be in contact with a trainee? Would it be fair to assume or to expect that there will be some difference in the conduct, the rate of attendance or the classroom performance of those students who are related to the trainees, as against those who are not?" He ends with the question, "Is there any way to measure the specific skills which are transmitted to the trainee as a result of the WTC effort . . . [or] the utility of these skills as they relate to the trainee's carrying on the tasks assigned to her in the school? And would these questions be relevant?" Interestingly Wilcox is broaching on the possibility that children's teachers, and even the institution training them, might be held accountable for the academic performance of the children themselves—a concept that more

than fifty years later is stirring up heated controversy throughout the teaching profession.

13. For a compelling and well-documented history of the educational conflicts at Ocean Hill–Brownsville (and mention of Preston Wilcox's role), see Jerald Podair, *The Strike That Changed New York: Blacks, Whites, and the Ocean Hill-Brownsville Crisis* (New Haven: Yale University Press, 2002).

14. In May 1968, however, as part of an experiment of "Learning through Action" initiated by Preston Wilcox, about forty Women's Talent Corps students volunteered to man Ocean Hill schools during the teachers' strike. (Wilcox had also tried to get members of the Women's Talent Corps Board of Trustees to volunteer to teach in Brownsville, with little success—see board minutes for the meeting on May 23, 1968, 2.) For the students the experience was mixed. As recorded in Pires-Houston's volume, "Our students were very warmly, though quietly, received, and promptly put to work. . . . While Rhody McCoy and his staff confirmed our impression that the students performed capably and confidently, the students themselves had many mixed reactions to the experience. Most of them were appalled at the physical condition of the schools; many of those who had been sympathetic to the parents and children of the community began to blame them for conditions. Others continued to blame the system, and many were just confused and distressed at what they saw and heard." The following August the college organized a two-day workshop on the subject of decentralization. Excerpted from the Second Annual Report and Evaluation of the Women's Talent Corps, prepared by Barbara Walton, 1967–1968 program, 20–22, in Laura Pires-Houston, "The Women's Talent Corps → The College for Human Services: An Historical Reconstruction Phase I–Crystal 3: Institutional Development and expansion–Pushing the Parameters of the Possible," Vol. IV, December 4, 1978, 25A.

15. "Profile of Audrey Cohen," College for Human Services, July 1983, Archive Folder #000750, 5; also personal communication from Clyde Griffin, Fall 2012. I have been unable to determine whether Cohen was acting alone or with others at this time.

16. Conversation with Nicholas Juravich, September 12, 2013.

17. "UFT Hails Breakthrough Program of Teacher Assistants," *United Teacher*, Vol. 8, No. 13, February 17, 1967.

18. A draft of a report roughly typed, probably by Audrey Cohen, with Dellie Bloom's handwritten corrections, Archive Folder #000058, fifth page.

19. Women's Talent Corps, Minutes of the Meeting of the Governing Board, November 8, 1965, Archive Folder #000653.

20. Dellie Bloom interview with Herbert Bienstock, Audrey Cohen College, May 15, 1992, Archive Folder #000082, 1–2.

21. Women's Talent Corps, Minutes of the Meeting of the Governing Board, February 15, 1966, Archive Folder #000654.

22. The minutes of a May 16, 1966, Meeting of the Women's Talent Corps Governing Board refers to ongoing delays with the proposal: "A letter from Sen. Robert Kennedy to OEO was the precursor to budget review meetings held in New York City with Mrs. Cohen and several members of the board in February. On OEO recommendation following suggested budget revisions, the proposal itself was revised to coincide with the budget changes and resubmitted to Washington in April. . . . In April a key OEO official from Washington called on Mrs. Cohen to specify two requisites for funding: 1) sponsorship by an organization with 'prior concern with poverty'; and 2) a program statement stressing the training institute as the core of the program. . . ." The minutes state that to accommodate the last requirement, the Forest Neighborhood House had agreed to nominal sponsorship of the Women's Talent Corps. See Archive Folder #000654.

23. GR interview with Diana Gordon, October 13, 2011, Morgan transcript, 2.

24. GR interview with Dawn Margolin, January 20, 2012, Morgan transcript, 16. Also see GR interview with Wendy Cohen, 3: "My mother always had a vision, and she had a vision for this place that, 'you know what, I can turn this into something.' And she did, and it turned out great."

25. GR interview with Franklyn Rother, May 10, 2013, Morgan transcript, 11.

26. GR interview with Diana Gordon, 4. In the draft of a "History" of the College Cohen referred favorably to Gordon: "Eventually I met a most incredible woman, Dini [sic] Gordon. . . . She was dedicated and concerned and willing to listen and understand and help. She came to believe in what we were trying to accomplish and it was through her good support that we finally were funded." Audrey Cohen, "The History of the College for Human Services" Chapter III (8/15/1977), 4.

27. GR interview with Diana Gordon, 5.

28. Western Union Telegram from Sargent Shriver to Audrey Cohen, July 15, 1966, Archive Folder #004904.

29. CAP-RDT FORM 2 and 3 of the Office of Economic Opportunity, Archive Folder #004903.

30. Speech delivered for HERS in Denver, CO, Archive Folder #000098, No. 3, 16.

31. Entry on John Lindsay in Wikipedia. http://en.wikipedia.org/wiki/John_Lindsay.

32. GR interview with Mark Cohen, 9.

33. A draft of a report roughly typed, probably by Audrey Cohen, with Dellie Bloom's handwritten corrections, Archive Folder #000058, second and sixth pages. In the archives is also a copy of a letter from Audrey Cohen to President Lyndon B. Johnson, (dated January 7, 1965), though there is no evidence that he responded. See Archive Folder #000654.

34. GR interview with Diana Gordon, 5–6.

35. GR interview with Dawn Margolin, 18–19.

36. Ibid., 20.

37. Ibid., 33.

38. GR interview with Mark Cohen, 11. GR interview with Wendy Cohen, 13.

39. GR interview with Mark Cohen, 11.

40. Ibid., 17.

41. Mesrop, "In the Beginning," 17.

CHAPTER 5. THE WOMEN'S TALENT CORPS (1965–1967)

1. GR interview with Laura Pires-Hester, June 21, 2011, Morgan transcript, 2–3.

2. Ibid.

3. Laura Pires-Houston, "The Women't Talent Corps → The College for Human Services: An Historical Reconstruction," Vol. 1: Phase I: Building and Transition (1966–1968), August 16, 1978, 12.

4. "Book on the History of the College," taped conversation between Alida Mesrop and Audrey Cohen—August 4, 1986, Archive Folder #000094, 12.

5. Pires Houston, "The Women's Talent Corps," 20.

6. See minutes of the Governing Board meeting of September 17, 1966: "A motion was made and carried to authorize the Women's Talent Corps to accept office space at 346 Broadway as a base of operations, through October 1967. The space has been offered rent-free by the federal government, which is moving into new quarters, and is convenient to all forms of transportation," Archive Folder #000654, 3.

7. Pires Houston, "The Women's Talent Corps," 20.

8. Women's Talent Corps, minutes of meeting of Board of Directors, October 26, 1966, Archive Folder #00654, 1.

9. Pires-Houston, "The Women's Talent Corps," 20–21.

10. Grant and Riesman, in *Perpetual Dream*, Chapter 5 (135), state that the Women's Talent Corps opened in 1965. This is misleading. Students were

not enrolled until 1966. In addition to the Pire-Houston's "Reconstruction" cited earlier, see "The College for Human Services: An Historical Perspective," in Archive Folder #000062.

11. Audrey C. Cohen, "The College for Human Services," *Teachers College Record*, Vol. 69, No. 7, 1968, 665; http://www.tcrecord.org, ID Number: 1966, 3.

12. Frank Riessman, *New Careers: A Basic Strategy Against Poverty*. With an Introduction by Michael Harrington. (New York: A Philip Randolph Educational Fund, November, 1967), inside front cover.

13. Riessman, *New Careers*, 18.

14. Indeed, the United Federation of Teachers' (UFT) archives provide evidence of the union's recognition of the Women's Talent Corps as a model training institution for paraprofessionals. In a *United Teacher* article in the January 1968 issue entitled "UFT Opens Doors for the Educational Assistant," Gladys Roth stated that "The seed [for the creation of the career position of educational assistant] was first planted in April 1967, when at the request of the UFT, Superintendent Donovan agreed to hire 75 teacher assistants trained by the Women's Talent Corps." (UFT Papers, Box 155, Folder 1). I am indebted to Nicholas Juravich for this information.

15. "Part III, Women's Talent Corps Program and Its Accomplishments in 1966–67," in the "Application for Extension of OEO Contract," the Women's Talent Corps, 1967, Archive Folder #004905, 10. In Cohen's *Teachers College Record* article the cycles are described somewhat differently: "Each training cycle of the Women's Talent Corps institute begins with four weeks of classroom orientation and academic work, followed by six months of combined academic and field training (20 hours field practicum, 10 hours seminar). This is a total of thirty weeks, the span of an academic year." See Audrey C. Cohen, "The College for Human Services," *Teachers College Record*, Vol. 69, No. 7, 1968, 665; http://www.tcrecord. org, ID Number: 1966, 4.

16. CAP-RDT Form 3, "Proposed Budget," of Proposal to Office of Economic Opportunity, Archive Folder #004903. The earnings for the Coordinator Teachers are taken not from this document but from news articles published in January 1967. See Mary Hornaday, "Talent Corps Graduates Sent Afield," *Christian Science Monitor*, January 23, 1967, page number illegible.

17. As the minutes of the meeting of the Board of Directors on October 26, 1966, make clear, fewer than expected of the first applicants to the program had incomes that low, and the Board discussed (without coming to a resolution at that point) whether "a greater degree of flexibility might not be desirable to permit selection of otherwise eligible women with incomes above $4,000," Archive Folder 0000654, 2.

18. Application for Extension of OEO Contract," the Women's Talent Corps, 1967, Archive Folder #004905, 9. See also Cohen, "The College for Human Services," *Teachers College Record*.

19. "Personal History Written by F.L.–Cycle I Trainee," in Appendix B of "Application for Extension of OEO Contract," the Women's Talent Corps, 1967, Archive Folder #004905.

20. "Personal History Written by L.C.–Cycle I Trainee," in Appendix B of "Application for Extension of OEO Contract," the Women's Talent Corps, 1967, Archive Folder #004905.

21. "Personal History Written by G.C.–Cycle I Trainee," 3, in Appendix B of "Application for Extension of OEO Contract," the Women's Talent Corps, 1967, Archive Folder #004905.

22. Mary Hornaday, "Talent Corps Graduates Sent Afield," *Christian Science Monitor*, January 23, 1967, page number illegible.

23. Pires-Houston, "The Women's Talent Corps," 24–25 and 134.

24. See Grant and Riesman, *Perpetual Dream*, 138. In another context the Coordinator Trainers were referred to as "reformist middle class ladies," a term that made Cohen and her colleagues cringe. See Joseph Featherstone, "The Talent Corps: Career Ladders for Bottom Dogs," *The New Republic*, September 13, 1969, 1, Archive Folder #000573 and Grant and Riesman, *Perpetual Dream*, 136.

25. Minutes of the May 16, 1966, meeting of the Governing Board of the Women's Talent Corps, 2, Archive Folder #000654.

26. Pires-Houston, "The Women's Talent Corps," 26–33. Other CTs included in Cycle I were Babette Drapkin, Ruth Ovryn, Barbara Prem, Marcia Smiegel, Mildren Stuart, and Myra Waldinger; in Cycle II Diane Cook, Ruth Jutson, Susan McCord, Lygia Rivers, Marie Nersoyan, and Lee Snider; and in Cycle III Jean Gant, Ellen Maslow, Gladys Williams Meyersand, Irene Wolf, Rose Saletan, Felicia Wright, and Micaela Hickey.

27. Email message to the author from Ellen Bloom Lubell, June 25, 2013.

28. GR telephone interview with Barbara Buchanan, June 25, 2013.

29. GR interview with Sylvia Hack and Judy Hozore, June 15, 2011, Morgan transcript, 41.

30. Oral History interview with Dodie Younger by Dellie Bloom, 10/10/1976; transcribed 3/14/1989, from Archive Folder #000173, 1 and 8.

31. There are no Student Progress Workbooks in the college's archives, but they are mentioned by Barbara Walton in her interview with Dellie Bloom, June 29, 1993, Archive Folder #000166, last page.

32. "Part III, Women's Talent Corps Program and Its Accomplishments in 1966–67," in the "Application for Extension of OEO Contract," the Women's

Talent Corps, 1967, Archive Folder #004905, 10–11. See also Cohen, "The College for Human Services," in the *Teachers College Record*. A transcription of a tape recording of Audrey Cohen's summary of the program describes the Orientation classes as follows: "The City of New York was one of the basic topics during this period . . . the various departments and their functions . . . the youth of the city . . . schools and . . . legal services in the city . . . welfare. Then there was the standard fare for potential job seekers . . . how to write a business letter, communications . . . speaking and writing . . . job interviews, . . . facing on-the-job situations." See fifth page of untitled manuscript, Archive Folder #000058.

33. Cohen, "The College for Human Services," *Teachers College Record*, printout, 9.

34. Oral History interview with Dodie Younger by Dellie Bloom, 10/10/1976; transcribed 3/14/1989, from Archive Folder #000173, 2.

35. GR interview with Laura Pires-Hester, June 21, 2011, Morgan transcript, 15.

36. Women's Talent Corps, "Application for Extension of OEO Contract," April 1967, Archive Folder #004905, Appendix D.

37. Cohen, "The College for Human Services," *Teachers College Record*, printout, 5.

38. Laura Pires Houston, "The Women's Talent Corps → The College for Human Services: An Historical Reconstruction" (Phase I: Crystal 3: Institutional Devlopment and Expansion—Pushing the Parameters of the Possible) Vol. IV, December 4, 1978, 16.

39. Grant and Riesman, *Perpetual Dream*.

40. Pires-Houston, "The Women's Talent Corps," 40–44.

41. Ibid., 57.

42. Ibid., 40–44.

43. Oral History interview with Dodie Younger by Dellie Bloom, 10/10/1976; transcribed 3/14/1989, from Archive Folder #000173, 8.

44. See profiles and resumes in Archive Folder 000751.

45. Patterson, *Grand Expectations*, 662–663.

46. James Sandquist, *Politics and Policy: The Eisenhower, Kennedy, and Johnson Years* (Washington, 1968), 285, cited in Patterson, *Grand Expectations*, 649.

47. Robert Hamlett Bremner, *Children and Youth in America: A Documentary History*, Vol. 1–3 (Cambridge, MA: Harvard University Press, 1974), 494.

48. Women's Talent Corps, "Application for Extension of OEO Contract," April 1967, Archive Folder #004905, 11.

49. Women's Talent Corps, "Application for Extension of OEO Contract," 21–22.

50. Ibid., 22.

51. See profile of Audrey Cohen Executive Director of the Women's Talent Corps, Archive Folder #000751, 2.

52. "My notes indicate that the grant was 'signed off' on 11/6/67." Pires-Houston, "The Women's Talent Corps," Vol. IV, 13.

53. The address on Audrey Cohen's resume in Archive Folder #000751, apparently written in 1968, is the first document I've seen containing the Varick Street address.

54. Cohen, "The College for Human Services," *Teachers College Record*, printout 2.

55. Ibid., printout 6–7.

56. Ibid., printout 7.

57. Ibid., printout 8 and 11.

58. Dellie Bloom, Observations, "Social Notes: the 60s and 70s," in Barbara Walton's file box labeled "History, '89–90," November 27, 1990, first page of unpaged document.

59. Ibid.

60. Ibid., second page of unpaged document.

61. Ibid.

62. Ibid.

63. Ibid.

64. Ibid., third page of unpaged document.

CHAPTER 6. TRIAL BY FIRE (1968–1972)

1. Audrey Cohen, in transcribed tapes that she did of herself, probably in 1978, of a discussion with an unidentified audience, Archive Folder #000097, Tape B, 4.

2. Patterson, *Grand Expectations*, 655.

3. Pires Houston, "The Women's Talent Corps" Vol. IV, 11.

4. Ibid., Vol. 1, 53–53a.

5. Ibid., Vol. 1, 53a–53b.

6. Ibid., Vol. 1, 53b.

7. Ibid., Vol. 1, 53.

8. Oral History interview with Dodie Younger by Dellie Bloom, 10/10/1976; transcribed 3/14/1989, from Archive Folder #000173, 3–4.

9. For background planning of the demonstration see Board of Trustees minutes of a meeting on September 23, 1967.

10. Pires Houston, "The Women's Talent Corps" Vol. IV, 13.

11. GR interview with Alida Mesrop, 6.

12. Pires Houston, "The Women's Talent Corps," Vol. IV, 12–13.

13. Dawn Cohen interview with Audrey Cohen, 24.

14. Ibid., 26.

15. Grant and Riesman, *Perpetual Dream*, 140.

16. Ibid.

17. Ibid., 140–141.

18. Louis Menand, Massachusetts Institute of Technology, chairman; Frank Chambers, Middlesex County College, and Richard C. Richardson Jr., Northampton County Area Community College, "Report on Talent Corps, Inc., New York City, concerning its application for a charter as a two-year college to be known as College for Human Services." Dated by hand 1969, from Archive Folder #002091, 1.

19. Freshman Curriculum Material, 1969, Unit II: Society, Archive Folder #003105.

20. Menand et al., 9.

21. In 1975 board member Israel Laster claimed that getting the right to grant the AA degree was the peak experience of his years on the board. See Dellie Bloom's interview with Israel Laster, December 16, 1975, Archive Folder #000128.

22. "Regents Charter School for Poor: 2-Year College Here Gives 'Human Service' Training," *New York Times*, May 26, 1970. http://select.nytimes.com/gst/abstract.html?res=F0061FFC3B5A157493C4AB178ED85F448785F9.

23. Oral History interview with Dodie Younger by Dellie Bloom, 8–9.

24. "New Way Up," *Vogue*, Vol. 152, No. 7, October 15, 1968, 98–99.

25. See curriculum vitae of Audrey C. Cohen, Archive Folder #000098, 4, and in Archive Folder #000751, 4–5.

26. "Education: Self-Made College," *Time* July 6, 1970, online at http://content.time.com/time/subscriber/printout/0,8816,878365,00.html, 1.

27. See curriculum vitae of Cohen, 3 and 4.

28. Dellie Bloom, transcript of telephone interview with Joseph Rhodes Jr., June 30, 1992, 2, Archive Folder #000053.

29. Audrey C. Cohen, "Women and Higher Education: Recommendations for Change," *Phi Delta Kappan*, November 1971, 164–167.

30. See the report on the legal service assistant program in Grant and David Riesman, *Perpetual Dream*.

31. "To Docket from Audrey Cohen," December 1970, Archive Folder #003021, 1. Typed at the top of the first thin yellow sheet of paper is "This and some of the following tapes are concerned with events in 1970 but may conceivably

be useful in the design of the book or the story of what happened at the College for Human Services." I am basing the chronology here on Cohen's memory of the sequence of events. In other accounts (see, e.g., Dellie Bloom's interview of Peter Houghteling, March 4, 1994, from Barbara Walton's file drawer labeled "History '89–92"), the sensitivity training session occurred after the strike.

32. "To Docket from Audrey Cohen," December 1970, Archive Folder #003021, 1–2.

33. Larry Neal, "Black Art and Black Liberation," in a special 1969 issue of *Ebony*, excerpted in Alexander Bloom and Wini Breines, *"Takin' it to the Streets": A Sixties Reader* (New York: Oxford University Press, 2003), 122.

34. Position paper circulated by SNCC "The Basis of Black Power," excerpted in Bloom and Breines, 117.

35. "To Docket from Audrey Cohen," 6 and 4.

36. Audrey Cohen, "Thoughts on the College." "On July 31st we reached the decision to ask for Bob Jackson's resignation." March 16, 1971, Archive Folder #003021, 2.

37. See a memo to Robert Jackson, from Audrey C. Cohen and Laura Houston, dated August 11, 1970, Re: Job Termination, Archive Folder #000661.

38. Cohen's memories of this period are roughly typed on a packet of thin yellow paper entitled "Thoughts on the College," hand-dated March 16th, 1971, Archive Folder #003021, 1.

39. Another set of reflections, "Tape 9," hand-dated 2/24, 1, Archive Folder #003021.

40. Undated two-page draft memo, Archive Folder #000661.

41. Cohen, "Thoughts on the College," 1.

42. On letterhead from Afram Associates Inc., Wilcox's community outreach organization, August 17, 1970, Archive Folder #000661.

43. From "Humanness in a Racist Society," a talk given at the Salvation Army Breakfast Meeting at the National Conference on Social Welfare, May 27, 1969, as cited in a petition by undersigned members of the first and second year faculty, August 18, 1970, Archive Folder #000662.

44. Memo to Faculty, Students, Staff and Administration, College for Human Services, from Preston Wilcox, Chairman, Board of Trustees, hand-dated August 20, 1970, Archive Folder #000661. Underlining is in the original.

45. These are estimates from Cohen, "Thoughts on the College," 4. The "Fourth Annual Report" of the College for Human Services for 1970, prepared by Barbara J. Walton (copyright 1972), states that "at its peak" the picket line outside the College reached some 50–75 persons," Archive Folder #000004, 48.

46. Cohen, "Thoughts on the College," 2–3.

47. Ibid. 4.

48. To Arthur Gelb, *New York Times*, from Audrey Cohen November 13, 1970, Archive Folder #000644.

49. The letter of resignation had been drafted earlier by Alida Mesrop, just in case Cohen might need it. See GR interview with Alida Mesrop, 7–8.

50. Nancy Moran, "Students Occupy Office of Training School's Chief," *New York Times*, September 3, 1970, 29.

51. The "Fourth Annual Report" of the College for Human Services for 1970, prepared by Barbara J. Walton (copyright 1972), Archive Folder #000004, 51.

52. Moran, "Students Occupy Office," 11.

53. Ibid., 29.

54. GR interview with Dawn Margolin, 18–19.

55. "Book on the History of the College," transcription of taped conversation between Alida Mesrop and Audrey Cohen. August 4, 1986, Archive Folder #000094, 20.

56. Cohen, "Thoughts on the College," 9.

57. The College for Human Services, minutes of the Board of Trustees Meeting, November 13, 1990, Archive Folder #000171, 1 and 2.

58. Preston Wilcox to Brother Kalu Kalu, December 22, 1970, 1, Archive Folder 000171.

59. Preston Wilcox to Brother Kalu Kalu, 1–2. See also Molefe Kete Asante, *The Afrocentric Idea* (Philadelphia: Temple University Press, 1987).

60. Dellie Bloom, Interview/Conversation with Kalu Kalu, taped 3/14/1991, 3, Archive Folder #000126.

61. College for Human Services, Minutes of the Board of Trustees' meeting on May 20, 1971, 7, Archive Folder #000666.

62. "The History of the College for Human Services," Tape No. 2, Alida Mesrop and Audrey Cohen, August 4, 1986, 5, Archive Folder #000094.

63. "History of the College," Mesrop and Cohen, 18–19.

64. Ibid., 3.

65. Memo to members of the Board of Trustees, College for Human Services, from Preston Wilcox, May 30, 1972, Archive Folder #000747. Typed onto the Afram Associates letterhead throughout 1972 is the statement "You can't be free if someone else lets you be free." The statement is identified as coming from Harlem subway graffiti at the time and may give an indication of Wilcox's conflicting feelings about white-led movements for social change. See Archive Folder #3000747.

66. Dellie Bloom, interview/conversation with Kalu Kalu, taped 3/14/1991, 3, Archive Folder #000126. A similar story of Preston Wilcox's complex relationship

with integrationist educational institutions founded in the 1960s can be found in the history of Manhattan Country School. See Augustus Trowbridge, *Begin with a Dream: How a Private school with a Public Mission Changed the Politics of Race, Class, and Gender in American Education* (New York: Xlibris, 2005), 104, 135, 190–192, 196–198. I am grateful to Frank Roosevelt for finding these references.

67. "Sixth Annual Report of the College for Human Services, 1972–1973" by Judith S. Hozore and Barbara J. Walton (New York: The College for Human Services, 1976), 42–44. Archive Folder #000006.

68. "Fifth Annual Report of the College for Human Services, 1971 Program," 1, Archive Folder #000005.

69. "Sixth Annual Report," 42–44.

70. Dellie Bloom, "Narrative Summary, 1970–1980," labeled c:/db-text/his. chr, in Barbara Walton's file box labeled "History '89–92," 1.

71. Audrey C. Cohen, "The Service Society and a Theory of Learning Linking Education, Work, Life." (New York: The College for Human Services, 1976, 1989, 1997), 6.

72. Cited in the "Sixth Annual Report," 45.

73. Ibid., 47.

74. Audiotapes recorded by Audrey C. Cohen, probably in 1972, in the presence of unidentified other persons, transcribed 11/3/1989 by Dellie Bloom whose notes are attached, Archive Folder #000097, 1–4, italics added.

75. "Sixth Annual Report," 47–48.

76. I am summarizing here comments by Gary Roth, 8/16/2012.

77. The competing pulls of integration and black power did tear at the soul of Preston Wilcox, but he had few followers at the college and eventually left.

78. Audrey C. Cohen, "A Feminist System of Education for a New Public Service," Chapter 8 of Alan Gartner, Russell A. Nixon, and Frank Riessman, eds., *Public Service Employment: An Analysis of Its History, Problems, and Prospects*, with an introduction by Michael Harrington (New York: Praeger, 1973), 83.

79. Cohen, "A Feminist System of Education," in *Public Service Employment*, 84.

80. Ibid., 85–87.

81. GR interview with Dawn Margolin, 8–10.

82. Ibid., 9.

83. GR interview with Dodie Younger, October 20, 2011, Morgan transcript, 21.

84. GR interview with Dawn Margolin, 10.

CHAPTER 7. REINVENTING HIGHER EDUCATION (1973–1974)

1. The Protestant Reformation of the sixteenth century led to proposals for secularizing the schooling of children, the eighteenth-century Enlightenment and the political revolutions that followed gave rise to an interest in applying scientific methods to instruction, and the Industrial Revolution of the mid-nineteenth century ushered in models of elementary education that were universal, compulsory, and publicly financed. For educational change during the Reformation, see James Bowen, *A History of Western Education*, Vol. II, (New York: St. Martin's Press, 1972), 346–400. For a brief overview of educational proposals during the French Revolution, see H.C. Barnard, *Education and the French Revolution* (Cambridge: Cambridge University Press, 1969). For the United States during the Industrial Revolution see Lawrence A. Cremin's introduction to *The Republic and the School: Horace Mann on the Education of Free Man* (New York: Teachers College Press, Classics in Education No. 1, 1957), 3–28; and Michael B. Katz, *Class, Bureaucracy, and Schools: The Illusion of Educational Change in America* (New York: Praeger, 1975).

2. For the story of Manhattan Country School's early years see Trowbridge, *Begin With a Dream*.

3. See, for example, Nora Harlow, *Sharing the Children: Village Child Rearing Within the City* (New York: Harper and Row, 1975).

4. Grant and Riesman, *Perpetual Dream*, 1 and 3.

5. Ibid., 2.

6. Metropolitan College of New York, "Guidelines for Constructive Actions," v. 5.2, 9/19/12.

7. Deborah Allen, "A History of the Dimensions," unpublished paper, June 10, 2013, 8.

8. Audrey C. Cohen, "The Third Alternative" (New York: Audrey Cohen College, 1975, 1988, 1997), 8. In that article the dimensions are clarified further: "Instead of focusing on the distinctions between the disciplines and choosing the one discipline that they will specialize in, our students learn to bring together relevant elements from the liberal arts, the social sciences, and business and professional research and practice and draw on them to achieve worthwhile purposes" (6).

9. For the curricular grid filled in with course titles, see http://www.mcny.edu/human_serv/bpscourse_new.php.

10. See Chapter 10.

11. The term *connective thinking* comes from Jaya Kannan, faculty member at MCNY from 2004 to 2011.

12. Dellie Bloom interview with Barbara Walton, June 29, 1993, Archive Folder #000166, seventh page of unpaged document.

13. I am indebted to Wendy Cohen for this observation, email correspondence, June 12, 2013.

14. Dellie Bloom interview with Barbara Walton, seventh to ninth pages of unpaged document.

15. Ibid., eleventh page of unpaged document.

16. Ibid., thirteenth, fifteenth, and sixteenth pages of unpaged document.

17. Dellie Bloom, "Narrative Summary, 1970–1980," c:/db-text/his.chr from Barbara Walton file box labeled HISTORY, with handwritten title, "History Text: Dellie '92"

18. "Sixth Annual Report," 55.

19. Audrey C. Cohen, "A Vision of Humanity for the Future," speech given at Sterling Forest Staff Retreat, January 1973, Archive Folder #000802, seventh page of unnumbered document.

20. See Dellie Bloom, "History Interview" with Alida Mesrop, 12.

21. Barbara Walton, "Origins of the Human Service Performance Grid (1973–1974)," Occasional Paper, Chapter I of Annual Report. August 1978, 2–3, Archive Folder #000166.

22. Ibid., 3. Walton also mentions Michael Eoner, who was primarily interested in research and left the process before the end of the year.

23. GR interview with Tom Webber, June 18, 2012, Morgan transcript, 15 and 3.

24. GR interview with Deborah Allen, June 23, 2011, Morgan transcript, 17 and 19.

25. Barbara Walton, "Origins" 4.

26. GR interview with Tom Webber, 7, and Walton, "Origins," 5.

27. Walton, "Origins," 5–6.

28. Dellie Bloom, summary of taped interview, August 24, 1991, Archive Folder #000163, 5.

29. Walton, "Origins," 7.

30. Ibid., 6–15.

31. Dellie Bloom interview with Steve Sunderland, 8/24/91, in Barbara Walton's file box labeled "History 89–92," second and third page of unpaged document. Dellie Bloom's summary of the interview appears in Archive Folder #000163.

32. Walton, "Origins," 9.

33. Ibid., 15–19.

34. Ibid., 19–20.

35. Ibid., 22–23.

36. Ibid., 24.

37. GR phone conversation with Deborah Allen, Fall 2012.

38. GR interview with Tom Webber, 7–9.

39. Walton, "Origins," 26.

40. Ibid., 26–27. See also Cohen's account of the breakthrough in Audrey C. Cohen, *The Service Society, and a Theory of Learning Linking Education, Work, Life*. Originally prepared for delivery at a symposium, "Policy Issues in Educating for New and Emerging Careers," held at Pennsylvania State University, May 5 and 6, 1976, and in 1989, with support from the Banbury Foundation, republished by the College for Human Services, 12.

41. "Competency Reorganization," notes by Debbie Allen, n.d. (February 7, 1974?) cited in Barbara Walton, "Origins," 27.

42. Cohen, "The Service Society," 14.

43. Dellie Bloom interview with Steve Sunderland, 8/24/91, in Barbara Walton's file box labeled "History '89–92," fifth and seventh page of unpaged document. Dellie Bloom's summary of the interview appears in Archive Folder #000163. Bloom interviewed Sunderland in Cincinnati, where he still lives, and between the car trip from the airport and the hours talking in his office the interview lasted about four hours.

44. GR interview with Tom Webber, 6.

45. Audrey C. Cohen, Laura Houston, and Alida Mesrop, "Human-Services Education: College for Human Services," in S.V. Martorana and Eileen Kuhns, *Managing Academic Change* (San Francisco: Jossey-Bass, 1975), 27.

46. Personal email from Tom Webber, February 18, 2013.

47. Dellie Bloom interview with Yolaine Armand, August 7, 1991, Archive Folder #000078, eighth page of unpaged document.

48. Ibid., fifth page and last four pages of unpaged document.

49. Ibid., seventeenth page of unpaged document.

50. Ibid., sixteenth and seventeenth pages of unpaged document.

51. GR interview with Tom Webber, 11 and 43.

52. Dellie Bloom interview with Steve Sunderland, Tape II, 8/24/91, in Barbara Walton's file box labeled "History '89–92," eighth and fourteenth page of unpaged document. Dellie Bloom's summary of the interview appears in Archive Folder #000163. Italics added.

53. From Audrey Cohen, "The Third Alternative," originally published in 1975 by the College for Human Services, published in 1997 by Audrey Cohen College, New York. Note 24, 28.

54. Dellie Bloom interview with Steve Sunderland, tenth page of unpaged document. Dellie Bloom's summary of the interview appears in Archive Folder #000163.

55. Dellie Bloom interview with Steve Sunderland, 8/24/91, Tape II, in Barbara Walton's file box labeled "History '89–92," fourteenth page of unpaged document. Dellie Bloom's summary of the interview appears in Archive Folder #000163.

56. See, for example, the extensive chronology of Dewey's full life at the Center for Dewey Studies: http://www.siuc.edu/~deweyctr/pdf/CHRONO.pdf.

57. Susan F. Semel and Alan R. Sadovnik, "The Contemporary Small-School Movement: Lessons from the History of Progressive education," *Teachers College Record*, Vol. 110, No. 9, September 2008, 1744–1771, 1749.

58. John Dewey, "My Pedagogic Creed," in Martin S. Dworkin, *Dewey on Education: Selections* (New York: Teachers College Press, 1975), 22.

59. For a brief overview of Dewey's synthetic impulses, see Grace Roosevelt, "Reconsidering Dewey in a Culture of Consumerism: A Rousseauean Critique," *Philosophy of Education Society Yearbook 2011*, 283–292.

60. John Dewey's lecture notes from 1892, cited by Robert B. Westbrook, *John Dewey and American Democracy* (Ithaca: Cornell University Press, 1991), 44.

61. John Dewey, *Democracy and Education* (New York: Free Press, 1944), 114.

62. John Dewey, *Experience and Education* (New York: Collier Books, 1974), 22 and 56–58.

63. John Dewey, "My Pedagogic Creed," in *Dewey on Education*, 20.

64. John Dewey, *The School and Society and the Child and the Curriculum*, ed., Philip W. Jackson (Chicago: University of Chicago Press, 1990), 189.

65. Dewey, "My Pedagogic Creed," in *Dewey on Education*, 28.

66. Audrey C. Cohen, "The Citizen as the Integrating Agent: Productivity in the Human Services," *Human Service Monograph Series*, Project Share, No. 9, September 1978, 37; also at http://www.mcny.edu/library/documents/cohenciti-zena.html#empowercon.

67. Dewey, "My Pedagogic Creed," in *Dewey on Education*, 19.

68. While the cohort model can be highly motivational for students, it can cause administrative challenges when accepting transfer students or if a student needs to repeat a semester. The model also puts some pressure on faculty because they must function as part of an integrated, interdisciplinary team. Both of these challenges have been encountered at MCNY in recent years. I am indebted to Gary Roth for reminding me of these administrative hurdles.

CHAPTER 8. THE COLLEGE FOR HUMAN SERVICES GAINS RECOGNITION (1975–1979)

1. Northeastern Illinois University Faculty Meeting (Lunch) October 1994, Archive Folder 3000093, 7. This was probably part of a Conference on Innovation in Higher Education that Cohen attended on October 16–17, 1974, where she delivered a paper on "A Strategy for Changing Higher Education." See curriculum vitae dated 12/79 in Archive Folder #000098, 3.

2. See curriculum vitae dated 12/79 in Archive Folder #000098, 5.

3. GR interview with Dawn Margolin, 2.

4. GR interview with Wendy Cohen, 13.

5. GR interview with Dawn Margolin, 17.

6. Ibid., 19.

7. Ibid., 4 and 12.

8. GR interview with Wendy Cohen, 12.

9. GR interview with Dawn Margolin, 12–13.

10. Ibid., 34.

11. GR interview with Wendy Cohen, 12.

12. Ibid., 6.

13. GR interview with Frances Pelzman, 18.

14. GR interview with Mark Cohen, 16.

15. Ibid.

16. GR interview with Alida Mesrop, 1.

17. Grant and Riesman, *Perpetual Dream*, 150.

18. Dellie Bloom, "History Interview" with Alida Mesrop, 15.

19. Jean Macht with Douglas A. Whyte, "Human Services: History and Recent Influences," Chapter 3 in Howard S. Harris and David C. Maloney, eds., *Human Services: Contemporary Issues and Trends* (Boston: Allyn and Bacon, 1998), 35–58. I am indebted to Professor Franklyn Rother for this reference.

20. The "generalist" approach was conceptualized by Dr. Harold McPheeters in 1973. See Macht and Whyte, "Human Services: History and Recent Influences," in *Human Services: Contemporary Issues and Trends*, 52.

21. In much of the human services literature the word "indigenous" is used to refer to the workers from low-income communities——a term that Cohen herself never used. See, for example, Macht and Whyte, "Human Services: History and Recent Influences," *Human Services: Contemporary Issues and Trends*, 50.

22. Franklyn Rother, email communication, September 26, 2013. See also Audrey C. Cohen, "Human Service," Chapter 27 of Arthur W. Chickering

and Associates, *The Modern American College* (San Francisco: Jossey-Bass, 1981), 512–519.

23. Grant and Riesman, *Perpetual Dream*, 151–152.

24. Ibid., 152.

25. See entry for "Crystal" on Wikipedia at http://en.wikipedia.org/wiki/Crystal.

26. Walton, "Origins," 25. Cohen later elaborated on the crystal image as follows: "A mineral crystal has unique properties. It shows us different aspects of the world around us, depending on how it is turned. It brings together differing views of the world and lets us see how they relate to each other. It breaks apart the light that comes into it, displaying it in colorful array, and then focuses it once more. And, like a living thing, a crystal grows in all directions." From Cohen, "The Service Society," 10.

27. Tom Webber remembers the term *crystal* being applied to the dimensions, but by 1976 the publications about the model show refer specifically to the crystals as competencies. See GR interview with Tom Webber, June 18, 2012, Morgan transcript 10.

28. Audrey C. Cohen, *The Citizen as the Integrating Agent: Productivity in the Human Services*. Human Services Monograph Series. Project SHARE, No. 9, September 1978. Downloaded from http://www.mcny.edu/library/documents/cohencitizena.html. See also Cohen, "The Service Society," 40–41.

29. For a sense of the contents of the *Purpose Handbooks*, see Archive Folders #3111–3213.

30. College for Human Services Policy Paper #2, Archive Folder #000062, hand-dated 1977. Emphasis in the original.

31. See MCNY's statements of Mission, Vision, and Values at http://www.mcny.edu/about/mission.php.

32. College for Human Services Policy Paper #2. Emphasis in the original.

33. Ibid.

34. See profile document, June 1977, Audrey C. Cohen, president, College for Human Services, Archive File #000750, 3.

35. College for Human Services Policy Paper #2.

36. Ibid., #3, Archive Folder #000062, hand-dated 1977.

37. GR interview of Tom Webber, 17.

38. See Archive Folders #002017–002066.

39. Cohen, "The Third Alternative," 9–10.

40. Ibid., 11–12.

41. Ibid., 12–15.

42. Ibid., 24–25.

43. Paolo Freire, *Pedagogy of the Oppressed* (New York: Seabury Press, 1974), 67–68.

44. Cohen, "The Citizen as the Integrating Agent." http://www.mcny.edu/library/documents/cohencitizena.html#empowercon, printout 2.

45. Ibid, printout 3.

46. Ibid., printout 2–3.

47. Ibid., printout 4.

48. Ibid., printout 25.

49. Audrey C. Cohen, "Human Service," Chapter 27 in Arthur W. Chickering and Associates, *The Modern American College* (San Francisco: Jossey-Bass, 1981), 514 and 528.

50. See, for example, Samuel Bowles, Richard Edwards, and Frank Roosevelt, *Understanding Capitalism: Competition, Command, and Change* (New York: Oxford University Press, 2005), 175–176.

51. See, for example, http://www.nationalhumanservices.org/what-is-human-services.

52. Cohen, "The Third Alternative," 27.

53. Ibid., 13.

54. Ibid., 1.

55. Ibid., 5. Emphasis added for clarity.

56. See the American Friends Service Committee web page at http://afsc.org/about.

57. Personal telephone conversation with Barbara Walton's daughter Frances Walton, February 19, 2013.

58. Cohen, "The Third Alternative," 27.

59. See Chapter 5.

60. Letter to Dr. [sic.] Audrey Cohen from Frank Newman, November 10, 1978, Archive Folder #000141.

61. Patricia McCormack, United Press International, "New College for Human Services gives courses in purposeful living," *Providence Sunday Journal*, November 5, 1978, E 23, Archive Folder #000141.

62. McCormack, "New College," E 23.

63. Robert Coles, "Telic Reforms," *New Yorker*, March 13, 1978, 134–141.

64. From a folder entitled "Alida's Intro" in a file box of Barbara Walton's papers in the MCNY Archives room but not included in the professionally indexed archives.

65. GR interview with Alida Mesrop, 18.

66. College for Human Services Policy Paper #1, hand-dated 1977, Archive Folder #000062.

67. Dellie Bloom interview with David Seeley, July 22, 1992, 11–12, from Barbara Walton's file drawer.

68. Ibid., 14–15.

69. Frank J. Prial, "A Degree Based on Skills, Not Credit," *New York Times*, May 5, 1975, http://query.nytimes.com/gst/abstract.html?res=9803E0D71E30E03ABC4C53DFB366838E669EDE.

70. Author unknown, "The Chronology of the College for Human Services Bachelors and Masters Programs," Archive Folder #000064, 1–2.

71. Ibid., 2–4.

72. Audrey C. Cohen Fact Sheet, "draft not used," 5/77, Archive Folder #000750, 1.

73. See the Lincoln University website, http://www.lincoln.edu/mhs/curric.html.

74. Prepared by Barbara Walton, "The College for Human Services: An Historical Perspective," Archive Folder #000062, 3.

75. See "Update on College for Human Services Review by New York State Department of Education, College for Human Services, February 13, 1978, Archive Folder #000064, 2.

76. Dellie Bloom, "Narrative Summary," 1970–1980, c:/db-text/his.chr, from Barbara Walton's file box labeled "HISTORY," 13.

77. ACC Diary tape, October 22, 1978, transcribed 7/1/89 by Dellie Bloom, Archive Folder #000099.

78. Dellie Bloom, "Narrative Summary," 1970–1980, c:/db-text/his.chr, from Barbara Walton's file box labeled "HISTORY," 17. See, for an overview of New York City's fiscal crisis in 1975, http://www.library.ca.gov/crb/95/notes/v3n1.pdf.

79. Dellie Bloom, "Narrative Summary," 18–19.

80. See Archive Index and Archive Folders #000362–000375.

81. Dellie Bloom, "Narrative Summary," 18–19.

82. Ibid., 19.

83. ACC Diary Tape, October 22, 1979, Dellie Bloom transcribed 7/1/89, in Barbara Walton's file drawer labeled "History '89–92," third page of unnumbered document.

84. Dellie Bloom, "History Interview with Alida Mesrop," Audrey Cohen College," October 4, 1990, Archive Folder #000139, 1–2.

85. Dellie Bloom's interview of Steve Sunderland, 8/24/91, in Barbara Walton's file drawer labeled "History '89–92," thirteenth page of unnumbered document. See also Dellie Bloom, "Narrative Summary," 1970–1980, c:/db-text/his.chr, from Barbara Walton's file box labeled "HISTORY," 19.

86. Ibid., fourteenth and twenty-first page of unnumbered document.

87. Ibid., seventeenth page of unnumbered document.

88. Ibid., Tape II in Barbara Walton's file drawer labeled "History '89–92," 4 and 17.

89. Ibid., sixteenth to nineteenth page of unnumbered document. At this point Sunderland's interviewer, Dellie Bloom, says, "I agree. I marvel at it."

90. Dellie Bloom's interview of Steve Sunderland, twenty-fourth page of unnumbered document.

91. Dellie Bloom, "Narrative Summary," 1970–1980, c:/db-text/his.chr, from Barbara Walton's file box labeled "HISTORY," 20–21.

92. Ibid., 21.

CHAPTER 9. CONSTRUCTIVE ACTIONS (1980–1989)

1. Dellie Bloom, "History Interview" with Alida Mesrop, Audrey Cohen College, October 4, 1990, 19, 2, and 18.

2. Dellie Bloom, "Narrative Summary," 2 and 18–20.

3. Dellie Bloom, "History Interview" with Alida Mesrop, 19.

4. Personal memories of the author.

5. Ibid., 1, 5, 2, and 22.

6. Dellie Bloom's notes from her October 4, 1990, interview with Alida Mesrop.

7. GR interview with Alida Mesrop, 15, 5, and 2.

8. Dellie Bloom, "History Interview" with Alida Mesrop, 19 and 29.

9. GR interview with Alida Mesrop, 17.

10. Dellie Bloom, "History Interview" with Alida Mesrop, 2 and 8–9.

11. Dellie Bloom, "History Interview" with Alida Mesrop, Audrey Cohen College, October 4, 1990, 27–29.

12. Report to the faculty, administration, trustees, students of the College for Human Services, by an evaluation team representing the Commission on Higher Education of the Middle States Association of Colleges and Schools, prepared after study of the institution's self-study report and a visit to the campus on September 30–October 3, 1984, 12 and 1. Currently found in Box #6, labeled Paul Lerman, Middle States but to be filed as Archive Folder #000224.

13. Julia D. Lisella, editor, "College Celebrates 20th Anniversary: Mayor proclaims May Tenth College for Human Services Day," in the *Human Service Bulletin*, a publication of the College for Human Services, Vol. 2., No. 2, New York, September, 1984, Archive Folder #000878, 1.

14. Audrey C. Cohen, May 10 speech, dated 5/4/84 (JL), Archive Folder #000878, 3–5.

15. Ibid., 7.

16. Ibid. Emphasis in the original.

17. Ibid., 8.

18. Ibid., 10 and 9.

19. *The College for Human Services Crystal IV Handbook*, January 1989, 18, Archive Folder #003168.

20. *The College for Human Services Crystal II Handbook*, January 1989, 19, Archive Folder #003143.

21. *The College for Human Services Crystal I Handbook*, January 1989, 18, Archive Folder #003121.

22. Cohen, May 10 speech, 9.

23. Ibid., 13.

24. GR interview with Clyde Griffin, March 7, 2013, Morgan transcript, 1.

25. Clyde Griffin Jr., Curricululm Vita, 2013, and GR interview with Clyde Griffin, March 7, 2013, Morgan transcript.

26. Notes on conversation/interview with Dr. Clyde Griffin Jr., by Dellie Bloom, taped October 18, 1991, Archive Folder #000144, 2.

27. Summary of conversation/interview with Dr. Clyde Griffin Jr., by Dellie Bloom, taped October 18, 1991, Archive Folder #000144, 1.

28. GR interview with Clyde Griffin, 19.

29. GR interview with Richard Grallo, June 10, 2011, Morgan transcript 6.

30. GR interview with Humphrey Crookendale, February 20, 2013, Morgan transcript, 12.

31. Ibid., 10.

32. Ibid.

33. GR interview with Anne Lopes, February 6, 2013, Morgan transcript, 2.

34. Ibid., 2–3.

35. GR interview with Humphrey Crookendale, 3–5.

36. I am indebted to Anne Lopes, in a phone conversation on March 2, 2014, for this information.

37. John Dewey, *Democracy and Education* (New York: Free Press, 1944), 150–151.

38. Cohen, "The Service Society," 11.

39. Ibid.

40. Ibid.

41. Cohen, speech at twentieth-anniversary dinner, 9.

42. Cohen, "The Citizen as the Integrating Agent," 14. Retrieved from Metropolitan College of New York website: http://www.metropolitan.edu/library/documents/cohencitizena.html.

43. Barbara J. Walton, ed., "The College for Human Services: An Applied Transdisciplinary Curriculum," (New York: College for Human Services, 1982), ii.

44. Jaya Kannan in personal conversation with the author and in numerous faculty presentations.

45. Anonymous, notes from faculty meeting of November 8, 1985, "More on the Plan of Action," page 4 of unpaged document, personally provided by Professor Clyde Griffin.

46. Cohen, "The Citizen as the Integrating Agent."

47. See Citizen Empowerment Charts in *Crystal* (or *Purpose*) *Handbooks*, Archive Folders #003111–003214.

48. Anonymously authored, "Report on the Constructive Action Documentation Project," hand-dated 1985, 1, personally provided by Professor Clyde Griffin.

49. "Report on the Constructive Action Documentation Project," 1 and 5.

50. Ibid., 5.

51. Zoe Ingalls, " 'Get Out There and Make Social Change,' That's the mandate given to students at the anything-but-everyday College for Human Services." *Chronicle for Higher Education*, September 2, 1980, 6–7.

52. Ingalls, "Get Out There," 6–7.

53. The above examples of Constructive Action documents were randomly culled from five file boxes trucked in from the college's storage facilities in New Jersey, Spring 2013.

54. Myrna Willis, August 1990, from "Success Interviews" by Dellie Bloom, August 7, 1990, Archive Folder #000162, 1–2.

55. Leonard Ampy, from "Success Interviews" by Dellie Bloom, August 7, 1990, Archive Folder #000162, 1.

56. Ibid., 2.

57. Ibid.

58. Theresa Rodrigues, from "Success Interviews" by Dellie Bloom, August 7, 1990, Archive Folder #000162, 1.

59. Ibid., 2.

60. Ibid.

61. Patricia Cross, August 1990, from "Success Interviews" by Dellie Bloom, August 7, 1990, Archive Folder #000162, 1.

62. Ibid., 2.

63. Ibid., 3.

64. Phone conversation with Anne Lopes on Sunday, March 2, 2014. According to an email exchange among Vinton Thompson, Beth Dunphe, and the author on March 7, 2014, the college applied for and received Higher Education Opportunity Program funding off and on between 1977 and 1993.

65. GR interview with Bernadette Smith, June 6, 2013, Morgan transcript, 23 and 2.

66. Ibid., 3–4.

67. Ibid., 15.

68. Personal communication from Bernadette Smith, July 26, 2013, URI Bernadette A Smith biography.doc.

69. GR interview with Wendy Cohen, 14.

70. Ibid., 22.

71. GR interview with Alida Mesrop, 22–23.

72. Email correspondence from Wendy Cohen, May 2, 2013.

73. "Audrey Cohen is Wed to Dr. R.M. Wharton," *New York Times*, Style Section, January 31, 1988. http://nytimes.com/1988/01/31/style/audrey-cohen-is-wed-to-dr-r-n-wharton.html.

74. The College for Human Services Board of Trustees, minutes of meeting on April 19, 1988, Archive Folder #000718, 2.

75. The College for Human Services Board of Trustees, minutes of meeting on October 4, 1988, Archive Folder #000718, 2.

CHAPTER 10. BEYOND VOCATIONAL EDUCATION

1. GR interview with Franklyn Rother, May 10, 2013, Morgan transcript, 10.

2. *New York Times*, Style, January 31, 1988. http://www.nytimes.com/1988/01/31/style/audrey-cohen-is-wed-to-dr-r-n-wharton.html?pagewanted=print&src=pm.

3. Videotape on CD of *McNeil/Lehrer Report* on Audrey Cohen, October 10, 1989, compliments of Beth Dunphe.

4. Cohen, May 10 speech, 7. Emphasis in the original.

5. Aristotle, *Politics*, trans. Ernest Barker (New York: Oxford University Press, 1958), 334. As the context makes clear, Aristotle envisioned an educational system that would create free-minded men whose lives were not limited to professional pursuits and who in their leisure time would be inclined to devote themselves to politics. The assumption was that the polity requires forms of knowledge and habits of mind that are different from the forms of knowledge and habits of mind required by the economy. Although liberal education's identification with the life of leisure has not withstood the test of time, its essential role in preparing young people for civic life remains one of its central, though contested, features today.

6. Stephen R. Greenwald, "The Challenge of the 'For-Profit' College to the Traditional College Model," Oxford Roundtable, Oxford University, July 30–August 4, 2000, 21.

7. See also Grace Roosevelt, "The Triumph of the Market and the Decline of Liberal Education: Implications for Civic Life," *Teachers College Record*, Vol. 108, No. 7, July 2006, 1404–1423.

8. Booker T. Washington, *Up from Slavery* (New York: Penguin, 1986), 220.

9. W.E. Burghardt Du Bois, *Dusk of Dawn: An Essay Toward an Autobiography of a Race Concept* (New York: Harcourt, Brace, 1940), 70–80, in Hugh Hawkins, ed., *Booker T. Washington and His Critics: The Problem of Negro Leadership* (Boston: D.C. Heath, 1962).

10. Personal recollection of Clyde Griffin.

11. See http://www.admissions.college.harvard.edu/about/learning/liberal_arts.html, italics added. I am indebted to both John Greene and Maxine McClintock for their contributions to my thinking here.

12. Personal correspondence with Reinhold Niebuhr's daughter, Elizabeth Sifton.

13. Jean-Jacques Rousseau, *Emile or On Education*, Book II, Barbara Foxley, trans. http://www.gutenberg.org/catalog/world/readfile?fk_files=3275614&pageno=39.

14. Faculty profile of Vanda Wark by Cecelia Knight, *The Crystallizer*, Vol. V, Issue IV, June 1997, 5.

15. Ibid.

16. Author's personal correspondence with Vanda Wark, April 2013.

17. The Purpose III Values dimension syllabus includes these elements as objectives for the course. See www.mcny.edu.

18. GR interview with Theodor Damian, May 13, 2013, Morgan transcript, 11.

19. Ibid., 10.

20. Ibid., 13.

21. Ibid., 18.

22. Faculty profile of Charles Gray by Frank Fusco, *The Crystallizer*, Vol. V, Issue IV, April 1996, 10.

23. GR interview with Charles Gray, June 10, 2013, Morgan transcript, 8.

24. Faculty profile of Steven Cresap by Suzanne Thomas, *The Crystallizer*, Vol. V, Issue I, June 1997, 6.

25. Steven Cresap, personal communication with the author, March 24, 2012.

26. See Chapter 9.

27. Deborah Allen, "A History of the Dimensions," June 2013, unpublished, 11–12.

28. GR interview with Louis Tietje, April 5, 2013, Morgan transcript, 6.

29. Ibid., 7.

30. Ibid., 8.

31. GR interview with Charles Gray, June 10, 2013, Morgan transcript, 7.

32. In public and private discourse at the college in the early 2000s Jaya Kannan used the term *connective thinking* to describe the kind of learning that she was encouraging her students to do.

33. GR interview with Franklyn Rother, May 10, 2013, Morgan transcript, 20 and 1.

34. Wildris R. Tejeda, Purpose VIII Constructive Action document under the direction of Professor Charles Gray, Audrey Cohen College, Spring 1994, 65, from the college's random CA document storage facility in New Jersey.

35. Purpose V Constructive Action document, name withheld, under the direction of Professor Jan Goldberg, Audrey Cohen College, Spring 1998, from collection of CA documents in office of Student Services, courtesy of Dona Sosa.

36. See, for example, Bettye Watford-Faison, Purpose V Constructive Action document under the direction of Professor Charles Gray, the College for Human Services, Summer 1991, 28, from the college's random CA document storage facility in New Jersey.

37. Pandora Wise, Purpose VII Constructive Action document under the direction of Professor Rosalia LaPena, the College for Human Services, Spring 1990, 33–34, randomly selectively from the college's CA document storage facility in New Jersey.

38. Shanese McFadden, student paper, December 2, 2013, p. 2.

CHAPTER 11. THE TRIUMPHS AND CHALLENGES OF LEADERSHIP (1990–1999)

1. Audrey C. Cohen, "Leadership and the New Service Ethic," draft of a speech for HERS, #3/CH/2–14–80, Archive Folder #000098, 15.

2. Alan R. Sadovnik and Susan F. Semel, eds., *Founding Mothers and Others: Women Educational Leaders During the Progressive Era* (New York: Palgrave, 2002), 254.

3. Ibid.

4. Ibid.

5. See Semel and Sadovnik, "The Contemporary Small-School Movement: Lessons from the History of Progressive education," in the *Teachers College Record*, Vol. 110, No. 9, September 2008, 1744–1771. Maria Montessori was often

criticized for her heavy-handed control over the use of her method, the training of the method's teachers, and the production of her didactic materials. See http://en.wikipedia.org/wiki/Maria_Montessori. I am grateful to Cathryn Harding for making this point.

6. See, for example, http://en.wikipedia.org/wiki/Founder's_syndrome. For an interesting commentary, see also Elizabeth Schmidt, "Rediagnosing 'Founder's Syndrome': Moving Beyond Stereotypes to Improve Nonprofit Performance," in *The Nonprofit Quarterly*, online at http://www.nonprofitquarterly.org/management/22547-rediagnosing-fo . . . me-moving-beyond-stereotypes-to-improve-nonprofit-performance.html. I am indebted to Beth Dunphe for this reference.

7. Sadovnik and Semel, *Founding Mothers*, 254.

8. Ibid., 72–73.

9. "Mildred Robbins Leet" Wikipedia entry, at http://en.wikipedia.org/wiki/Mildred_Robbins_Leet and "Mildred Robbins Leet (1922–2011) at http://www.mildredrobbinsleet.org/.

10. GR interview with Wendy Cohen, 7.

11. GR interview with Dona Sosa, April 10, 2013, Morgan transcript 17.

12. GR interview with Humphrey Crookendale, 21.

13. Dellie Bloom interview with David Seeley, July 22, 1992, from Barbara Walton's file drawer, 3.

14. A memo to Audrey Cohen from C. Helman, subject titled "Leet and Stookey interview" [by Terry Lunsford of College for Human Services California campus], dated 2/19/80, Archive Folder #000159, 3.

15. Dellie Bloom interview with David Seeley, 11.

16. Ibid., 3–4.

17. College for Human Services Board of Trustees, minutes of meeting on June 18, 1991, Archive Folder #000721, 4–5.

18. Dellie Bloom interview with David Seeley, 12 and 2–3.

19. Ibid., 5 and 27–28.

20. Ibid., 10.

21. Ibid., 10 and 20.

22. Sadovnik and Semel, *Founding Mothers*, 254. See also Semel and Sadovnik, "The Contemporary Small-School Movement," 1744–1771.

23. GR interview with Humphrey Crookendale, 4.

24. GR interview with Richard Grallo, June 10, 2011, Morgan transcript, 11–12 and 3.

25. Ibid., 2.

26. GR interview with Anne Lopes, 10.

27. Ibid., 9.

28. Ibid., 9–10.

29. Ibid., 18–20; GR interview with Lou Tietje, April 5, 2013, Morgan transcript, 29.

30. GR interview with Anne Lopes, 16–17.

31. Audrey C. Cohen, "Leadership and the New Service Ethic," draft for HERS speech #3, CH/ 2/14/80, 1, Archive Folder #000098.

32. Ibid., 3.

33. Dellie Bloom interview with David Seeley, 32.

34. Ibid., 20.

35. Fiscal Officer Lincoln Roney's records show that space was rented in the Bronx, Queens, and Staten Island from 1994 onward. There were prior rentals starting at least in 1992 for which records could not be located.

36. College for Human Services, Board of Trustees minutes of meeting on March 19, 1991, Archive Folder #000721, 3.

37. GR interview with Theodor Damian, May 13, 2013, Morgan transcript, 6–7.

38. GR interview with Sylvia Hack, June 15, 2011, Morgan transcript, 37.

39. Dellie Bloom interview with David Seeley, 24 and 25.

40. GR interview with Clyde Griffin, 9.

41. Dellie Bloom interview with David Seeley, 25–26.

42. GR interview with Tom Webber, 28–29.

43. Report by Clyde Griffin in College for Human Services Board of Trustees minutes for meeting on January 20, 1988, Archive Folder #000718, 8.

44. GR interview with Clyde Griffin, 4. For an extensive report by Griffin on the implementation of the College for Human Services curricular model in a New York City high school, see the College for Human Services Board of Trustees minutes for the meeting on December 6, 1988, Archive Folder 3000718, 2–6.

45. I am grateful to Anne Lopes, in a phone conversation on March 2, 2014, for this information.

46. Dellie Bloom conversation/interview with Janith Jordan, January 10, 1991, Archive Folder #000125.

47. GR interview with Clyde Griffin, 8.

48. Ibid., 7.

49. Ibid., 11.

50. Ibid., 12.

51. Ibid., 11–13.

52. Ibid., 13–15, and in a conversation on June 13, 2014.

53. Ibid., 14.

54. Ibid., 8.

55. The College for Human Services, minutes of meeting on March 19, 1991, Archive Folder #000721, 5.

56. GR interview with Ralph Wharton, May 16, 2013, Morgan transcript, 4. See also Mark Pitsch, "The Outsider. Breaking the Mold: The Shape of Schools to Come," *Education Week*," January 25, 1995, 23 ff.

57. Jeffrey Mirel, "Unrequited Promise: Tracing the Evolution of New American Schools from Feisty Upstart to Bulwark of the Education Establishment," *Education Next*, Summer 2002, Vol. 2, No. 2. http://educationnext.org/unrequited-promise.

58. From Barbara Walton's file drawer, Dellie Bloom, "Informal conversation with Alida," Thursday, July 9, 1992, 1 and 2.

59. Mark Pitsch, "The Outsider," 23 ff.

60. See Audrey Cohen, "A New Educational Paradigm," *Phi Delta Kappan*, June 1993.

61. Audrey Cohen and Janith Jordan, "Audrey Cohen College System of Education: Purpose-Centered Education," in S. Stringfield, S. Ross, and L. Smith, eds., *Bold Plans for School Restructuring: The New American Schools Designs* (Mahwah, NJ: Erlbaum, 1996), 36.

62. See selections from John Dewey's *The School and Society* (1900) and *The Child and the Curriculum* (1902) in Martin S. Dworkin, ed., *Dewey on Education: Selections* (New York: Teachers College Press, 1959).

63. Cohen and Jordan, "Audrey Cohen College System of Education" in *Bold Plans*, 45 and 50.

64. Susan Bodilly, "Lessons Learned: RAND's Formative Assessment of NAS's Phase 2 Demonstration Effort," Chapter 11 of Sam Stringfield, Steven M. Ross, and Lana Smith, eds., 296/*Bold Plans for School Restructuring: The New American Schools Designs* (Mahwah, NJ: Erlbaum, 1996), 296 and 301–311.

65. The idea to have the college renamed may have come indirectly from Cohen's husband. In 1991 Ralph Wharton decided to establish a special fund at Columbia Presbyterian Medical Center for neurological research into the emotional and mental stresses that accompany illness and disease. In thinking about what to name the research fund, Wharton reasoned that institutions attract more interest and are easier to identify if they carry the name of a person or a place. After some deliberation, he decided to name the fund the Nathanial Wharton Fund, after his father who had also been a noted professional in the medical field. See GR interview with Ralph Wharton, May 16, 2013, Morgan transcript, 7.

66. Personal email message to Grace Roosevelt from Wendy Cohen, 5/20/2013.

67. Dellie Bloom's observations Re: Name change, 5/11/92, Archive Folder #000053.

68. Audrey Cohen, "The College for Human Services Name Change Announcement Speech," May 8, 1992, 3–5, Archive Folder #000889.

69. Dellie Bloom's observations Re: Name change, 5/11/92, Archive Folder #000053. In another place Bloom reflects that "From past experience, Audrey seems to have decided that resentment at decisions by fiat was less unsettling than resentment that mistook consultation for the right to make the decision. The way the name change was presented as a 'fait accompli' had the advantage of speed, forthrightness and surprise, with no opportunity for a challenge to the name change to coalesce." Dellie Bloom interview with Faye-Ran-Mosely, 5/13/92, Archive Folder #000125.

70. GR interview with Elaine Azen-Lampl, 5.

71. GR interview with Ralph Wharton, 5–6 and 8–9.

72. Personal email correspondence with Wendy Cohen, 5/20/2013.

73. GR phone interview with Alida Mesrop, 1–2.

74. GR interview with Ralph Wharton, 9 and 16.

75. Personal communication with Laura Pires-Hester, June 15, 2013.

76. GR interview with Dawn Margolin, 3–4.

77. GR interview with Wendy Cohen, 25.

78. Ibid., 25–26.

79. Audrey Cohen College Board of Trustees minutes of meeting August 16, 1994, Archive Folder #000725, 3.

80. Dellie Bloom's notes on lunch conversation with Mark Wille, March 18, 1992. From Barbara Walton's file drawer, "HISTORY" 1989–1992, 3, 1, and 2.

81. GR interview with Annie LaRock, February 15, 2013, Morgan transcript, 10 and 5.

82. Pitsch, "The Outsider," 23–26.

83. GR interview with Humphrey Crookendale, 9.

84. Eulogy delivered by Wilbert A. Tatum on Tuesday, March 19, 1996, at the Memorial Service for Audrey Cohen from file box labeled "Archives" in the Office of the President Storage Room, #1139.

85. Untitled eulogy delivered on Tuesday, March 19, 1996, at the Memorial Service for Audrey Cohen from file box labeled "Archives" in the Office of the President Storage Room, #1139.

86. Letters of condolence from file box labeled "Archives" in the Office of the President Storage Room, #1139.

87. William H. Honan, "Audrey Cohen, 64, Innovative Educator, Dies," *New York Times*, March 12, 1996. http://www.nytimes.com/1996/03/12/nyregion/audrey-cohen-64-innovative-educator-dies.html?pagewanted=print&src=pm.

88. GR interview with Dawn Margolin, 4, 7, 19, and 4.

CHAPTER 12. MCNY IN THE NEW MILLENNIUM (2000–2014)

1. Email communication with Steven Cresap, June 28, 2013, 10:29 A.M.

2. Personal conversation with Lou Tietje, Spring 2013.

3. "I treated the college's money as if it were my household money. Not one cent was used in a way that could raise any questions," Mesrop affirmed. GR phone interview with Alida Mesrop, June 21, 2013, Morgan transcript, 4.

4. GR phone interview with Alida Mesrop, 5–6.

5. Among the condolence notes that Alida Mesrop received after Cohen's death was one from Edwin Jay Siegel, a man who never attended the college but who—on seeing the ad in the subway—proceeded to change his life. "I picked up my pen and resumed writing poetry that I had put off since 1979. Now forty-two years old, I have been refining a talent once given up." He was terribly sorry, he continued, "that I was not able to say 'Thank You' to Ms. Cohen" while she was alive. "My love goes with her always. Thank You." See folder of condolence letters in box on top of filing cabinets in Office of the President Storage Room, Rm. #1129. The message is also printed in *The Crystallizer*, Vol. 5, Issue I, April 1996, 4.

6. Greenwald's name was first introduced to the Board of Trustees at their September 15, 1992, meeting, Archive Folder #000722.

7. Most of the information in this and the following paragraphs is based on the author's personal recollections of the events of those years.

8. The term was used by Clyde Griffin at the Faculty Council meeting where the decision to institute a ranking system was approved.

9. GR interview with Bernadette Smith, Esq., June 6, 2013, Morgan transcript, 7.

10. The Barbara Goleman Senior High School web page, at http://bghs.dadeschools.net/abo-ghshhistory.asp.

11. GR interview with Stephen Greenwald, June 21, 2013, Morgan transcript, 17. At its peak, in the fall of 2003, student enrollment at the Bronx site was 361 students. I am grateful to Vinton Thompson, in an email message dated March 7, 2014, for this information.

12. GR interview with Theodor Damian, 7.

13. GR interview with Stephen Greenwald, 7.

14. See Chapter 11.

15. At its peak, in the fall of 2003, student enrollment at all four college sites was 1,591 students. I am grateful to Vinton Thompson, in an email message dated March 7, 2014, for this information.

16. GR phone interview with Alida Mesrop, 4.

17. GR interview with Bernadette Smith, Esq., June 6, 2013, Morgan transcript, 7.

18. See the Wikipedia entry on EDMC at http://en.wikipedia.org/wiki/EDMC.

19. GR interview with Bernadette Smith, Esq., 11.

20. Unarchived file drawer for MCNY Board of Trustees 2007 in folder labeled Board Correspondence, 2007, in the Office of the President's Storage Room, Rm. 1129.

21. GR interview with Bernadette Smith, Esq, 10.

22. Ibid., 9.

23. Ibid., 10.

24. Ibid., 10–12.

25. GR phone interview with Loretta Robinson, July 15, 2013, Morgan transcript, 4.

26. Ibid., 12.

27. Ibid., 15

28. GR phone interview with Daniel Gregoire, July 20, 2013, Morgan transcript, 11.

29. Ibid., 21 and 23.

30. GR notes from phone interview with Ethel Perez, July 14, 2013, Morgan transcript, 2.

31. GR phone interview with Maria Martin, July 16, 2013, Morgan transcript, 12

32. GR notes from phone interview with Millie Arroyo, July 11, 2013.

33. Wendy Cohen's remarks prepared for installation ceremony of Vinton Thompson, December 3, 2009, from personal files labeled WC Speech VINTON small edits doc 12 1 copy.doc

34. An address by Dr. Vinton Thompson at the installation ceremony for the Fourth President of Metropolitan College of New York, Thursday, December 3, 2009, pdf., 6. See alsoYouTube clips at http://www.youtube.com/watch?feature=player_embedded&v=waRCjfPBO_Y.

35. Niccolò Machiavelli, *The Discourses*, Book III, Chapter 1, http://www.constitution.org/mac/disclivy3.htm.

36. Discussion draft CA guidelines VTDA v3 7–16–2012.docx

37. GR interview with Stephen Greenwald, 16.

38. GR personal memories of accreditation visit by NCATE to MCNY, Spring 2010.

39. Audrey Cohen College Board of Trustees minutes of meeting on September 15, 1992, Archive Folder #000722, 3.

40. See Alida Mesrop's outline for the book, Archive Folder #000094, 8–9.

41. Alida Mesrop states that Cohen herself "just decided that it wasn't working." GR phone interview with Alida Mesrop, June 21, 2013, Morgan transcript, 16.

42. See, for example, Grant and Riesman, *Perpetual Dream*," 135–176.

43. Pitsch, "The Outsider," 23.

44. See, for example, Alan Gartner and Frank Riessman, "The Paraprofessional Movement in Perspective," *Personel and Guidance Journal*, Vol. 53, No. 4, December 1974, 253–256; and Teri Wallace, "Paraprofessionals," Prepared for the Center on Personnel Studies in Special Education, July 2003, COPSSE Document No. IB-3, http://www.copsse.org, 6–8.

45. The contrasts between George H. W. Bush and George W. Bush's foreign policies have been frequently noted; a fruitful area of scholarship might also be their different policies regarding education.

SOURCES AND ACKNOWLEDGMENTS

1. See Alida Mesrop's outline for the book, Archive Folder #000094, 8–9.

2. A taped and transcribed conversation between Alida Mesrop and Audrey Cohen, August 4, 1986, Archive Folder #000094, 7–8.

INTERVIEWS

INTERVIEWS BY SYDELLE (DELLIE) BLOOM
(FROM MCNY ARCHIVES)

Leonard Ampy, Yolaine Armand, Audrey Cohen, Patricia Cross, Clyde Griffin, Kalu Kalu, Israel Laster, Alida Mesrop, Fay Ran-Mosley, Joseph Rhodes, Theresa Rodrigues, David Seeley, Steven Sunderland, Barbara Walton, Mark Wille, Myrna Willis, and Dodie Younger.

INTERVIEWS BY GRACE ROOSEVELT
(CONDUCTED BETWEEN JUNE 2011 AND
SEPTEMBER 2013)

Deborah Allen, Millie Arroyo, Elaine Azen-Lampl, Dawn Cohen Margolin, Mark Cohen, Wendy Cohen, Humphrey Crookendale, Theodor Damian, Richard Grallo, Charles Gray, Clyde Griffin, Melvina Goodman, Dinni Gordon, Steven Greenwald, Daniel Gregoire, Sylvia Hack, Judy Hozore, Annie La Rock, Maria Martin, Alida Mesrop, Lorraine Montenegro, Frankie Pelzman, Ethel Perez, Laura Pires-Hester, John Rodgers, Loretta Robinson, Franklyn Rother, Bernadette Smith, Dona Sosa, John Stookey, Lou Tietje, Vanda Wark, Tom Webber, Ralph Wharton, and Dodie Younger.

BIBLIOGRAPHY

Alinsky, Saul. *Rules for Radicals: A Pragmatic Primer for Realistic Radicals.* New York: Vintage Books, 1989.

Allen, Deborah. "Book Proposal," unpublished paper, February 24, 1992.

Allen, Deborah. "A History of the Dimensions," unpublished paper, June 10, 2013.

Aristotle. *Politics*. Translated by Ernest Barker. New York: Oxford University Press, 1958.

Asante, Molefe Kete. *The Afrocentric Idea*. Philadelphia: Temple University Press, 1987.

Audrey Cohen College, *Catalogue*, 1999.

Baker, Al. "In One School, Students are Divided by Gifted Label—and Race." *New York Times*, January 12, 2013. http://www.nytimes.com/2013/01/13/education/in-one-school-students-are-divided-by-gifted-label-and-race.html?pagewanted=1&_r=0.

Barnard, H.C. *Education and the French Revolution*. Cambridge: Cambridge University Press, 1969.

Bender, Marylin. "Meeting of 2 Housewives Was Start of a Business." *New York Times*, August 29, 1960, section on food, fashions, family, furnishings, p. 10.

Bloom, Dellie. "Narrative Summary, 1970–1980." Unpublished paper, undated.

Bodilly, Susan. "Lessons Learned: RAND's Formative Assessment of NAS's Phase 2 Demonstration Effort." Chapter 11 of *Bold Plans for School Restructuring: The New American Schools Designs*, edited by Sam Stringfield, Steven M. Ross, and Lana Smith. Mahwah, NJ: Erlbaum, 1996.

Bowen, James. *A History of Western Education*, vol. II. New York: St. Martin's Press, 1972.

Bowles, Samuel, Richard Edwards, and Frank Roosevelt. *Understanding Capitalism: Competition Command, and Change*. New York: Oxford University Press, 2005.

Bremner, Robert Hamlett. *Children and Youth in America: A Documentary History*, vols. 1–3. Cambridge, MA: Harvard University Press, 1974.

"Brother Preston Wilcox," in *AframSouth Inc*. http://www.aframsouth.net/legacy.htm, p. 1.

Bulletin for The College. Announcements for 1949–1950, University of Pittsburgh. Vol. 45, No. 2.

Burdick, Eugene, and William J. Lederer. *The Ugly American*. New York: Norton, 1999.

Clark, Kenneth B. *Dark Ghetto: Dilemma of Social Power*. Wesleyan, CT: Wesleyan University Press, 1989.

Cohen, Audrey C. "The College for Human Services." *Teachers College Record*, vol. 69, no. 7, 1968, 665. http://www.tcrecord.org, ID Number: 1966.

Cohen, Audrey C. "Women and Higher Education: Recommendations for Change." *Phi Delta Kappan*, November 1971, 164–167.

Cohen, Audrey C. "A Feminist System of Education for a New Public Service." Chapter 8 of *Public Service Employment: An Analysis of Its History, Problems, and Prospects*, edited by Alan Gartner, Russell A. Nixon, and Frank Riessman, with an introduction by Michael Harrington. New York: Praeger, 1973.

Cohen, Audrey C., Laura Houston, and Alida Mesrop, "Human-Services Education: College for Human Services," in *Managing Academic Change*, edited by S.V. Martorana and Eileen Kuhns. San Francisco: Jossey-Bass, 1975.

Cohen, Audrey C. "The Third Alternative." New York: Audrey Cohen College, 1975, 1988, 1997.

Cohen, Audrey C. "The Service Society and a Theory of Learning Linking Education, Work, Life." New York: College for Human Services, 1976, 1989, 1997.

Cohen, Audrey C. "The Citizen as the Integrating Agent: Productivity in the Human Services." *Human Service Monograph Series.* Project Share, no. 9, September 1978, 37. http://www.mcny.edu/library/documents/cohencitizena. html#empowercon.

Cohen, Audrey C. "Human Service." Chapter 27 of *The Modern American College*, edited by Arthur W. Chickering and Associates. San Francisco: Jossey-Bass, 1981.

Cohen, Audrey. "A New Educational Paradigm." *Phi Delta Kappan*, June 1993.

Cohen, Audrey. "Empowerment: Toward a New Definition of Self-Help." In *Human Services: Contemporary Issues and* Trends, edited by Howard S. Harris and David C. Maloney. Boston: Allyn and Bacon, 1996, 319–328.

Cohen Audrey, and Janith Jordan. "Audrey Cohen College System of Education: Purpose-Centered Education," in *Bold Plans for School Restructuring: The New American Schools Designs*, edited by S. Stringfield, S. Ross, and L. Smith. Mahwah, NJ: Erlbaum, 1996.

Cohen, Audrey C. "A Vision of Humanity for the Future." Speech given at Sterling Forest Staff Retreat, January 1973. Archive Folder #000802.

Cohen, Audrey C. "Leadership and the New Service Ethic." Draft of a speech for HERS, #3/CH/2–14–80. Archive Folder #000098.

Cohen, Audrey. Draft of a long article to be published in the periodical *Forum* under Audrey Cohen's name entitled "The History of the College for Human Services." Undated. Archive Folder #000093.

Cohen Mark I., and Lorna Hahn. *Morocco: Old Land, New Nation.* New York: Praeger, 1966.

Cohen, Wendy. "A Purpose-Centered Life." Speech to the Graduating Class of 2008, Metropolitan College of New York, June 2008.

Cohen, Wendy. Remarks prepared for installation ceremony of Vinton Thompson, December 3, 2009, from personal files labeled WC Speech VINTON small edits doc 12 1 copy.doc.

Coles, Robert. "Telic Reforms." *New Yorker*, March 13, 1978, 134–141.

Cremin, Lawrence A. *The Republic and the School: Horace Mann on the Education of Free Men*. New York: Teachers College Press, Classics in Education No. 1, 1957.

Dewey, John. "My Pedagogic Creed," in *Dewey on Education: Selections*, edited by Martin S. Dworkin. New York: Teachers College Press, 1975.

Dewey, John. *The School and Society* and *The Child and the Curriculum*. Philip W. Jackson, ed. Chicago: University of Chicago Press, 1990.

Dewey, John. *Democracy and Education*. New York: Free Press, 1944.

Dewey, John. *Experience and Education*. New York: Collier Books, 1974

Dillard, Annie. *An American Childhood*. New York: Harper, 1988.

Du Bois, W.E. Burghardt. *Dusk of Dawn: An Essay Toward an Autobiography of a Race Concept*. New York: Harcourt, Brace, 1940. In *Booker T. Washington and His Critics: The Problem of Negro Leadership*, edited by Hugh Hawkins. Boston: Heath, 1962.

Edsall, Thomas B. "The Reproduction of Privilege." *New York Times*, March 12, 2012. http://campaignstops.blogs.nytimes.com/2012/03/12/thr-reproduction-of-privilege/?pagemode=print.

"Education: Self-Made College." Time, July 6, 1970. http://content.time.com/time/subscriber/printout/0,8816,878365,00.html.

Faludi, Susan. "Facebook Feminism, Like It or Not." *The Baffler*, no. 23, 2013. http://thebaffler.com/past/facebook_feminism_like_it_or_not.

Finch, Caleb E., and Thomas B.L. Kirkwood. *Chance, Development, and Aging*. New York: Oxford University Press, 2000.

Freire, Paolo. *Pedagogy of the Oppressed*. New York: Seabury Press, 1974.

Garson, G. David. "Economic Opportunity Act of 1964." http://wps.prenhall.com/wps/media/objects/751/769950/Documents_Library/eoa1964.htm.

Gartner, Alan, and Frank Riessman. "The Paraprofessional Movement in Perspective." *Personel and Guidance Journal*, vol. 53, no. 4, December 1974, 253–256.

Gitlin, Todd. *The Sixties: Years of Hope, Days of Rage*. New York: Bantam Books, 1993.

Goodman, Paul. *Growing Up Absurd: Problems of Youth in the Organized System*. New York: Vintage, 1962.

Grant, Gerald, and David Riesman, *The Perpetual Dream: Reform and Experiment in the American College*. Chicago: University of Chicago Press, 1978.

Greenwald, Stephen R. "The Challenge of the 'For-Profit' College to the Traditional College Model." Oxford Roundtable, Oxford University, July 30–August 4, 2000.

Halberstam, David. *The Fifties.* New York: Random House, 1993.

Hanover Research. "2010–2011 Annual Graduation Survey Analysis Prepared for Metropolitan College of New York." March 2012.

Harlow, Nora. *Sharing the Children: Village Child Rearing Within the City.* New York: Harper & Row, 1975.

Harrington, Michael. *The Other America: Poverty in the United States.* New York: Macmillan, 1962.

Hoffman, Marilyn. "Spare Time Made Profitable." *The Christian Science Monitor,* January 15, 1964.

Holt, John. *How Children Fail.* New York: Dell, 1964.

Honan, William H. "Audrey Cohen, 64, Innovative Educator, Dies." *New York Times,* March 12, 1996. http://www.nytimes.com/1996/03/12/nyregion/audrey-cohen-64-innovative-educator-dies.html?pagewanted=print&src=pm.

Hornaday, Mary. "Talent Corps Graduates Sent Afield." *Christian Science Monitor,* January 23, 1967.

Hozore, Judith S., and Barbara J. Walton. "Sixth Annual Report of the College for Human Services, 1972–1973." New York: College for Human Services, 1976.

Ingalls, Zoe. "'Get Out There and Make Social Change,' That's the Mandate Given to Students at the Anything-but-Everyday College for Human Services." *Chronicle for Higher Education,* September 2, 1980, 6–7.

Illich, Ivan. *Deschooling Society.* New York: Harper & Row, 1970.

Katz, Michael B. *Class, Bureaucracy, and Schools: The Illusion of Educational Change in America.* New York: Praeger, 1975.

Knight, Louise W. *Jane Addams: Spirit in Action.* New York: Norton, 2010.

Kohl, Herbert. *36 Children.* New York: Signet Books, 1967.

Kozol, Jonathan. *Death at an Early Age: The Destruction of the Hearts and Minds of Negro Children in the Boston Public Schools.* New York: Bantam Books, 1967.

Lagemann, Ellen Condliffe. *A Generation of Women: Education in the Lives of Progressive Reformers.* Cambridge, MA: Harvard University Press, 1979.

Machiavelli, Niccoló. *The Discourses.* Book III, chapter 1. http://www.constitution.org/mac/discllivy3.htm.

Macht, Jean, with Douglas A. Whyte. "Human Services: History and Recent Influences." Chapter 3 in *Human Services: Contemporary Issues and Trends,* edited by Howard S. Harris and David C. Maloney. Boston: Allyn and Bacon, 1998.

McClintock, Maxine. *Letters of Recommendation*. New York: Collaboratory for Liberal Learning, 2013.

McClintock, Robert. *Enough: A Pedagogic Speculation*. New York: Collaboratory for Liberal Learning, 2012.

McCormack, Patricia. "New College for Human Services Gives Courses in Purposeful Living." *Providence Sunday Journal*, November 5, 1978.

McKay, Matthew, Martha Davis, and Patrick Fanning. *Messages: The Communication Skills Book*. Oakland, CA: New Harbinger Publications, 2009.

Menand, Louis, Frank Chambers, and Richard C. Richardson Jr. "Report on Talent Corps, Inc., New York City, Concerning Its Application for a Charter as a Two-Year College to Be Known as College for Human Services." Dated by hand 1969.

Mesrop, Alida. "In the Beginning." An unpublished draft of a book to be entitled "From Dream to Reality: The Biography of a College." Undated.

Mirel, Jeffrey. "Unrequited Promise: Tracing the Evolution of New American Schools from Feisty Upstart to Bulwark of the Education Establishment." *Education Next*. Summer 2002, vol. 2, no. 2. http://educationnext.org/unrequited-promise, p. 1 of 11.

Moran, Nancy. "Students Occupy Office of Training School's Chief." *New York Times*, September 3, 1970.

Neal, Larry. "Black Art and Black Liberation," in *"Takin' it to the Streets": A Sixties Reader*, edited by Alexander Bloom and Wini Breines. New York: Oxford University Press, 2003.

Neill, A.S. *Summerhill: A Radical Approach to Child Rearing*. New York: Hart, 1960.

"New Way Up." *Vogue*. Vol. 152, no. 7, October 15, 1968, 98–99.

Obst, Lynda Rosen., ed. *The Sixties: The Decade Remembered Now, By the People Who Lived It Then*. New York: Random House/Rolling Stone, 1977.

Patterson, James T. *Grand Expectations: The United States, 1945–1971*. New York: Oxford University Press, 1996.

Pires Houston, Laura. "The Women's Talent Corps → The College for Human Services: Historical Reconstruction, Volume I," August 16, 1978.

Pires Houston, Laura. "The Women's Talent Corps → The College for Human Services: An Historical Reconstruction" (Phase I: Crystal 3: Institutional Development and Expansion—Pushing the Parameters of the Possible), vol. IV, December 4, 1978.

Pitsch, Mark. "The Outsider. Breaking the Mold: The Shape of Schools to Come." *Education Week*, January 25, 1995, p. 23 ff.

Podair, Jerald. *The Strike That Changed New York: Blacks, Whites, and the Ocean Hill-Brownsville Crisis*. New Haven: Yale University Press, 2002.

Prial, Frank J. "A Degree Based on Skills, Not Credit." *New York Times*, May 5, 1975, http://query.nytimes.com/gst/abstract.html?res=9803E0D71E30E03A BC4C53DFB366838E669EDE.

Ramer, Donna K. "Wendy Cohen and Her Mother, Audrey Cohen, Founder of Metropolitan College of New York." *The HBAdvantage*, Winter 2011. www. hbanet.org.

"Regents Charter School for Poor: 2-Year College Here Gives 'Human Service' Training." *New York Times*, May 26, 1970. http://select.nytimes.com/gst/ abstract.html?res=F0061FFC3B5A157493C4AB178ED85F448785F9.

Riessman, Frank. *New Careers: A Basic Strategy Against Poverty*. With an Introduction by Michael Harrington. New York: A Philip Randolph Educational Fund, November, 1967.

Roosevelt, Grace. "The Triumph of the Market and the Decline of Liberal Education: Implications for Civic Life." *Teachers College Record*, vol. 108, no. 7, July 2006.

Roosevelt, Grace. "Reconsidering Dewey in a Culture of Consumerism: A Rousseauean Critique." *Philosophy of Education Society Yearbook 2011*, 283–292.

Rousseau, Jean-Jacques. *Emile, or On Education*, Book II. Translated by Barbara Foxley. http://www.gutenberg.org/catalog/world/readfile?fk_files=3275614&pageno=39.

Sadovnik Alan R., and Susan F. Semel, eds. *Founding Mothers and Others: Women Educational Leaders During the Progressive Era*. New York: Palgrave, 2002.

Sandberg, Sheryl. *Lean In: Women, Work, and the Will to Lead*. New York: Knopf, 2013.

Schiff, Karenna Gore. *Lighting the Way: Nine Women Who Changed Modern America*. New York: Hyperion, 2006.

Schmidt, Elizabeth. "Rediagnosing 'Founder's Syndrome': Moving Beyond Stereotypes to Improve Nonprofit Performance." *Nonprofit Quarterly.* http://www.nonprofitquarterly.org/management/22547-rediagnosing-fo . . . me-moving-beyond-stereotypes-to-improve-nonprofit-performance.html.

Schrecker, Ellen. *The Lost Soul of Higher Education: Corporatization, the Assault on Academic Freedom, and the End of the American University*. New York: New Press, 2010.

Semel, Susan F., and Alan R. Sadovnik, "The Contemporary Small-School Movement: Lessons from the History of Progressive Education," in the *Teachers College Record*, vol. 110, no. 9, September 2008, 1744–1771.

Sosa, Dona, ed. *The Crystallizer*, vols. I–VI. New York: College for Human Services, 1983–1997.

Spar, Debora L. *Wonder Women: Sex, Power, and the Quest for Perfection*. New York: Sarah Crichton Books, 2013.

Stringfield, Sam, Steven M. Ross, and Lana Smith, eds. *Bold Plans for School Restructuring: The New American Schools Designs.* Mahwah, NJ: Erlbaum, 1996.

Tavernise, Sabrina. "Education Gap Grows Between Rich and Poor, Studies Say." *New York Times,* February 9, 2012. http://www.nytimes.com/2012/02/10/education/education-gap-grows-between-rich-and-poor-studies-show.html?_r=1&pagewanted=print.

Tietje, Louis. "Experience and Purpose: Thoughts on Purpose-Centered Education at Metropolitan College of New York." http://www.studyplace.org/wiki/MCNY_purpose.

Trowbridge, Augustus. *Begin with a Dream: How a Private School with a Public Mission Changed the Politics of Race, Class, and Gender in American Education.* XLibris, 2005.

"UFT Hails Breakthrough Program of Teacher Assistants." *United Teacher,* vol. 8, no. 13, February 17, 1967.

U.S. Department of Education, National Center for Education Statistics, 2012 IPEDS Data Feedback Report on Metropolitan College of New York.

Wallace, Teri. "Paraprofessionals." Prepared for the Center on Personnel Studies in Special Education, July 2003, COPSSE Document No. IB-3. http://www.copsse.org, pp. 6–8.

Walton, Barbara J. "Fourth Annual Report of the College for Human Services for 1970." New York: College for Human Services, 1972.

Walton, Barbara. "Origins of the Human Service Performance Grid (1973–1974)." Occasional Paper, Chapter I of Annual Report. August 1978.

Walton, Barbara J., ed. "The College for Human Services: An Applied Transdisciplinary Curriculum." New York: College for Human Services, 1982. Archive Folder #000432.

Walton, Barbara. "The College for Human Services: An Historical Perspective." Archive Folder #000062.

Washington, Booker T. *Up from Slavery.* New York: Penguin, 1986.

Westbrook, Robert B. *John Dewey and American Democracy.* Ithaca: Cornell University Press, 1991.

Zenz, Cassandra. "Wilcox, Preston (1923–2006)." http://www.blackpast.org/?q=aah/wilcox-preston-1923–2006, p. 2.

INDEX

Note: Italicized numbers indicate illustrations